Samuel Richardson's
Fictions of Gender

Samuel Richardson's Fictions of Gender

TASSIE GWILLIAM

STANFORD UNIVERSITY PRESS

STANFORD, CALIFORNIA

1993

Stanford University Press
Stanford, California
© 1993 by the Board of Trustees of the
Leland Stanford Junior University
Printed in the United States of America
CIP data are at the end of the book

To Frank Stringfellow
&
Nicholas Gwilliam Stringfellow

Acknowledgments

Many people have contributed to the thinking of the person who wrote this book, and I am pleased to have the chance of recording their names in print, although most of them, I hope, already know my gratitude and the pleasure they have brought me. Jean Frantz Blackall and the late Walter Slatoff gave scrupulous attention to the prose style and the argument of an earlier version of this work, and Harry Shaw has been a continuing source of support, both intellectual and personal, throughout its composition. Neil Hertz's influence and assistance have been more important than he can know. I would also like to thank the members of the intellectual and social community out of which this book originally grew: Robert Chibka, Jane Dickinson, Anne Posel, Christopher Pye, Paul Sawyer, Anita Sokolsky, Stephen Tifft, Melissa Zeiger, and the members of the Cornell University Feminist Theory Reading Group, 1981–85. Karen Swann, Veronica Kelly, and Beth Newman have read and commented (helpfully) on various drafts over the years; Lauren Berlant's assistance at a critical juncture was only one of her many generous acts; and Mihoko Suzuki has been a canny, indefatigable reader and rereader as well as the source of practical assistance and friendship. I am grateful too to Susanne Wofford for her generosity. Zack Bowen, Hermione de Almeida, George Gilpin, Frank Palmeri, and Lindsey Tucker have been exemplary friends and colleagues.

An earlier version of Chapter One—"*Pamela* and the Duplicitous Body of Femininity"—appeared in *Representations* 34 (1991): 104–33; some of the material contained in Chapter Two appeared in a different form in " 'Like Tiresias': Metamorphosis and Gender in *Clarissa*," *NOVEL: A Forum on Fiction* 19, no. 2 (Winter 1986): 101–17.

I want to thank the Gwilliam-Gansers and the Stringfellows, superb family members all. My parents, Marjorie and Frank Gwilliam, not only have offered unstinting support of all kinds, they have also been models of what it means to love your work. My debt to them long predates this book. Frank Stringfellow has made me happy; it is to him, and to Nicholas Gwilliam Stringfellow, that I dedicate this book.

T. G.

Contents

A Note to the Reader

Quotations from *Pamela* are from the following two editions: *Pamela, or, Virtue Rewarded*, ed. T. C. Duncan Eaves and Ben D. Kimpel (Boston: Houghton Mifflin, 1972); and *Pamela* [Volume 2] (London and New York: Dent Dutton, 1978). The first is a reprint of the first (1740) edition of *Pamela*, with the letters of praise and Richardson's response to criticism (the "Introduction to the Second Edition") added. The second is Richardson's continuation of *Pamela* (1741), usually referred to as "Part 2." Quotations from *Pamela* cite simply the page number: "I have been in Disguise indeed ever since my good Lady, your Mother, took me from my poor Parents" (p. 62).

Quotations from *Clarissa* follow the text of the third edition: *Clarissa. Or, the History of a Young Lady*, 8 vols. (New York: AMS Press, 1990; rpt. of 3d ed., 1751). After the volume and page number, though, I also cite the page number for the equivalent passage in the widely available and inexpensive Viking Penguin *Clarissa*, edited by Angus Ross (Harmondsworth, Eng.: Penguin, 1985), a lightly modernized version of the first edition (1747–48). I have also indicated in notes those passages I quote that do not appear in the first edition. Quotations from *Clarissa* appear as in the following example: "And hence it is, that a mischief which would end in simple robbery among men rogues, becomes murder if a woman be in it" (V: 314) (896).

For *The History of Sir Charles Grandison*, I use the Oxford Clas-

sics paperback based on the first edition of 1753–54, edited by
Jocelyn Harris (Oxford: Oxford Univ. Press, 1986), which re-
prints the 1972 three-part edition in a single volume. The cita-
tions are to part number and page number. "The best of men, they
said, loved to have difficulties to conquer. Their brother, generous
as he was, was a *man*" (1.423).

In the texts of all three novels, Richardson occasionally uses
square brackets along with parentheses; in order to distinguish
Richardson's brackets from my own in quotations, I have added
the words "brackets in original" where necessary.

Samuel Richardson's
Fictions of Gender

Introduction

If "masculinity" and "femininity" have increasingly come to be recognized as fictions about bodies, fiction itself has always had its place in the construction of gender. Novels have notoriously offered models for extravagant and transgressive behavior, particularly on the part of young women; anxiety about the effect of novel reading on female behavior seems to have been born at the same moment as the novel. More pervasively, fiction, like any network of representations, tends both to embody and to naturalize particular ideologies, including ideologies of gender and sexuality. That fiction which takes as its subject the constitution of masculinity and femininity, however, necessarily renders visible, if only intermittently, the problems and anxieties of gender construction. Because gender and sexuality are explicitly contested in the fiction of Samuel Richardson, his works offer an extraordinarily rich—and immense—textual field for the investigation of both gender and sexuality.

"Gender" is a term used to distinguish social and cultural sexual identity from biological sex.[1] According to Joan Scott, "Gender becomes a way of denoting 'cultural constructions'—the entirely social creation of ideas about appropriate roles for men and women. Gender is, in this definition, a social category imposed on a sexed body."[2] Gender has been crucial for feminists interested in prying "nature" apart from "culture" and in rendering the categories of masculinity and femininity problematic; the use of this concept also allows the relational nature of male and female identity—their interdependence—to emerge more powerfully.

While the developing distinction between "gender" and "sex" has thus been extremely useful, the relation between "gender" and the more psychoanalytically inflected concepts of sexuality and sexual difference, as well as the relation between "sex" and sexuality, have been less clear-cut and more troubling. In the words of Parveen Adams, "Sex can be thought of in biological terms; gender can be thought of in sociological terms. To introduce psychoanalytic theory is to complicate things because we have to make room for one more reality, this time psychical reality. . . . It is not surprising that psychoanalysis seems to have nothing to say about sex and gender. What psychoanalysis speaks about is sexuality."[3] Because this investigation of Richardson looks both at the construction of gender and at the operation of sexuality, my view of the relations among sex, sexuality, and gender in these fictional works requires some elaboration. Psychoanalytic theory suggests that sexual identity is created through the process of sexual differentiation, which occurs in a relation to the sexed body, or at least in relation to perception of / fantasies about the sexed body; further, psychoanalytic theory claims that sexual identity is always unstable because of the presence of repressed desires and repressed identifications in the unconscious. Although some sociologically grounded gender theory attempts to derive the basis of gender wholly from culture, psychoanalytic theory, even Lacanian / feminist psychoanalytic theory, recognizes the fact that sexuality cannot be fully detached from biology or removed from the physical. If gender theory at its most reductive sometimes suggests that masculinity and femininity are simply imposed from without by a monolithic "culture," psychoanalysis reminds us that physical and psychical components interact with culture and language to create those constructs or operations.

Much recent feminist theory, however, moves back and forth between discussions of gender and discussions of sexuality, reading the different registers as compatible, in fact open to being fruitfully juxtaposed. In part, this process of juxtaposing involves an investigation of the impact of gender construction on sexuality, and vice versa. It also involves defining the particular, local manifestations of that abstract entity known as "the body." The precise fit between these various components remains a problem, however. It is probably not adequate to assume, for example, that "gender" can represent the "outside" or what is culturally imposed and "sexuality" the "inside" or psychological and bodily responses of the human subject; indeed, an important aspect of my project is to examine how fantasies and metaphors of inside and outside, of imposed and intrinsic elements bear on the construction of sexuality and gender in Richardson's work.

My interest in defining (if sometimes indirectly) aspects of an eighteenth-century understanding of gender leads me to take a close look at sexuality. Sexuality is a medium through which ideas about gender are formed and played out, and as Eve Sedgwick remarks, "What *counts* as sexual is . . . variable and itself political."[4] The place of Richardson's fiction in the history of gender thus includes the meaning attached to particular forms of sexual expression as well as the psychic meaning of masculinity and femininity. Some readers may regard my account of sexual and psychic meanings as abstract or dehistoricized; the historicist critique of psychoanalytic or psychological criticism has always been that it ignores context and flattens out historical specificity. But even though I believe, and have tried to demonstrate, that the sexual and more generally psychic meanings I investigate do depend on cultural and historical contexts, I also assume that certain aspects of sexuality are more than local, and that they help to create the human subject in similar ways at different times and in different cultures. That is, my analysis assumes that there are transhistorical forces in human subjectivity. Nevertheless, the project is also shaped by the (ambiguous) presence of a human author, Samuel Richardson, who is located in a specific historical period and social milieu, and who himself influences as well as reflects the conceptualization of gender and sexuality.

There has been a great deal of interest on the part of feminist critics, as well as others, in Richardson's attitudes toward women, in his (and his novels') beliefs about the proper role and place of women, and, to a lesser degree, in his attitudes toward men, particularly rakes.[5] If gender and sexuality are constructs, however, it is worth focusing the investigation more specifically on the process of their construction in a fictional world.[6] Not only does this approach allow us to see the process of that construction at work at a specific moment, and in a rich body of writing, but it also allows us to see Richardson's representation of women and men in a conceptual or theoretical framework, not simply as the product of a somewhat contradictory set of beliefs about role and propriety. As a result of this focus, I have given only limited attention to the debates about women's education and role that appear in the novels and in Richardson's correspondence.[7] Instead, I am pursuing the meanings attached to "masculinity" and "femininity," the embodiment of sexuality, and the way that the categories of gender are created and contested in the novels. In seeing the novels from this angle, I am following out a trail laid down by Richardson himself; that is, the novels often explicitly theorize gender and sexuality, in part simply by worrying the question of what makes a man and what makes a woman, and in part by offering a kind of catalog of the meanings, fantasies, and metaphors attached to the sexed body.[8]

The sexed body in literature and art is perhaps most notoriously female. The women's bodies that appear and that are the site of extensive fantasies in Richardson's novels, however, are often not merely or solely female bodies—because there is no natural "body" to find or represent. The women's bodies in these novels most characteristically appear under wraps of some kind; veiled, disguised, cloaked, and hidden, they are also metaphorized in terms that confuse and conflate these wrappings—or surfaces— with the "depths" that lie beneath. The male body is also constantly at issue in the representation of women and the female body. The insistence on exposing and penetrating female bodies— of finding what exists beneath the surfaces applied by art, culture, or nature—engages the question of sexual difference in its radical sense; the female body is often probed or viewed for the information it is presumed to contain about the male body. At times it seems that Richardson's novels are fragments of an immense epistemological quest to "know" women, to define women's bodies, and to establish the meaning of femininity. But what emerges, both in Richardson's own statement of his enterprise as a writer and in the novels themselves, is also a search—less directed, less overt—for the meaning of masculinity, a search that shadows the open investigation of femininity. One of my interests here is to bring that covert search out into the open.

The doubleness of this quest by Samuel Richardson creates some interesting effects that tend to disrupt and complicate the reading of gender in his fiction, transforming the mode of his thought in which, as Simone de Beauvoir has memorably formulated it, man is the "self" and woman is the "other."[9] This model takes maleness as the standard from which femaleness is a deviation: "Humanity is male and man defines woman not in herself but as relative to him."[10] Thus investigation of gender difference tends to focus on woman as the marked term, the one who differs. As Ludmilla Jordanova writes, "There is a notable asymmetry at work in terms like 'gender' and 'the body' as a result of which we as scholars, like the writers and artists we study, focus more on women than on men. . . . The very idea of gender leads more directly to women than to men. . . . By a variety of means we have come to see women as the problematic sex, indeed as *the* sex."[11] Thomas Laqueur notes that

it is *always* woman's sexuality that is being constituted; woman is the empty category. Woman alone seems to have "gender" since the category itself is defined as that aspect of social relations based on difference between sexes in which the standard has always been man. . . . It is probably not possible to write a history of man's body and its pleasures because the historical record was created in a cultural tradition where no such history was necessary.[12]

A related mode of thinking appears in the "tradition that defines male sexuality as obvious, uncomplicated, and iterable, and female sexuality as mysterious."[13] While Richardson's work does not stand in opposition to this pervasive and constitutive mode of thought—its very absorption in the question of femininity ensures a certain complicity—its method of investigating femininity tends to call masculinity into question, to trouble masculinity's equanimity and obviousness. This tendency to disturb the ideological stability of gender, and to disrupt the boundaries between male and female, particularly by disturbing the internal coherence of each category, is a fundamental quality not only of Richardson's fiction but also of Richardson's myth of his origin as a writer.

The origin of Richardson's writing, as he reports, is in women. When Richardson's Dutch translator, Johannes Stinstra, asks, "From whom you have acquired such accurate acquaintance of nature, the various inborn qualities and manners of mankind?," the very stories Richardson employs in answering the question suggest that, in his experience, knowledge of "mankind" originates in the penetration of and control over women's secrets:

I was not more than Thirteen when three of these young Women [in a group he read to while they sewed], unknown to each other, having a high Opinion of my Taciturnity, revealed to me their Love-Secrets, in order to induce me to give them Copies to write after, or correct, for Answers to their Lovers' Letters: Nor did any of them ever know, that I was the Secretary to the others. I have been directed to chide, and even repulse, when an Offence was either taken or given, at the very time that the Heart of the Chider or Repulser was open before me, overflowing with Esteem and Affection; and the fair Repulser dreading to be taken at her Word, directing *this* Word, or *That* Expression, to be softened or changed.[14]

Through writing, the young Richardson is free to range across the boundaries of gender difference without endangering his privileged status as male. He sees deeper into the women than their lovers themselves do, and not only is he privy to the love secrets of three women (secrets each keeps from the other women), he is himself a secret from their lovers—a man writing love letters to other men without guilt or anxiety.[15] The overflowing hearts—open only to him—signify a knowledge and power that are gendered as well as generic; Richardson is privy to three sets of secrets that, in his telling, are essentially indistinguishable, categorized simply as feminine "Love-Secrets." The image of hearts on display for the youthful connoisseur and amanuensis also betokens the presence of the female body in a state of desire; these hearts are erotically charged. In Richardson's myth of the origin of writing and knowledge, knowledge of *a* woman implies knowledge of women, and knowledge of women implies knowledge of "mankind."

Johannes Stinstra seems satisfied with Richardson's explanation of how he has "come to the full knowledge of the woman's heart, and his [*sic*] deepest recesses," but he is unable to comprehend Richardson's shift to the knowledge of "the mysteries of unrighteousness, in the heart of a Rake, a Libertine, a wanton and sly Lovelace."[16] Stinstra appears to take the "man" of "mankind" more literally than does Richardson, and to insist on fuller disclosure, wider experience. Richardson's reply suggests a double and oddly circuitous route for his literary knowledge of his own sex:

You think, Sir, you can account from my early Secretariship to young women in my Father's Neighbourhood, for the Characters I have drawn of the Heroines of my three Works. But this Opportunity did little more for me, at so tender an Age, than Point, as I may say, or lead my Enquiries, as I grew up, into the Knowledge of the Female Heart. And knowing something of that, I could not be an utter Stranger to that of Man. Men and Women are Brothers and Sisters: They are not of different Species.[17]

Stinstra's assumption that Richardson merely copied from young women for his characters clearly irritated the writer, who insists on the gravity and breadth of his research into the female heart as well as the applicability of its lessons to knowledge of "Man." While he admits that observing women has been important for his development, Richardson claims that women themselves lack adequate knowledge of their own "nature," and that only one who can see simultaneously from the inside and the outside is able to understand them; thus women require the intervention of a writing man to show them their meaning. Women seem to function as sites for his identification rather than being important for what they can *tell* him. In a letter to his favorite female correspondent, Lady Bradshaigh, Richardson stakes out the knowledge of women as a masculine preserve, even as a preserve restricted to the most discriminating of male writers:

Indeed, my good Lady B, one too generally finds, in the writings of even ingenious men, that they take up their Characters of women too easily, and either on general Opinions, or particular acquaintances. Shakespeare knew them best of all of our writers, in my humble opinion. He knew them better than they knew themselves; for, pardon me for saying, that we do not always go to women for *general* knowledge of the Sex. Ask me now with disdain, my dear Lady B, if *I* pretend to know them? No, I say—I only guess at them: And yet I think them not such mysteries as some suppose. A tolerable knowledge of men will lead us to a tolerable knowledge of women.[18]

Richardson seems to reverse the trajectory of knowledge he traced out for Stinstra: In that letter to a man, knowing men was a reflex of knowing women; in this letter to a woman, knowing women is a reflex of knowing men. Richardson's statements about knowing women are ultimately also (and, on occasion, primarily) about knowing men. Knowledge of men, whether it is target or route, however, fatally lacks the power of generation that knowledge of women offers; although Richardson denies that women are "mysteries," and further denies to women general knowledge of their own sex, his identification across the lines of gender with "the Sex" is clearly the source and origin of his writing. But this reflexive basis itself produces a kind of anxiety about originality that is tinged with anxiety about gender. Richardson's denial that he copied his heroines from the young women for whom he wrote letters, and his criticism of other writers for using "general Opinions" about women *or* "particular acquaintances" among women for their characters, suggest the wish to demonstrate that, as he elsewhere insists, he "wrote not *from* women; but *for* them."[19] He claims to be both near enough and far enough from women to maintain his perspective on them.

These assertions of objectivity and originality only partially conceal an uneasy truce between absorption in women and superior knowledge of them. As Thomas Laqueur notes about the anxiety over "effeminacy" in the Renaissance, "Being with women too much or being too devoted to them seems to lead to the blurring of what we would call sex."[20] The pose of the uninvolved, superior male observer is undermined by the close identification with women that seems to be required for the knowledge Richardson claims. The fact that knowledge of women is almost always shadowed by or tied to knowledge of men also calls into question the independence and detachability of the male subject. As demonstrated by the circuitous routes to knowledge of men that Richardson describes, he depends on femininity as the model for talking about mankind, and on the sexual signification of women's bodies to define male sexuality. The representation of women, female bodies, and femininity, which appears so often to be the focus of the texts, at times seems partly intended to cover for an investigation of men, male bodies, and masculinity.

In the letter quoted earlier, Richardson tells Stinstra that his knowledge of men is based on the analogy of female and male hearts, for, as he asserts, "Men and Women are Brothers and Sisters"; on closer inspection it develops, however, that "man" is a category that breaks down. Richardson goes on implicitly to distinguish his wicked male characters from those who are "Brothers" to women: "As to the Knowledge I seem to have had of the Wicked Hearts and Actions of such Men as Lovelace, which engages your Wonder, I have always been as attentive to the Communication, I may say to the profligate Boastings, of the one Sex, as I have been to the Disguises of the other."[21] The difference between men and women is characterized as the difference between "Boastings" and "Disguises"; this odd attempt at a balanced opposition suggests the pervasiveness of the view that men and women must always be somehow paired and opposed. But if one member of the pair ceases to be a single entity—if it splits—"opposition" becomes less adequate as a way of defining the relation between entities; at the same time, "male" and "female" themselves are revealed as less complete, less natural, and less satisfying—as fragments, not wholes. Despite the apparent certainty and security with which Richardson claims to approach "the one Sex" and "the other," it is clear in his fiction that the very process of examining the constitution of either troubles both.

Thomas Laqueur argues for the origin in the eighteenth century of the notion that men and women are "opposite," a notion that marks a shift from a "one-sex / two genders" model to the belief that men and women belong to "two incommensurable sexes." According to Laqueur, "The notion, so powerful after the eighteenth century, that there was something concrete and specific inside, outside, and throughout the body that defined male as opposed to female, and provided the foundation for the attraction of opposites, was absent in the Renaissance."[22] In the "one-sex" model female "organs of generation" were simply inversions of male organs; creating a stable world in the face of this difference in degree (rather than in kind) required strict policing of *gender* differences.[23] The shift to the "two-sex" model, in which gender difference reflects organic difference, was not, however, absolute or conclusive, particularly in the course of the eighteenth century. Richardson's fiction can be seen as a proving ground or battlefield for this shift; the novels do much to test the conflicts both between and within the two models.

The intersection between the analytical categories of "sexual difference" and "constructions of gender," as well as the intersection between male and female, appears most prominently in Richardson's fiction through the motif of cross-dressing, through the presence of characters whose gender affiliation comes under attack or into question, through instances of cross-gender identification, and through signs of castration. The transgressions of gender illustrated by these heterogeneous but related manifestations signal anxiety about maintaining the purity of each gender—most of these crossings smack of violation—but they also at times reveal a powerful if fugitive longing for genuine transformation of sex and body, and for some way across a divide that seems artificial. This often positively inflected longing, it is important to note, is

principally gendered male, though the characters explicitly cas-
tigated for violating their gender roles are primarily female; in the
last novel, however, male sexual aggression is ambiguously punished by castration. Each novel, in fact, features a woman who is
perceived by the heroine as masculine and who is tinged with homosexuality; in *Pamela* and *Clarissa* the diabolically maternal Mrs.
Jewkes and Mrs. Sinclair are deeply implicated in the rape or attempted rape of the heroines, while in the considerably less
fraught world of *Sir Charles Grandison*, hearty Miss Barnevelt
briefly and openly expresses her desire for the heroine, Harriet Byron. Mrs. Jewkes and Mrs. Sinclair, for their violations of gender
role, invite a revulsion and horror that are in excess of the response
to their actions against the heroine. Their "unnatural," "deviant"
behavior makes them almost more horrific to their victims than
are the rapists, actual or potential, themselves. The representation
of these characters serves as veiled warning to women of the consequences of taking on masculinity, and offers them as scapegoats
and covers for the transgressions of male characters.

Same-sex desire is expressed directly primarily by women in
the novels, and by women who are masculine in one way or another.[24] In *Pamela*, where Mrs. Jewkes initially appears as a kind
of masculine monster, the reassertion of gender proprieties and the
return of Mr. B to ownership of his desires eventually make Mrs.
Jewkes, like Miss Barnevelt in *Grandison*, merely a ridiculous
anomaly. The link between gender transgression and same-sex desire, represented as inevitable and perhaps constitutive for these
women, is broken in the cases of the male characters.[25]

Although the boundaries of femininity are more explicitly and
heavily policed in the social sphere than are those of masculinity,
transformations in one gender are also linked to the other, so that
both masculinity and femininity are involved in any gender
transgression. Male characters seem, on the face of it, to be allowed more sartorial freedom and freedom to experiment with
gender than are female characters; the instances of male cross-
dressing in the novels, whether actual or imaginary, have an ambiguous but often powerfully generative effect. The meanings of

these various gender transgressions depend partly on the gender of the transgressor, but in addition the presence of gender crossing as an integral component of Richardson's project—the overlap between Richardson and Lovelace as men identifying with women, most notably—controls the way particular forms of gender transgression appear in the novels. The erotic and sometimes sadistic component of male cross-dressing and disguise is certainly frowned on, but male cross-dressing itself, interestingly enough, is not explicitly proscribed as unnatural, and its ties to homosexuality are either ignored, denied, or displaced onto such figures as Mrs. Jewkes. Lovelace's identification with women, which has a floating relationship to his disguises and imaginary cross-dressing, is the most complex of these various crossings, as well as the one that most involves Richardson himself. This association between Lovelace and Richardson almost ensures that Lovelace's employment of gender crossing will eventually be punished; Richardson must finally detach himself from his hero/villain. Lovelace uses cross-gender identification as a conscious tool to gain power over women, but, for a variety of reasons, this willful form of gender transgression rapidly evades his control, not only opening him to the power Clarissa wields, but sapping his own "imperial" will. This slippage occurs in part because of the implications that gender transgression has for sexuality.

Although such male transgressions of gender may initially be figured as fruitful—a method of gaining, not losing—and female transgressions simply anathematized, Richardson's last novel, *Sir Charles Grandison*, offers a kind of fantasied closure to these transformations. The novel presents a violent transformation of the male body, a transformation that epitomizes lack of control, lack of will, and, simply, lack: castration. Castration is not a gender transgression in the same sense as are the other examples I have been sketching, but castration does, in a certain conceptual scheme, turn men into "women."[26] The price exacted for gender transgression comes to overlap the price exacted for sexual transgression in this punishment; that is, these castrations punish sexual transgressions by enforcing a kind of gender transformation, while some of the gender transformations themselves call down violent punishments on the body, most notably in the case of Mrs. Sinclair and more equivocally in the case of Lovelace.

Sir Charles Grandison's query—"Can there be characters more odious than those of a masculine woman, and an effeminate man?" (3.247)—implies a balance and opposition between male and female transgressions of gender roles that Richardson's work itself seems to evade. The "masculine woman" is a far more important figure in these novels than is the "effeminate man," although femininity, I will argue, is present in some important form in the male protagonists of all three novels. The excoriation of masculine women, coupled with the intermittent celebration of male identification with femininity, suggests that the dangerous elements of masculine desire are being displaced onto women.

My approach to Richardson's work aims to demonstrate that the borders, frontiers, and crossing points reveal most about gender, and that the disruption of the categories of masculinity and femininity from within reveals most about sexuality. The individual discussions of the novels engage the questions of gender and sexuality through the examination of these border zones and disrupted categories, and through a form of (necessarily selective) close reading that tries to echo what might be called Richardson's close writing; it is, in part, Richardson's precise, almost disorientingly minute registering of the shift and flux of thought that allows the unsettled, unsettling nature of desire and sexual difference to emerge. That refusal to settle itself forms a recurrent theme; although for each of the novels I define a particular shape for the investigation of gender, in each case I also try to establish what gets left over, unabsorbed and unresolved. Some of the surfeit from each novel finds its way into the succeeding work, where it often supplies Richardson with the impetus to correct and redefine himself, but some remains intractable. That node of intractable material about the meaning of masculinity and femininity is one of the principal subjects of this study.

In a recent critique, Eve Sedgwick has pointed to "a damaging bias toward heterosocial or heterosexist assumptions" inherent in the concept of gender. She sees the bias as "built into any gender-based analytic perspective to the extent that gender definition and gender identity are necessarily relational between gender. . . . The ultimate definitional appeal in any gender-based analysis must necessarily be to the diacritical frontier between different genders."[27] One of the aims of this study is to demonstrate, through a reading of Richardson, the unstable and fictional nature of the construction of masculinity and femininity, and to show the fragility of their structural, definitional dependence on one another—thereby undermining and going beyond the contrastive (and heterosexual) model of gender.

In broad terms, it could be said that each of the following chapters seeks to investigate a particular turn of gender construction, and a particular mode of the reiterative story of sexual difference. The first chapter, on *Pamela*, looks at a problem in the constitution of femininity: the problem of duplicity. Because *Pamela* moves insistently toward a form of public rapprochement between opposing ideologies of gender and sexuality, my discussion calls on eighteenth-century discourse about those ideological positions to elucidate Richardson's project. The chapter on *Clarissa* shifts to a more intricate analysis of fantasies about sex and gender; in particular, I focus on the double reading of masculinity and femininity in the form of masculinity reading itself through the feminine. The final chapter, on *Sir Charles Grandison*, examines Richardson's attempt to solidify masculinity in the person of the "good man." Richardson's turn away from what engaged him in *Clarissa*—which is also a turn toward comedy, the consolidation of masculine power over women, and domestic harmony—returns him, in part, to the compromises of *Pamela*. After the intense tragedy of *Clarissa*, this last novel depicts a world where gender and sexuality are tied to the social sphere. But, as my reading makes clear, the reconstitution of domestic harmony in *Grandison* takes place only at the cost of considerable damage to the fluidity and daring that elsewhere characterize Richardson's investigation of gender and sexuality. *Grandison* may represent Richardson's most far-reaching attempt to solve the problems of gender, but the methods he uses only create the problems anew.

Pamela and the Duplicitous Body
of Femininity

Pamela is a novel split by Samuel Richardson's impulse to reproduce or mimic contradictory aspects of the ideology of gender, particularly the ideology of femininity. Its narrative is, in part, constituted by—and even promotes—the attributes of femininity it explicitly repudiates. The novel seems to set itself against hypocrisy and duplicity, as well as disruptions of gender identity, but it cannot do without them, perhaps because feminine duplicity operates as the perfect cover for masculine identification. In fact, feminine duplicity's transforming powers and numerous attractions pervade a novel that represents itself as the defender of female truth and virtue.

Duplicity, of course, is one of the cardinal sins in the traditional model of femininity that Richardson both employs and questions; it recurs as a basis for attacks on women throughout history.[1] Although the dichotomy between body and mind has been attributed to both genders, women have been seen as most duplicitously responsible for and most damagingly constituted by that split. In the Restoration and the eighteenth century, the accusations of feminine duplicity, while traditional in nature, also directly reflect contemporary concerns. Katharine Rogers sees the Restoration impulse to attack women's deployment of artifice as part of a more general "stripping away of idealization" arising from the "neoclassical emphasis on reason as opposed to misleading appearance and sentimental illusion."[2] According to Rogers, the examination of women's deceptive appearance revives the classical philosopher Lucretius's "conviction that, since romantic love is irrational, *no* woman's attractiveness can survive a keen analysis by reason";[3] Lucretius directs the man who would escape love to the dressing room, thus becoming a source of the "lady's dressing room" poems so popular in the Restoration and the early eighteenth century.[4] On the other hand, historians and literary critics have also seen in the course of the eighteenth century a movement away from the overt misogyny of using women to exemplify monstrous physicality and toward what has been called the "Cult of True Womanhood." This ideological change has been linked to women's presumed loss of productive work and an increase in leisure under capitalism, and thus to the new status of women as "consumers rather than contributors to the household economy."[5] Marlene LeGates argues, for example, that the idealization of womanhood enabled the shift to capitalism: "The idea of the morally superior woman contributed an ideological prop to the family seen as a means of social consolidation in an increasingly class-conscious society." Further, in its literary manifestation, according to LeGates, "the drama of the aggressive male checked by the virtuous female is paradoxically a reaffirmation of the patriarchal authority of the family."[6] Ruth Bloch describes the change in sex roles in terms of a movement from an emphasis on "differences in degree" in the sixteenth and seventeenth centuries, to a promotion of "differences in kind" in the eighteenth and nineteenth centuries. In the eighteenth century, she perceives an increasing separation of male from female imagery and activities, as well as a stronger contrast between male "rational" and female "affective styles."[7] These broad alterations in roles to some degree penetrate all levels of discourse, but at times the apparent transformations seem simply to reorient, rather than diminish, anxieties about women's deceitful display.

In the details of representations of femininity in the eighteenth century we can see over and over again the attempt to settle unsettling questions about duplicity. The meaning of the female body is reorganized and reshaped, but that body's uncertainty, its doubleness or multiplicity, repeatedly troubles representation. Richardson's works engage directly with this question, and *Pamela* is itself the problematic embodiment of a reinscription of its meaning. Nancy Armstrong depicts *Pamela* as a novel that alters the meaning ascribed to woman's divided nature; in Armstrong's reading, *Pamela* describes and promotes the rejection of the female aristocratic ornamental body—the female body as spectacle—in favor of the ideal of a woman whose "depths" were more valued than her "surface."[8] This change, says Armstrong, "redirects male desire away from the surface of the female body and into its depths."[9] But this presumably beneficial change, and Armstrong's depiction of it, depend on the same metaphors—the body as surface and the soul or metaphysical self as depths—that Armstrong suggests the eighteenth century was rejecting, the same metaphors that are used elsewhere to posit a disfiguring fault in the female subject.[10] In fact, the finding of value in "inner" qualities does not transform existing ideologies of femininity as much as it reinscribes them. In my view *Pamela*, as well as the reactions it provoked, illuminates instead a complex interaction and confusion between surface and depths, and evidences the persistent attractions of the body under the purportedly new ideology of femininity.[11]

To describe femininity in terms of surface and depths is always to employ a problematic metaphor, one that refuses the resolution it seems to promise. This irresolution arises in part because the female *body* is itself persistently represented as double both in its accretion of artificial, alluring surfaces and in its liability to transformation by age or disease; even the division is subdivided. If the female body is itself figured as being split between surface and depths, then this fragmented body ceases to be available as one of the two contrasting terms in the conventional dichotomy between body as "surface" and soul as "depths." The female body's multiplicity also disrupts the supposedly originary distinction between the sexes; one half of the original couple is already so fractured that it can only with difficulty be recuperated to unify a symmetrical pair.

These metaphors for women's bodies reproduce and support the accusations of duplicity to which women were so frequently subject; they explain the unsettling effects women seem to have by purporting to settle certain contradictions in the ideology of femininity. In the eighteenth century, thus, the hostility to feminine duplicity operates symbiotically with covert requirements that women behave in ways that could be construed as duplicitous; that is, women's behavior and bodies were supposed to provoke desire, but women were forbidden to provoke desire intentionally or to be conscious of their desirability. Thus the woman who is metaphorized in terms of surface and depths could easily be seen as the duplicitous agent of the division in herself. But metaphors that attribute multiplied bodies or selves to women tend also to reinforce anxieties about feminine abilities to cover and conceal a "true self" (or lack of self)—or a "true body" (or body's lack)—through arts of dress, cosmetics, and performance.[12] The metaphors themselves, as metaphors of doubleness, are always haunted by the ghost of duplicity and hypocrisy, the characteristic moral flaws of women.

What lies beneath—and the question of beneath what—is not only problematic in itself, but peculiarly resistant to representation, as a mid-century attack on women demonstrates:

Take [woman] as Nature made her *naked*, or look upon her stript of her borrowed Feathers, and she'll be but little amiable, if at all; nothing desirable: She'll be, perhaps, rather an Antidote against Love. True Love is grounded on *Virtue*, not on these low, mean, sordid Outsides: Shadows, Vanities, Fooleries all! Ask *Travellers*, if you'll not believe me; they'll tell you, when they converse with Women, whose Custom is always to go naked as they were born; they have no amorous Fancies, no Desires, they rather loath the Thoughts of them, they detest a *Woman* as a *Beast*, shall I say! why they are so much alike, they scarcely make any Difference between them; so little are they provoked *by seeing all*. A laced Show, a Silk Stocking, or a rich Petticoat, will tempt thee more, and make thee mad, after THAT which they were not moved for when they saw Hundreds of them.[13]

This diatribe, which leaves the reader in the classic pose of the fetishist solaced by shoe, stocking, or petticoat, conflates two surfaces—body and clothing—apparently to contain the horror of absence in the female body. In this energetic description of revulsion it is not entirely clear whether the woman's body or her "borrowed Feathers" are the "low, mean, sordid Outsides." The passage gestures vestigially to virtue as what is ideally contained by the woman, but the nausea provoked by the undifferentiated nature of the female body swamps the passage, receding only with the return of the gaze to clothing.

When metaphors and images of surface and depth—or any terms of doubleness—are used to describe women, the disorienting divisions can threaten to disclose the unstable relation of surface to depths. As a consequence, the use of these metaphors can ultimately provoke a restabilization that denies women depths or attempts to render invisible what has been revealed when a "surface" is removed and the depths uncovered. The long misogynist tradition that sees women as empty creatures of show attempts to clarify the relation of surface to depths by depicting women as hollow containers; there should be nothing left after the surface or clothing or makeup is peeled away. But as this passage shows, the nothing that is revealed can be extremely ambiguous.

Woman's duplicity underwrites—and undermines—other varieties of metaphorical language too. For example, when John Locke, in the *Essay Concerning Human Understanding*, compares women to eloquence, he does so in such a way that women's duplicity, their physical attractions—and masculine investment in both—seem as palpably present as eloquence itself: "*Eloquence*, like the fair sex, has too prevailing beauties in it to suffer itself ever to be spoken against. And it is in vain to find fault with those arts of deceiving wherein men find pleasure to be deceived."[14] This tendency of the female body to take over, to become an alternate subject, reinforces the sense of its deceptive powers.

But Locke's perception of man's pleasure in being deceived by the fair sex as much as by eloquence opens another path for the investigation of duplicity as well as offering an explanation for certain of the effects of *Pamela*. If some of the duplicities attributed to women, for example, are actually the product of masculine desire and identification, and not inherent, both sexual difference and duplicity change their meanings.[15] In Richardson's fictions, for example, the woman is produced to some degree by an imaginative transvestism on Richardson's part, which sometimes gives the effect of a masquerade. However, this masquerade, because it is seen as primarily an attribute of femininity, seems for many readers to revert to the female character who is its object, rather than originating in its male author. Feminine hypocrisy and duplicity are thus convenient fictions potentially covering masculine identification with femininity.

Although the ideology of sexual difference seems to require that masculinity and femininity be mutually exclusive categories, efforts to taboo and proscribe resemblances between the sexes show how pervasive and persistent the belief in such resemblances and identifications is. The eighteenth century produces innumerable examples of the taboo and its attendant anxiety. As a newspaper commentator in 1738 wrote: "There is nothing more observable than that the same Qualities, which are extremely decent and ornamental to one Sex, are very misbecoming and reproachful in the other, as it is encroaching upon the Boundaries, assign'd to each, for a proper Distinction and Discrimination between us."[16] Richardson himself at times tries to construct a utopian model of sexual difference as the basis for a symmetrical, reciprocal, and mutually responsive relation between men and women. But his novels' acuteness about the social realities of that relation, and the inherent contradictions between symmetry and hierarchy, identification and opposition, repeatedly break down these attempts, despite their narrative and ideological power. Like Richardson's own shifting statements of his origin as a writer, the representation of the "opposition" of the sexes founders on the multiplying fissures and crossovers in the two categories, male and female.

Masculine desire as the identification with the feminine has left its traces in the plot and action of *Pamela* as well as in its narration and authoring.[17] *Clarissa* articulates and thematizes this problematic aspect of desire;[18] in *Pamela* masculine desire as identification troubles the text and refuses assimilation. Richardson, in privileging his identification with the feminine, embeds his novels so deeply in his own duplicitous desires that they cannot break free.

The numerous readers who have attacked Richardson's heroine and his novel for hypocrisy, and who confuse text and woman, are not simply misguided; instead they are responding to the troubling confusions and contradictions in the novel itself. Even Fielding's attacks on Pamela's hypocrisy in *Shamela* are only echoes of similar attacks by Mr. B in the novel. But why should feminine duplicity in a work of fiction represent a threat, represent power, and thus provoke contempt? To accuse a woman or a book of hypocrisy, duplicity, and disguise is to pick up a double-edged sword; although the accusation seems primarily to denigrate and devalue women, it also attributes to the woman the power to repel investigation and penetration. If women are constituted by duplicity, there is no sure way to know when one has arrived at some kernel of "truth," or even if there is a kernel to find. The reading of the novel and/or woman as hypocritical and duplicitous derives from the text's refusal to give up duplicity's transforming and responsive powers. Feminine duplicity is too fruitful to abandon, and femininity is too closely intertwined with duplicity for Richardson to eliminate duplicity once its usefulness has ended. Feminine duplicity, among other allurements, allows masculinity a way to understand itself.

ॐ

The attractions of the veiled female body prop up and eroticize Edward Young's description of how woman should allow her wit to be "discovered" or uncovered by man:

> Naked in nothing should a woman be;
> But veil her very wit with modesty:
> Let man discover, let not her display,
> But yield her charms of mind with sweet delay.[19]

In fact, that metaphorical body eclipses the "charms of mind" that ostensibly concern the poet. Young covertly acknowledges the woman's planning and participation in the scenario of intellectual delights for the male voyeur, thereby making his pleasure dependent on her. Man's pleasure resides in the foreplay; those charms of mind, and the woman's submissive activity, seem to gain their value from the veil and from the delay in revelation, not from any inherent properties. But there is a paradox in the relation of surface to depths: The woman is not supposed to be naked in anything, but once her charms of mind are yielded up, will she not be unclothed?[20] Or does modesty remain a veil inseparable from the modest body?[21]

The problems suggested by this passage—problems of metaphors that turn into bodies, of the requirement of feminine unselfconsciousness joined to a masculine obsession with effect, of fruitful duplicity—inform as well much of the conduct literature of the late seventeenth and eighteenth centuries. If one reads the descriptions of feminine behavior in conduct books it is possible to glimpse the cultural machinery necessary to construct this duplicitous female body.[22] Such literature, like Richardson's fiction, provides a view of how a woman is imagined to construct herself under the ideological constraints of her culture. Dr. James Fordyce, for example, celebrates the ideal woman's management of contradictory traits: "There are not perhaps on earth many objects of more dignity or attraction than that female, who, though endowed with beauty, and skilful in dress, yet discovers nothing conceited on either score, no conscious attention to herself when taken notice of for either."[23] The ideal woman must not only construct herself for a vigilant—and perhaps capricious—male gaze, she also must not *see* herself as the object of the gaze she courts; her skill in dress must be unreflecting, her response to responses inattentive. John Gregory, in *A Father's Legacy to his Daughters*, directly confronts the problem for a woman of *seeming* to be modest while encouraging admiration, but he also explicitly justifies duplicity. Deliberate concealment lures the masculine imagination: "A fine woman shews her charms to most advantage, when she seems most to conceal them. The finest bosom in nature is not so fine as what imagination forms."[24] Gregory's analogy of the concealed bosom reveals the matter—reveals the body as well as the canny use of it—that other writers on feminine propriety themselves tend to gloss over; he engages in revelation pragmatically, in the service of his daughters. In writing this *Art of Love* for women he openly describes what Mary Wollstonecraft attacked as a "system of dissimulation,"[25] but his openness is not unreflecting misogyny; rather than simply exposing or requiring feminine calculation he offers rules for its use, and does so by offering two viewpoints, one the woman's, the other that of the man looking at her.[26]

Gregory elsewhere reveals the tendency of masculinity to see itself reflected in the mirror of the retiring woman:

One of the chief beauties in a female character is that modest reserve, that retiring delicacy, which avoids the public eye, and is disconcerted even at the gaze of admiration. . . . When a girl ceases to blush, she has lost the most powerful charm of beauty. That extreme sensibility which it indicates, may be a weakness and incumbrance in our sex, as I have too often felt; but in yours it is peculiarly engaging.[27]

The absence of the desired sign—in this case, the blush—signals loss or lack. However, the loss belongs not to the woman but to her male observer; significantly, it leads the observer to consider his own resemblance to the blushing woman. The "masculine" woman, who no longer blushes, is not the object of the man's identification; the writer bypasses the obvious resemblance and identifies instead with the extreme sensibility of the (absent) girl who blushes under the gaze of admiration. The same quality, which in his sex is a "weakness and incumbrance," becomes in hers "peculiarly engaging." Gregory seems to express a kind of nostalgia for his sex's own renounced or emasculating sensibility, and to reorient that nostalgia as desire for the woman's vanished blush, the vanished woman's blush.[28]

Masculine investment in—and identification with—feminine wiles emerges repeatedly in these accounts; many desires are disallowed, but women's desire to seduce and entrap men is actually celebrated. Fordyce, in *Sermons to Young Women*, warns against open aggression, but covertly endorses the use of covert wiles:

To get into men's affections, women in general are naturally desirous. They need not deny, they cannot conceal it. The sexes were made for each other. . . . When you show a sweet solicitude to please by every decent, gentle, unaffected attraction; we are soothed, we are subdued, we yield ourselves your willing captives. But if at any time by a forward appearance you seem resolved, as it were, to force our admiration; that moment we are upon our guard and your assaults are vain.[29]

The man in this scenario offers himself up as ready, even eager victim, happily instructing women to capture him. He predicates all on his own sex's absolute desirability, but he also implicitly presents himself as a dupe; both strategies he attributes to women are tacitly assumed to be aggressive in aim, but the woman who triumphs conceals her aggressive intentions from her willing victim by masquerading as a submissive female. Although her purpose cannot be completely concealed from the penetrating man, because he already knows her purpose, she can deflect accusations of activity by not appearing "forward." Fordyce implies that femininity is duplicitous, but accepts that duplicity as the price voluntarily paid by men for women's submissive focus on their desires, desires that may themselves partake of a version of femininity.

The effect of inversion or parody in Fordyce's identification with the feminine is explicit in the description of female "force" and "assaults," and male "captivity" and "yielding," culminating in oblique descriptions of the guarding of a masculine citadel. Fordyce first plays the compliant woman, seduced by (feminine) wiles; but as soon as the seducer reveals her aggressive wish to capture/captivate him, he turns into a retreating virgin. This fantasy of seduction seems to show the two figures contending for the feminine position; Fordyce's woman fails to seduce when she ceases to conceal her presumed masculinity and aggression. Fordyce's sexual scenario briefly allows both men and women to be feminine, though it forbids overt masculinity to women.

Joan Riviere defines "womanliness" as something that "could be assumed and worn as a mask, both to hide the possession of masculinity and to avert the reprisals expected if she was found to possess it." Riviere questions the distinction between "genuine womanliness and the 'masquerade,'" seeing them as identical.[30] If femininity is a mask, it is "a mask, behind which man suspects some hidden danger,"[31] and it is, for a woman, a dangerous tool that can be turned back on her in the form of accusations that she is duplicitous, hypocritical, or a usurper of masculine prerogative. Luce Irigaray offers "mimicry"—her subversive version of the masquerade of womanliness—as a strategy that, through "playful repetition," can make visible "the operation of the feminine in language."[32] Whether femininity as masquerade hides masculinity or conceals what Irigaray calls "the feminine in language," it seems to be associated with concealment and duplicity, thus, strangely but consistently, containing its opposite.

Femininity as masquerade destabilizes sexual difference by threatening to reveal the possibility of cross-gender identification.[33] In fact, in a move that reveals the need to contain the threat perceived behind the masquerade, a woman's impropriety is characterized as femininity's perverse "opposite," female masculinity. Fordyce gives a picture of the unnatural woman: "Paint to yourself, by way of contrast, a woman who talks loud, contradicts bluntly, looks sullen, contests pertinaciously, and instead of yielding, challenges submission. . . . How forbidding an object! Femininity is gone: Nature is transformed: Whatever makes the male character most rough, and turbulent, is taken up by a creature, that was designed to tranquillize and smooth it."[34] Lack of submission in a woman deforms nature and overturns sexual difference, threatening all by unnaturally mingling genders. The focus on feminine transgression polices both male and female gender roles because the two are represented as reciprocating, but women are held responsible for initiating the dislocation. Richard Allestree, in *The Ladies Calling*, laments women's

virile Boldness, which is now too common among many even of the best Rank. Such a degenerate age do we now live in, that every thing seems inverted, even Sexes; While men fall to the Effeminacy and Niceness of women, and women take up the Confidence, the Boldness of men. . . . Nor is that {i.e., women's boldness] design'd to terminate in it self, but it is to carry them on, till they arise to a perfect Metamorphosis, their Gesture, their Language, nay somtimes their Habit too being affectedly masculine.[35]

The enabling dream of symmetry is disturbed; the woman's meta-morphosis disrupts and interrupts the circuit of mutual dependence by mirroring back a distorted parody of masculinity rather than the desired endorsement, complementarity, and support. The masquerade of femininity induces fears that femininity, when exposed, will contain a lurking masculinity. Careful control and constant vigilance are needed to keep femininity from straying into masculinity's province—because that is where it came from.

Duplicitous femininity will always evade control because not only are the metaphors of the body that support accusations of it fragmented, but so is the body itself; the female body's multiplicity refuses assimilation to the binary oppositions in the service of which it is invoked. Once femininity's doubleness is extolled for its ability to provoke pleasure or to create identification, the woman's power to use duplicity—her body's multiplicity—for her own ends has been set in motion and cannot be recalled. Thus the need to scapegoat feminine duplicity alternates and combines with the desire to invest it with transforming and magical powers.

Richardson's personal involvement with feminine duplicity emerges in his accounts of early epistolary masquerades, first at the age of eleven when, "assuming the Style and Address of a Person in Years," he wrote a moral expostulation to a flighty widow, and later, at thirteen, when he wrote love letters for young women in his neighborhood. Richardson presents these imitations of the voices of others as (another) buried genesis of his career as a writer, and as a source for his knowledge of the human heart. Mimicry and performance thus link Richardson to Pamela; to some readers, however, femininity's disruptive duplicities mar both writers, and the perception of the duplicity of one is used to attack the duplicity of the other. Pamela as character has been called an "artless miss" with "a Machiavellian side" and concealed goals. According to Bernard Kreissman, who catalogs and contributes to the attacks on *Pamela*, "An attentive reading of the novel reveals behind the Pamela who minces across its pages the Shamela whom Fielding exposed."[36] The anonymous eighteenth-century author of "Critical Remarks on Sir Charles Grandison, Clarissa, and Pamela" remarks that "Pamela is a pert little minx whom any man of common sense or address might have had on his own terms in a week or fortnight."[37]

Both Kreissman and the anonymous writer are responding not only to the formal problems created by this particular first-person narrator but also to effects engendered by the project of representing femininity.[38] Kreissman offers *Shamela* as the correct reading of *Pamela*—Shamela as the truth about Pamela—but he does so in terms that uncover something other than he seems to intend. Using the language of undressing as sexual exposure and humiliation, Kreissman says that Fielding "exposes" the Shamela inside the "mincing" Pamela. In contemptuously claiming that he or any other man of common sense and address could succeed where Mr. B so signally failed, the author of "Critical Remarks" also proclaims what is essentially a wish to penetrate a text. This eagerness to expose, penetrate, or triumph over Pamela (or *Pamela*) suggests that woman or novel poses a threat that requires exposure and redress.

To defuse and avoid some of the problems these readings raise, formalist critics have focused their discussions of the novel on issues of narration. This shift away from exposing the duplicities of the novel produced far more interesting analyses of the novel than seemed possible before, but until recent feminist and materialist criticism of the novel emerged, it has also tended to obscure both the sexual and political threat, *and* the uneasy analysis of femininity, that *Pamela* does offer.[39] Both Kreissman's pleasure in observing Fielding's exposure of Pamela as Shamela, and the anonymous critic's faith that he could easily seduce Pamela, respond to something disturbing about the novel. Kreissman aligns himself with Fielding against Pamela/Shamela, and the anonymous critic pushes aside B; both men identify with another man's desire in order to defuse what they interpret as a feminine threat.

The anti-*Pamela* literature sees the relation of Richardson to his heroine, for example, as an obvious but perverse self-reflection.

For Kreissman, "Richardson in telling the story of Pamela un-wittingly has given us a self-portrait. He is a Pygmalion whose Galatea is modeled on what he perceives in the mirror of his own vanity; he invests her with his complete repertoire of virtues, she is his own reflection, his alter ego. The result is not only the por-trait of Pamela but also of the man."[40] Kreissman quotes Aurelien Digeon's parallel observation: "One feels that his view of the world is the same as hers, narrow and conventional. In painting her he has laid bare the secret of his own soul."[41] Covertly present in these attacks is the belief that Richardson's identification with Pamela renders his representation of her morally reprehensible, not only because he himself is morally reprehensible, but because he has transgressed the boundaries of gender. Richardson's novel becomes a perverse spectacle of a man looking in the mirror and seeing himself as a woman, or pretending to be a woman, or seeing the woman in himself. None is acceptable.

Richardson's supposedly too close relation to women also ap-pears in the conventional contrast of Richardson's "femininity" with Fielding's "masculinity." For example, Martin Battestin says that while the relation between Richardson and Fielding "could hardly be called a marriage . . . from the rude and often hilarious conjunction of Richardson's feminine sensibility and Fielding's robust masculinity, the modern novel was born."[42] This account figures the birth of the novel (in *Shamela* and *Joseph Andrews*) as the result of a generative sexual assault on Richardson's receptive and vulnerable "sensibility." Battestin's slighting analysis not only devalues femininity itself, it evidences distaste for the ap-parent presence of both sexes in one body (of writing). Thus gen-der confusion seems to be part of *Pamela*'s very constitution, be-cause part of its author's constitution. There is a strong sense that Richardson, by the fact he has written a novel under cover of fem-ininity, has already created a kind of scandal.

The disruptive effects on readers of the novel's problematic gender and its connection with feminine duplicity are reflected in early praise of *Pamela*. In celebrating *Pamela*, these writers find themselves unable to extricate surface from depths, body from text, or author from heroine. The relation of surface to depths— and of woman to text—gets out of control in the discourse. In one of the laudatory passages with which Richardson prefaced the second edition of *Pamela*, William Webster focuses on the transparency of Pamela's language. Pamela, he says, "pours out all her Soul . . . before her Parents without Disguise; so that one may judge of, nay, almost see, the inmost Recesses of her Mind. A pure clear Fountain of Truth and Innocence, a Magazine of Virtue and unblemish'd Thoughts" (p. 7). In a novel so vigilant about the surveillance and penetration of the female body, this picture of the mind is necessarily tinged by the woman's body that supports it; other (gendered) recesses are inevitably suggested by those Webster cites. Webster's relief at the absence in those recesses is instructive in light of the problem of the feminine masquerade; there is, in fact, nothing to see, only reassuring transparency. Webster urges Richardson to leave *Pamela*'s language simple, direct, and "natural":

I could wish to see it [*Pamela*] out in its own native Simplicity . . . and, should you permit such a murdering Hand to be laid upon it, to gloss and tinge it over with superfluous and needless Decorations, which, like too much Drapery in Sculpture and Statuary, will but incumber it; it may disguise the facts, marr the Reflections, and unnaturalize the Incidents. . . . No; let us have *Pamela* as *Pamela* wrote it; in her own Words, without Amputation or Addition. . . . The flowing Robes of Oratory may indeed amuse and amaze, but will never strike the Mind with solid Attention. (Pp. 7–8)[43]

"Amputation" sticks out like a sore thumb in this passage. The rest of Webster's language defends the natural text / natural body from the decorations that will "marr the Reflections" (ruin the didacticism and, perhaps, the book and woman as mirrors) by blocking the viewer's access to the body/text. But by proscribing "Amputation," Webster attributes to the body/text a phallic power that needs to be protected from castration. The invocation of sculpture and statuary also undermines Pamela's artlessness by let-

ting in through the back door the idea that *Pamela*/Pamela is a
nude and thus an art object, not self-created. Webster's whirling
metaphors confuse woman with novel, and radically confuse both
with the woman's body. Pamela in this passage becomes a statue
disturbingly come to life. The question of the text's sex—the need
to sex the text—troubles Webster's desire to praise the woman and
the novel for their transparency, their lack of duplicity.

Webster later counters his own celebration of *Pamela*'s naked
charms, valorizing disguise when he moves to define the novel's
artistic effects; when he moves, in fact, from feminine text to male
author: "Yet, who could have dreamt, he should find, under the
modest Disguise of a *Novel*, all the *Soul* of Religion, Good-
breeding, Discretion, Good-nature, Wit, Fancy, Fine Thought,
and Morality?" (p. 9). The (probably feminine) covering of
"*Novel*" here modestly falls away to reveal a plenitude of (presumably masculine) virtues. Rather than concealing "native Simplicity," here the (discarded) drapery or disguise sets off the attractions
of what it covers. The pleasure, like the pleasure in Young's cou-
plets, now resides in the power of unveiling the riches concealed
in a humble genre, and, it appears, the pleasure and power of finding the man behind, or inside, the woman—the novelist behind
the novel. The ultimate source of all the virtues Webster uncovers
is thus not Pamela, but Richardson: "Where, and how, has he [the
author] been able to hide, hitherto, such an encircling and all-
mastering Spirit. . . . The Comprehensiveness of his Imagination
must be truly prodigious!" (p. 10). Richardson as the invisible,
omnipotent, and masculine creator, whose gaze penetrates reader
and character, but who himself remains unknowable and unknown, is the reassuring final source and image of the artlessly
artful woman. The voyeur who sees into Pamela's recesses does not
find the woman's body (which might reveal either reassuringly or
threateningly that there is nothing there to see); instead he comes
before the mystified, disembodied presence of God the author, a
presence that encircles and masters reader, text, and woman. Webster makes Richardson the *deus ex machina* of the novel, showing
him in control of the seductive body of the woman and the text.

But the narrative voice seems always to be subverting that transcendence by its refusal to be disembodied and by its inseparability from the metaphors of the body.

Richardson invokes duplicity and hypocrisy in his representation of Pamela. Although these terms, along with disguise, are repudiated by Pamela and by the novel's support of her honesty, Pamela's constitution of her self is shown as directly dependent on forms of duplicity and disguise.

When, early in the novel, Pamela decides she will have to return to her family, she prepares for her departure by dressing in clothes "fit for [her] Condition" as a daughter of the Andrews family:

There I trick'd myself up as well as I could in my new Garb, and put on my round-ear'd ordinary Cap; but with a green Knot however. . . . A plain Muslin Tucker I put on, and my black Silk Necklace, instead of the *French* Necklace my Lady gave me, and put the Ear-rings out of my Ears; and when I was quite 'quip'd, I took my Straw Hat in my Hand, with its two blue Strings, and look'd about me in the Glass, as proud as any thing.—To Say Truth, I never lik'd myself so well in my Life. (p. 60)

This description can be read as a spectacle that breaks down the coherence of the narrative in order to create a picture, or what one critic disparagingly calls "a fashion plate."[44] But Pamela herself fixes the scene as an illustration by framing herself in the mirror. Pamela's assumption of her role as country girl partakes of the masquerade of femininity in Luce Irigaray's sense, in part because her transformation—what the motherly housekeeper Mrs. Jervis calls her "metamorphosis"—is both playful and powerful.

Annette Kuhn suggests that "clothing as performance threatens to undercut the ideological fixity of the human subject," and particularly the fixity of gender.[45] Pamela's disguise of herself as the country girl disrupts her identity and is later echoed by Mr. B's transvestite disguise as the maidservant Nan. Mrs. Jervis and Mr. B both fail to recognize Pamela in her country garb, and B then takes her (or pretends to take her) for Pamela's perhaps more amenable, more natural, rural sister. When that game ceases to amuse and he "recognizes" her as Pamela, he asks: "Who is it you put your Tricks upon? I was resolved never to honour your Unworthiness, said he, with so much Notice again; and so you must disguise yourself, to attract me, and yet pretend, like an Hypocrite as you are" (p. 62). Mr. B accuses her of the linked transgressions of disguise and hypocrisy, assuming, characteristically, that her self-transformation must be in the service of her desire for him. Pamela repudiates the accusation of disguise and hypocrisy, but she lets slide the question of desire:

I was out of Patience, then; Hold, good Sir, said I; don't impute Disguise and Hypocrisy to me, above all things; for I hate them both, mean as I am. I have put on no Disguise—What a-plague, said he, for that was his Word, do you mean then by this Dress?—Why, and please your Honour, said I, I mean one of the honestest things in the World. I have been in Disguise indeed ever since my good Lady, your Mother, took me from my poor Parents. (p. 62)

Pamela's response to B's attack itself evades not only desire but other aspects of the problem of disguise. Essentially she makes a claim for the present honesty of her dress, but bolsters that claim by making disguise a property of her past. The rhetorical value of disguise is greatest when disguise is being removed. The "real," undisguised Pamela stands before Mr. B; the other version has been the creation of external forces, specifically B's mother, whose clothes she has been wearing. (Thus, even the disguise she admits to has a female filiation.) The earlier embodiment of "Pamela" does not thereby become false, but the emphasis is wholly on the validity and truth of the present version. Disguise is thus displaced into the past, and onto clothing, away from the female body itself onto something that can be put on and taken off.

In fact Pamela is making a claim for self-definition and self-representation, even though she anchors this claim in her identity as the daughter of "poor Parents." If she can choose to represent herself in her "round-ear'd Cap," she can define her clothing's use rather than being defined by it. The eighteenth-century fear that clothes were ceasing to function as a reliable guide to status, and especially to status and virtue in women, is here confronted through a reversal. The usual anxiety was that women servants, in wearing the cast-off clothes of their mistresses, were becoming indistinguishable from their mistresses. Pamela rejects her mistress's clothes in favor of those she has made herself, apparently following society's edict against sumptuary presumption, but she is actually using clothes as a part of a performance. Although it is a performance as herself, the meaning of that self has been put in doubt. While Terry Castle sees costume as ideally representing "an inversion of one's nature,"[46] it is clear that here Pamela's "costume" is actually a kind of double reversal—it underlines and almost parodies the "poor Pamela" who has no power except in her virtue.

In rejecting clothes given her by Mrs. B in favor of clothes that she herself has made, Pamela marks her repudiation of a role because of its sexual danger, but her pleasure in herself and her appearance shows that this rejection is not a renunciation of her own body. Since she does eventually replace her mistress Mrs. B, Pamela's repudiation of Mrs. B's clothing is a step on the road to becoming her own version of Mrs. B. But that move takes place, to some extent, on her own terms; she is, of course, rejecting the clothes partly because they are conveyed to her by Mr. B. The "stockens" of his mother that B gives Pamela in the first pages of the book are transformed by passing through his hands into emblems of sexual commerce; by asserting her control of clothing she refuses B's version of the relations between the sexes and the classes.[47]

Pamela's control of the masquerade remains explicitly in the service of family and virtue—it is not a naked assertion of her own independence. The fact that Pamela "disguises" herself in order to resist Mr. B's sexual encroachments also underscores the novel's claim that she manipulates her image for heroic and necessary reasons, not because she is duplicitous. But Pamela's pleasure in her garb is so clearly superfluous to these claims that the claims begin to seem to excuse rather than justify.

The novel asserts Pamela's lack of hypocrisy all along, even while showing the heroine engaged in equivocal transformations of self. But *Pamela* also ritually expels hypocrisy, only to represent its irrepressible return. In fact, Richardson seizes the return of hypocrisy as an opportunity to reorient Pamela's disguise so that it can be shown to serve masculine authority and patriarchal power as well as to demonstrate the ambiguous reformation of that power and authority.

In the last half of the book, for example, Mr. B's sister arrives to see for herself what her brother has been up to. Lady Davers encounters Pamela, who is now (secretly) married to B, and she attacks Pamela by accusing her of theatricality: "And I'll warrant, my little Dear has topp'd her Part, and paraded it like any real Wife; and so mimicks still the Condition!—Why, said she, and turn'd me round, thou art as mincing as any Bride! . . . Pr'ythee, Child, walk before me to that Glass, survey thyself, and come back to me, that I may see how finely thou canst act the Theatrical Part given thee!" (p. 322). Like B when he sees Pamela in her country apparel, Lady Davers wants Pamela to acknowledge her duplicity; Lady Davers thinks she can effect this acknowledgment if she forces Pamela to confront her image *as image* in a mirror. Lady Davers assumes that the mirror's revelatory properties will strip away Pamela's artificiality and artfulness, and that Pamela will be unable to sustain her performance once it has been exposed as a performance. Pamela's earlier appropriation of the mirror's power suggests that this attempt at exposure is doomed to fail, although it now becomes clear that Pamela is no longer just performing the part of her "self," because the construction of that self is dependent on others' definitions of her. Lady Davers's wish to catch Pamela out in her lines—to disrupt the performance—clashes with Pamela's own positive sense of being something she does not appear to be, of embodying not a shameful but a triumphant doubleness: "If, said I, to attend your Ladyship at Table, or even kneel at your Feet, was requir'd of me, I would most gladly do it, were I only the Person you think me; but, if it be to triumph over one who has received Honours, that she thinks requires her to act another Part, not to be utterly unworthy of them, I must say, I cannot do it" (p. 323). If Pamela were single (in both senses of the word), she would do what Lady Davers requests, but since she is Pamela B or Pamela *and* B, she would be falsifying herself and devaluing B to accede to those demands. Pamela asserts that her identity with and her indebtedness to B control her actions, and that therefore Lady Davers has no power over her. Earlier, in the scene of the country garb, Pamela has identified herself and her virtue with her parents against B, but she now identifies herself with the newly reformed Mr. B against Lady Davers, who herself now speaks for B's apparently disowned family (and class) pride. Thus doubleness is again valorized; the terms used to castigate women are converted by Pamela, and by circumstances, into praiseworthy qualities. The covert possession of masculinity in the feminine masquerade may have ominous implications for women, but here the possession *by* the masculine—Pamela's marriage to and identification with B—is presumed to create an untroubled pairing in Pamela herself, and thus to defuse duplicity's threat.

The structure of this scene recalls Webster's description of Richardson as the effaced masculine power behind the feminine text; Pamela's feminine theatricality can also be peeled away to reveal Mr. B's "all-mastering Spirit" and to produce a similarly reassuring effect. B's presence as an aspect of Pamela calls up notions of theatricality and doubleness but assimilates them to a male figure. This masculine presence in feminine duplicity suggests that Richardson's own investment in Pamela may not be a simple matter of a male author seeing himself as a female character, as Bernard Kreissman suggests when he describes Pamela as Richardson's "own reflection, his alter ego." In fact, Richardson's relation to his heroine seems often to be represented in the novel through the relation of B to Pamela; the relation appears sometimes as B's identification with Pamela and sometimes as Pamela's identification with B.

With his conversion B ceases to perceive Pamela as duplicitous and hypocritical, but Lady Davers briefly takes over his position. Accusations of duplicity and hypocrisy retain a place in the novel, but Lady Davers, not B, makes them. In her mouth the accusations become ludicrous, almost farcical. Although Lady Davers continues for a while to reproach Pamela for her duplicity, she then replays in miniature B's conversion to Pamela-worship. As in B's conversion, Lady Davers moves from total opposition to Pamela to a desire to be a part of Pamelism, to be a Pamelist.[48] Duplicity and hypocrisy are qualities—or accusations—that seem to be deeply embedded in the economy of the novel, and they consistently resurface in new permutations, often to be again banished. That the final accusation against Pamela of duplicity ends up in the mouth of a woman indicates its lessening force and its loosening grasp on the imagination.

Pamela's displaced duplicity continues to haunt the novel, a ghost that cannot be laid to rest; it finds a new home as the attribute of another character, a woman who functions (briefly) to threaten B's happiness with Pamela. Sally Godfrey, whom B has seduced, impregnated, and abandoned, seems to be the monitory example of what Pamela might have become, but she also seems to represent what some readers have thought Pamela is: a canny manipulator using her virginity to buy her way into the upper classes. Sally fails, Pamela succeeds, but it then emerges that even Sally is not quite the figure she seems to be; the schemer was Sally's mother, not Sally herself, and Sally has nobly repudiated whatever she might have gained from B by sailing to America and a new identity. Duplicity is thus further split between these two women; the mother schemes, the daughter weakly succumbs to desires and then suffers—although she escapes the usual fate of seduced maidens by escaping the country and leaving her own daughter behind. The effort to find a scapegoat, a woman who can fully embody the duplicity and masquerade of femininity, is again thwarted or diluted; Sally Godfrey's mother is not even a character in the novel. Duplicity and disguise must continue to circulate without being either fully embodied or fully expelled. Richardson seems to back away from possibilities, as if to settle on either would upset the delicate balance necessary to his project.

Sally Godfrey embodies Pamela's averted fate and thus heightens the value and the effect of Pamela's triumphant virtue.[49] Pamela also manages to fulfill what Sally (or her mother) dreamed of; and Pamela succeeds without trying, or without appearing to try. The novel seems to endorse the feminine vigilance and unconsciousness so central to the conduct books, but again the difference between the woman as hypocrite and the woman as ideal figure of innocence is obscured. Pamela's success, as much as her innocence in using her virginity and beauty, distinguishes her from Sally; but it is easy to see how the line separating the woman who performs for an audience without knowing it from the woman who consciously performs for that male audience can blur. But that line is effaced and crisscrossed in its inception—blurred by a masculine investment irreparably divided between judgment and identification.

Even a brief scene from one in the series of "attempts" Mr. B makes to seduce or rape Pamela illuminates the issues of feminine performance and masculine investment. Despite the scene's restricted compass, it elicited an extravagant attack in *Pamela Censured*, indicating the disorienting power of the double presence of masculinity and femininity in one figure, particularly when desire and the female body are at stake.

During this early "attempt," in which Mr. B tells Pamela she will be blameless if he rapes her, Pamela has such a hairbreadth escape that she leaves a bit of her dress caught in the door. She reports: "I just remember I got into the Room; for I knew nothing further of the Matter till afterwards; for I fell into a Fit with my Fright and Terror, and there I lay, till he, as I suppose, looking through the Keyhole, spy'd me lying all along the Floor, stretch'd out at my Length" (p. 42). Pamela portrays herself prostrate and unconscious—absent from the scene—while imagining Mr. B at the keyhole; she offers a glimpse of what her unconscious presence, stretched out on the floor, might look like to Mr. B. The syntax reinforces Pamela's double state; she at once experiences her prostration and reports the gaze that observes it. Tania Modleski describes the implications of what she calls the "Man-in-the-closet plot device" so frequently used in *Pamela*: "As readers we are at the same time with Pamela in her supposed isolation, and with Mr. B watching and judging her. We possess the guilty knowledge that Pamela must lack; we experience a split consciousness in order to be reassured that a whole one is possible."[50] But this scene, along with the responses to it, points to an effect more complex than the creation of a split consciousness in the reader and its suppression in the character. Pamela does not know she is being watched because she is literally unconscious, but she represents the gaze of the man watching her, and she represents her body under that gaze. Because Pamela is temporarily "absent" in unconsciousness, Mr. B's consciousness and gaze briefly supplant hers as the governing forces of the scene. But Mr. B, although he is here a watcher, is produced through—and subject to—Pamela's hypothesis of his presence, and he cannot be separated entirely from her. This lack of separation between Mr. B and Pamela can be reread in terms of a male identification with woman as spectacle. Mr. B here is not simply the voyeur of Pamela; he is identified with her through the medium of her voice. The man who identifies with woman as spectacle is himself constructed through the gaze of the Other, and is not in control of the gaze.

Pamela Censured responds to this brief scene with almost violent distaste. Richardson is the primary target of the attack, but in the course of defining the scene's effects, *Pamela Censured* (perhaps unwittingly) pays tribute to the disturbing power of the female body as spectacle: "And here the author (fearing lest his Male Readers should have no Entertainment . . .) contrives to give us an Idea of *Pamela*'s hidden Beauties, and very decently to spread her upon the Floor, for all who will peep thro' the Door to surfeit on the Sight."[51] *Pamela Censured* accuses the author of using his heroine as a spectacle for the greedy eyes of male reader-voyeurs, but itself supplies added details of that spectacle: "The Young Lady by thus discovering a few latent Charms, as the snowy Complexion of her Limbs, and the beautiful Symmetry and Proportion which a Girl of about fifteen or sixteen must be supposed to shew by tumbling backwards . . . has her Laces cut, and all the pretty little necessary Things that the most luscious and warm Description can paint, or the fondest Imagination conceive."[52] The discoverer of the "latent Charms" is, of course, *Pamela Censured*. Richardson does not dwell on Pamela's snowy limbs or on the symmetry and proportion of the body tumbling backwards onto the floor. But the body alone is not the determining element in the scene; the posture of the audience, placed at the keyhole, creates the pornographic effect: "How artfully has the Author introduced an Image which no Youth can read without Emotion! The Idea of peeping through a Keyhole to see a fine Woman extended on a Floor, in a Posture that must naturally excite Passions of Desire, may indeed be read by one in his grand *Climacteric* without ever wishing to see one in the same Situation, but the *Editor* of *Pamela* directs himself to the *Youth* of both Sexes."[53] Up until this point the reader has been male, a stand-in for Mr. B, subject to an uncontrollable drive to reproduce the scene. As the didactic claims of the novel receive attention, however, the audience becomes male and female, and feminine duplicity and masculine manipulation reenter the scene:

Therefore all the Instruction they can possibly receive from this Passage is, first, to the Young Men that the more they endeavour to find out the hidden Beauties of their Mistresses, the more they must approve them and for that Purpose all they have to do, is, to move them by some amorous Dalliance to give them, a *transient View* of the Pleasure they are afterwards to reap from the *beloved Object*. And secondly, to the young Ladies that whatever Beauties they discover to their Lovers, provided they grant not the last Favour, they only ensure their Admirers the more; and by a Glimpse of Happiness captivate their Suitor the better.[54]

Pamela Censured tries to resolve the brief confusion of Mr. B and Pamela by dividing the readers' responses along the lines of gender, but there is a residue that can only be taken care of by scapegoating that female figure, unconscious on the floor, as a duplicitous and canny user of her body. Pamela's unconscious self-exposure teaches young ladies deliberately to "discover" their "hidden Beauties" in order to captivate men. The exposure of the female body to the eyes of a voyeur seems inevitably to become the responsibility of the woman. *Pamela Censured* tries to rationalize and reorganize the scene by supplying additional voyeuristic details and by attaching to Pamela's consciousness the exposure that occurs in the scene. But this double move, which also includes an attack on the author, merely reproduces the uncertainty of the scene itself.

Richardson rings changes on the keyhole scene in an effort to settle the problems raised by the presence of B at the keyhole or in the closet. Late in the first novel, and again in the continuation of *Pamela*, Richardson transposes the scene to place Pamela herself at the keyhole. Near the end of Part 1 she observes B and Lady Davers through the keyhole, and in Part 2 she watches from her closet a reenactment of a scene from her past; her maidservant Polly and Jackey, Lady Davers's nephew (here called Mr. H, presumably to reinforce the parallel to Mr. B), appear in place of Pamela and Mr. B:

I heard a kind of rustling and struggling, and Polly's voice crying, "Fie—How can you do so!—Pray, Sir."

This alarmed me much, because we have such orderly folks about us; and I looked through the key-hole; and, to my surprise and concern, saw Mr. H.—foolish gentleman!—taking liberties with Polly, that neither became him to offer, nor, more foolish girl! her to suffer . . . the girl sometimes encouragingly laughing, as at other times, inconsistently, struggling and complaining, in an accent that was too tender for the occasion. (p. 186)

Polly, even more than Sally Godfrey, enacts Pamela's repressed hypocrisy; Polly is radically double-voiced, her behavior at odds with her speech, and her words at odds with her tone. She is the scapegoat for hostility to Pamela's social rise; she embodies precisely those characteristics of which Pamela must be shown to be free. Polly's hypocrisy also softens the novel's revolutionary edge and placates the forces of conservatism. Yes, it says, most maidservants (if not most women) are like that, but Pamela was not and is not.[55]

The scene's structure also defuses the narrative threat of the earlier voyeurism. Instead of Pamela's original position—complicit in the production of herself as the object of voyeurism—she is here a fully conscious observer whose revoked identification with Polly allows her an absolute moral superiority.

By displacing Pamela's hypocrisy onto this minor figure, whom she herself castigates, Richardson aims at reinforcing Pamela's untainted nature; by defusing the voyeurism of the keyhole scenes, he reinforces his narrative's untainted nature. But the resemblance between Pamela at the keyhole and Mr. B at the keyhole can easily backfire. Rather than inducing the kind of amnesiac reading that Richardson sometimes seems to aim at in *Pamela*, Part 2—that is, a reading that retrospectively grants Mr. B virtuous motives for suspect acts—the insistence on the virtue of Pamela's voyeurism suggests that Richardson's investment in scenes of voyeurism is not primarily moral or didactic.

The galvanizing effect of the original scene at the keyhole, registered by *Pamela Censured*, does not derive only from the spectacle of the disheveled, unconscious woman spread on the floor, or even from the possibility of viewing her through a keyhole. The excitement generated by this scene comes from the representation of Pamela seeing herself as a man would see her through the keyhole, itself perhaps the fantasy of a man imagining himself a woman being watched by a man.

In Mr. B's culminating attempt to rape Pamela, Richardson most explicitly confronts the conjunction of feminine duplicity and cross-gender identification. Richardson literalizes and embodies in Mr. B both the masculine identification with the feminine and the feminine duplicity that have been haunting the text. This embodiment—which is neither final nor complete—forms part of the same pattern as Pamela's positive assertion of her doubleness, a doubleness informed by Mr. B, when she confronts Lady Davers. Richardson seems to see the rapprochement of the opposing figures under the sign of patriarchy as the only way out of the double binds facing femininity.

In this scene Pamela is closeted with Mr. B, who wears the

clothes of the servant Nan, and with Mrs. Jewkes, whom Pamela sees as having an ambiguous gender and a perverse sexuality.[56] As the scene builds to its climax of averted rape, a complete dislocation of gender definitions seems to take place. This radical confusion enables the reorientation that follows; first, feminine alliances and the maternal are devalued and replaced by a movement toward the paternal. The paternal is represented initially by Mr. B's link with the idea of the Father, and then by Pamela's identification of B with her own father, whom he eventually displaces.

In her letter to her parents about the attempted rape, Pamela proleptically identifies herself as part of B by signaling her obedience to the rules of master-servant relations, rules she has elsewhere seen as broken by B's sexual advances. Pamela worries about the ethics of telling her "little history," since she perceives herself as no longer its sole owner: "Do you think *Nan* could hear me talk of my Master's Offers? No, no, said [Mrs. Jewkes]; she was dead asleep. I'm glad of that, said I; because I would not expose my Master to his common Servants; and I knew *you* was no Stranger to his *fine* Articles" (p. 175).[57] Solidarity with the master (her future husband) here begins to replace class and gender solidarity via a distinction between "common" and uncommon servants; Pamela will not expose Mr. B to his common servants, although she is content to describe his actions to Mrs. Jewkes as one who already knows them. While she worries about exposing B to himself, she is physically exposing herself to B. Pamela's disclosure of B's deeds thus explicitly parallels the exhibition of her body; in fact Pamela suggests that neither is actually a display if one has the right audience. But Pamela's "unconscious" exposure of herself to Mr. B recirculates the issue of feminine duplicity because, as in the keyhole scene, there are too many openings for the voyeurist: The man masquerades as a woman to be privy to a female conversation that endorses his desire by focusing on his desire; a woman undresses for the viewer's visual pleasure but without being aware (or without acknowledging) that she is doing so. The scene's covert fulfillment of the voyeur's desire is a force that the narrator's voice cannot abolish because the voice's body reproduces the voyeur's desire too precisely.

The letter Pamela writes to her parents about the attempted rape shows the effects of oscillation and double vision—the danger of duplicity. Pamela's narrative moves between her lack of knowledge at the time the scene occurred and her retrospective comprehension of events. But Pamela also fuses or confuses the moment of experience and the moment of writing. Richardson tries to enforce the distinction between the two moments as a way to protect Pamela's reputation, but it does not hold up. Because the situation of telling is presented as all female, Pamela's innocence is supposed to be protected; her belief that only women are present allows Richardson to claim she is free of coyness and coquetry. But while Pamela believes that she is telling her story to one female servant (Mrs. Jewkes) in the presence of another (Nan), she also implicitly conveys to the reader her later knowledge that her body and her story have created an enticing visual and aural spectacle for Mr. B. These two versions of the scene achieve a temporary suspension, with Nan / Mr. B as one Janus-faced figure and Mrs. Jewkes as another. Pamela's belief in Mrs. Jewkes's masculinity distracts attention from and displaces the fact that Nan *is* male. Mrs. Jewkes tends to take over Mr. B's position as sexual villain; part of the scene's sleight of hand involves the transfer onto Mrs. Jewkes of the most vicious aspects of Mr. B's desires.

As the scene reaches its culmination, gender becomes more and more significant because the interpretation of each gesture, each tremor depends on the sex of the performer. "Nan's" transformation from drunken maidservant to seducing master occurs in a landscape of shifting signs and shifting pronouns: "But, I tremble to relate it, the pretended She came into Bed; but quiver'd like an Aspin-leaf; and I, poor Fool that I was! pitied her much.—But well might the barbarous Deceiver tremble at his vile Dissimulation, and base Designs" (p. 176). At the moment when opposition—moral and sexual—seems to define Pamela's relation to B, the two are united in their trembling as well as, for an instant, in their gender. Pamela trembles to tell, and B ("She") trembles ambiguously with lust, anticipation, or, as Pamela retrospectively imagines, knowledge of *his* own duplicity. The bed contains three people, but they may be three women; one man and two women; one man, one hermaphrodite, and one woman; or two hermaphrodites and one woman.

Because sex and gender are in question, the gender of the audience also becomes an issue. Pamela wants to protect the paternal eye from certain kinds of sexual knowledge: "What Words shall I find, my dear Mother, (for my Father should not see this shocking Part) to describe the rest, and my Confusion, when the guilty Wretch took my Left-arm, and laid it under his Neck, as the vile Procuress held my Right; and then he clasp'd me round my Waist!" (p. 176). As the pronoun shift is completed—"Nan" consistently becomes "he" in the *description* before Pamela in the scene recognizes that "Nan" is Mr. B—Pamela tries to recreate for herself a female audience by excluding her father as reader. But this insistence on a female audience, specifically a maternal reading audience, merely presages the paradoxical reentry of the paternal; at the moment of her father's exclusion, the awful voice of God the Father at the Day of Judgment sounds: "Said I, Is the Wench mad! Why, how now, Confidence? thinking still it had been *Nan*. But he kissed me with frightful Vehemence; and then his Voice broke upon me like a Clap of Thunder. Now, *Pamela*, said he, is the dreadful Time of Reckoning come, that I have threaten'd" (p. 176). The shift from sexual threat to the invocation of patriarchal power takes place against the ground of a reshuffling or dislocation of gender. Pamela's virtue triumphs over Mr. B's transgressive desires but does so on the basis of Pamela's identification with B himself and with B's patriarchal power.

As B begins to align himself with Pamela—and Pamela with B—Mrs. Jewkes, who has been the other focal point of gender confusion, retreats into her "natural" state of servitude and into her "natural" gender.[58] Mrs. Jewkes almost literally shrinks; from the monstrously hermaphroditic and monstrously maternal presence of the novel's first half she becomes an overweight, vulgar, but essentially unthreatening female servant. Without B's mastery—and B's desires—inflating her, and without the burden of Pamela's search for a substitute mother, Mrs. Jewkes dwindles and becomes (uncomfortably) feminine and (awkwardly) servile.

Mr. B and Pamela begin to bridge their differences by turning away from the confusion of genders represented by Mrs. Jewkes, and by turning toward the father. This bridging allows a benign reading of sexual difference. The intervention of the idea of the father, and B's increasing identification with the figure of the father, signal the shift. Pamela begins to reassess Mr. B by using her own father as index and touchstone:

But sure, at least, he [B] must be sincere for the *Time*!—He could not be such a practised Dissembler!—If he could, O how desperately wicked is the Heart of Man!—And where could he learn all those barbarous Arts?—If so, it must be native surely to the Sex!—But, silent be my rash Censurings; be hush'd, ye stormy Tumults of my disturbed Mind; for have I not a Father who is a Man!—A Man who knows no Guile! Who could do no Wrong!—How then can I think it is native to the Sex? (p. 189)

B's disguise as Nan seems first to reveal and then dispose of the masculine body's own potential for disguise; and now B's link with Mr. Andrews again brings up, only to deny, the possibility of masculine duplicity. B's newly revealed sincerity is underwritten by Mr. Andrews's guilelessness, simply on the basis of their common gender and Pamela's desire. Pamela and B meet triumphantly as the former possessors of ambiguous and duplicitous bodies.

Although *Pamela* seems to offer the integration and transformation of male and female principles in the union between Pamela and B, the novel actually only reinscribes the problems it appears to have settled. In the first part of the novel, not only does Pamela embody a disturbing conjunction of masculine and feminine, and behave in ways that Mr. B can label as duplicitous, she also engages in activities that threaten to usurp masculine privilege. In the first part of the novel, for example, Pamela's letter writing provokes B's complaint that "you mind your Pen more than your Needle" (p. 55). Her letters even create a kind of paper pregnancy,

suggesting that she is self-fertilizing, capable of producing offspring without Mr. B:[59] "But I begin to be afraid my Writings
may be discover'd; for they grow large! I stitch them hitherto in
my Under-coat, next my Linen" (p. 120). Pamela here almost literally embodies femininity's fruitful duplicity; she conceals in her
clothing the material results of her resistance to Mr. B, keeping
"depths" of self-representation in a separable "surface" that is both
part of her and not part of her.

    Richardson attempts to "solve" the disturbing aspects of fem-
ininity and masculinity that *Pamela* brings up by shifting the
meaning of spectacle in the novel's second half. Mr. B's identification with Pamela as spectacle ceases to be a disruptive force in
her narrative when Mr. B begins to treat Pamela as a spectacle for
other people's voyeurism and admiration in the mutually reinforcing transformation of B and Pamela. For example, Mr. B presents
to his neighbors the edifying tableau of Pamela's reunion with her
father in a scene that requires Mr. B to exhibit authorial control
and a talent for stage-managing (pp. 249–50). B exhibits Pamela
to the others at a moment when her absorption in her emotions is
so intense that she becomes unconscious of her audience, just as
she was when spied upon from the closet or through the keyhole.
Through the realized presence of an audience and a (male) stage
manager Richardson seeks to separate those functions—and the
authorial function—from Pamela, who earlier seems to be author,
object, and audience. But Mr. B's new legitimacy as editor and
coauthor of the heroine's text, while it brings B's identification
with Pamela out from underground and out from its disruptive
place in her narrative voice, also reinforces Pamela's position as Mr.
B's representative. Masculine identification with the feminine essentially moves out into the open, to be celebrated in Mr. B's uxo-
rious displays of his wife's beauties and virtues. But this movement of masculine identification into the open, a movement that
seems to free the feminine from duplicity, actually depends on the
novel's continued investment in the feminine hypocrisy and duplicity that have constituted its narrative and its heroine.

    The consolidation of masculine and feminine seems at first intended to exorcise feminine duplicity and dissimulation, but the second half of the novel makes clear instead that Pamela, her body, and the body of her text have become integrated into the patriarchal family of Mr. B. Thus the self-display and putative deception so dangerous to Mr. B in the unmarried Pamela are transformed into positive attributes to be used in the service of the husband. Ellen Pollak describes the difference for eighteenth-century culture between the unmarried woman who uses art and the married woman who dissembles:

The very art of managing appearances—for which the coquette and prude are criticized—is actively encouraged in the wife. . . . As long as a woman subjected herself to social, legal, and economic dependence on a man by becoming his wife . . . conniving attempts on her part to gain advantage within the limits of that dependency were condoned. Dissimulation on the part of women was not only permissible when it remained interior to a masculine desire, but it was often necessary to sustain the desired relationships of power.[60]

Within the system of propriety Mr. B can now—and does—call on Pamela to serve his own (amended) desires, but Richardson presents Pamela's education in this new service as highly problematic. Richardson's recuperative plot attempts to show the reform and softening of the patriarchal family, but it refuses—or is unable—to eliminate the contradictions or the pain. When Mr. B lectures Pamela about her attempt to placate him on behalf of his sister, Pamela first reproduces his remarks and then reduces them to a list of rules that mimics the advice given by conduct books. B's requirements for a wife's behavior can barely be distinguished from requests for dissimulation:

Then I must have been morally sure, that she preferr'd me to all Men; and, to convince me of this, she must have lessen'd, not aggravated, my Failings; she must have borne with my Imperfections; she must have watch'd and study'd my Temper; and if ever she had any Points to carry, any Desire of overcoming, it must have been by Sweetness and Complaisance; and yet not such a slavish one, as should make her Condescension seem to be rather the Effect of her Insensibility, than Judgment of Affection.

. . . And if I was not always right, that yet she would bear with me, if she saw me set upon it. . . .

This would be so obliging a Conduct, that I should, in Justice, have doubled my Esteem for one, who, to humour me, could give up her own Judgment; and I should see she could have no other View in her Expostulations, after her Compliance had passed, than to rectify my Notions for the future; and it would have been impossible then, but I must have paid the greater Deference to her Opinion and Advice in more momentous Matters.

. . . That therefore she would draw a kind Veil over my Faults; that such as she could not hide, she would extenuate. (Pp. 367–68)

Pamela's list of "rules" derived from Mr. B's pronouncements suggests the ambivalence Richardson felt about the system he seems bound to uphold—not only for religious reasons, but perhaps because at this point he sees no alternative:

23. That a Woman gives her Husband Reason to think she prefers him before all Men. *Well, to be sure this should be so.*

24. That if she would overcome, it must be by Sweetness and Complaisance; *that is, by* yielding, *he means, no doubt.*

25. Yet not such a slavish one neither, as should rather seem the Effect of her Insensibility, than Judgment or Affection! . . .

30. That if the Husband be *set* upon a wrong Thing, she must not dispute with him, but do it, and expostulate afterwards.—*Good-sirs! I don't know what to say to this!—It looks a little hard, methinks!—This would bear a smart Debate, I fansy, in a Parliament of Women.* (Pp. 370–71)

The last rule in the list that Pamela thus internalizes should make them "all very tolerable": "That a Husband who expects all this, is to be incapable of returning Insult for Obligation, or Evil for Good; and ought not to abridge her of any Privilege of her Sex" (p. 372). Pamela concludes by telling her parents that "after all, you'll see I have not the easiest Task in the World," but she cheerfully proposes to do her best, believing she will not "willfully err" (p. 372). Pamela plans to submit, but her response to B's authoritarian designs—the tinge of mimicry and her faintly subversive commentary on the "rules"—suggests that she will retain a distance between her judgment and her behavior; her outward conformity will not always match her inward perceptions.

Feminine duplicity in *Pamela* is not simply produced out of the contradictory behavior of a modest eighteenth-century woman, although that model clearly contributes to the portrait; Richardson's novel further locates in masculine identification with women a source and a rationale for what is codified or categorized as feminine duplicity. The complaints many readers have voiced about the shadowy, uncertain representation of Mr. B, who seems at times less a character than a reflex of Pamela's consciousness, may derive directly from the effects of Richardson's invocation of a dynamic, reciprocal model of gender knowledge. That is, as he locates within the heroine's voice qualities and positions associated with masculinity, Richardson essentially excludes, for much of the novel, any but an indirect and partial depiction of the "hero." The last half of *Pamela* presents strategies of coping with this difficulty and of reasserting the clarity of gender difference. That reassertion requires the scapegoating of Mrs. Jewkes as avatar of gender instability and representative of the violence of male desire, as well as the rehabilitation of Mr. B through association with the figure of the beneficent father. This restructuring, which allows for a celebration of reformed masculinity and enables the marriage between Pamela and B, does not entirely succeed in erasing the evidence of gender trouble. Although Pamela has been triumphantly cleared of the sins of duplicity and hypocrisy, they continue to circulate in the novel, irrepressible and apparently unkillable elements of the eighteenth-century ideology of femininity.

"Like Tiresias":
Knowing the Sex in *Clarissa*

While congratulating himself on his successful plotting against Clarissa, Lovelace pauses to consider the sources of his intimate connections with women and with femininity:

But I was *originally* a bashful mortal. Indeed I am bashful still with regard to this Lady. Bashful, yet know the Sex so well!—But that indeed is the *reason* that I know it so well:—For, Jack, I have had abundant cause, when I have looked into *myself*, by way of comparison with the *other* Sex, to conclude, that a bashful man has a great deal of the soul of a woman; and so, like Tiresias, can tell what they think, and what they drive at, as well as themselves. (III: 106) (440–41)

The particular contours of the novel's fascinated analysis of masculinity and femininity are perfectly caught by this passage. In it, Lovelace moves easily between moments of identification and of differentiation. At once a voyeur comparing woman with himself, and the possessor of "a great deal of the soul of a woman," he plays with the definitions of gender. Identifying with women as a prelude to seduction or rape, Lovelace looks within to uncover what is female—like a woman—in himself, and in his comparison of interiors he names bashfulness as the link.[1] But the bashfulness that causes him to identify with women also encourages him to be the reverse of bashful with women; he uses self-inspection to promote the penetration of others. Lovelace displays—to Belford, to the reader, and to himself—his purported resemblance to women in order to represent his power over them as a natural, uninterrupted extension of self-knowledge.[2]

Lovelace asserts that his incorporation of masculinity and femininity in his own person gains him a privileged insight; he, "like Tiresias," knows women from inside and out. Lovelace's claims to special knowledge resemble Samuel Richardson's often celebrated insight into the female heart in his fiction. Although Richardson marks his own project as superior because morally justified, *Clarissa* is structured by two interpenetrating designs: that of Lovelace to "know" and display Clarissa for his own purposes, and that of the novel to know and display Clarissa for moral ends. The novel itself seeks to exhibit a complete, authoritative view of gender and sexuality at the same time it develops the case against Lovelace's imperial assertions of his intimate knowledge of both sexes. Richardson thus claims for his fiction and tries to give to his readers precisely that knowledge and power he denies to Lovelace—in particular, knowledge and understanding of Clarissa, the exemplar to her sex. But Richardson's project is mimed and mirrored by Lovelace's project; the endless examination of Clarissa's body and soul is performed as much by the novel as by Lovelace, so that the two enterprises, although their purposes are sharply at odds, blur and run together.[3]

It is, in part, the extent to which Lovelace shares the *details* of Richardson's identification with women that produces the novel's fascination and makes it both a minefield and a litmus test of issues of gender and sexuality.[4] The novel seems to offer an epic battle between the opposed forces of masculinity and femininity—and that, indeed, is how many critics have perceived it[5]—but Lovelace's predatory, incorporative desires and the images of division, self-division, and transformation instead reveal the extent to which the purportedly opposed forces are disrupted from within, as well as threatened from without by cross-gender identifications.

If *Pamela* presents a woman with a double voice, a woman who courts the dangers of duplicity, eventually speaking not only for herself but also for patriarchal power, *Clarissa* in contrast shows a

man with a double voice: Lovelace claims to speak for women, as
well as to be able to test the meaning and extent of femininity in
another. Although femininity—exemplary femininity under pressure—is the central subject of *Clarissa*, as it is of *Pamela*, in *Clarissa* the subject is, in part, mediated and undermined by that op-
positional male voice. This mediation produces a reciprocal analysis of masculinity, although masculinity's status as the "self" and
femininity's as the "other," in Simone de Beauvoir's terms, make
this analysis more circumstantial, less direct in form than the one
aimed at femininity. In some sense, Lovelace's obsession with the
meaning of Clarissa's sex and gender both justifies and produces
his interest in his own sex.[6]

As I have suggested in my discussion of *Pamela*, the woman
who incorporates a masculine voice while standing in opposition
to masculine desires seems to perform a potentially threatening or
irritating masquerade. But the threat that Pamela represents is
partly defused by her fully explored assent to masculine impera-
tives; when Pamela and B merge into a married couple under the
control of a reformed B, Pamela ceases to disrupt the social order.
In *Clarissa*, Richardson thematizes and reverses Pamela's problematic masquerade by producing a masculine figure who explicitly
seeks to incorporate femininity as well as to investigate it. Paradoxically, Richardson's most "masculine" protagonist is also the
man most overtly obsessed and influenced by femininity. While
readers of *Pamela* have characterized as "effeminate" Richardson's
identification with his heroine, a parallel structure, evident in
Lovelace's trials of Clarissa, is recognized as one of the later novel's
fascinations. By locating disguise, duplicity, and transformation
in the villain/hero, Richardson frees Clarissa from the accusations
of hypocrisy and duplicity that dogged Pamela, and apparently
frees the heroine's voice and body from the disruptive effects of
masculinity. But Lovelace's perverse investigation of femininity,
however much it is marked off from Richardson's celebration of
Clarissa, not only threatens the stability of Richardson's own enterprise by the resemblance of the two, it also introduces—or re-
introduces—the problems of gender and sexual difference that

Pamela attempted to solve through a reconciliation with the status quo. The transformation of Pamela's threatening duplicity into the approved doubleness of Pamela/B seems designed to ease or erase the problematic of femininity. But while *Clarissa* thematizes and foregrounds femininity in a new way, the novel's reintroduction of the problem in a new body and a new voice—Lovelace's— suggests femininity's importance and its insolubility for Richardson.

Clarissa offers a more complex and more explicitly theorized analysis of gender and sexuality than does *Pamela*. Lovelace formulates his trials of Clarissa as conclusive experiments on the nature of femininity and the female body; he both brings to bear on her his knowledge of women as a category and uses her to attempt to complete his understanding of that category.[7] And although Lovelace's purpose and presuppositions in this epistemological quest are anathematized, it is through his quest and his trials of Clarissa that Richardson attempts to reify femininity. Clarissa is exemplar of and to her sex; she functions as the quintessence of femininity and as an inimitable example, fitting into the category of woman, but transcending it. However, Clarissa thwarts the aims of Lovelace's experiments and disrupts Richardson's investigation of gender by complicating the category of femininity in the same way masculine identification with the feminine complicates the category of masculinity. Richardson's portrayal of the sexual opposition between his protagonists is thus repeatedly disturbed and reordered by the questioning of the categories that seem to underpin the struggle.

Richardson's investigations of gender in his fiction speak to concerns that appear in many Restoration and eighteenth-century discussions of the sexes; admonitions against crossing gender boundaries, intense scrutiny of the behavior proper to each sex, and the shoring up of barriers between the sexes are all strategies that underscore the crucial status of gender divisions—and signal anxiety about them. Policing of borders and margins in order to maintain distinctions, however, focuses attention on the meaning of those borders and margins.[8] The attempts to fix those borders, and to insist on the naturalness of the borders, tend, however, to distract attention from the constitution of the categories whose boundaries are being demarcated. Richardson's unironic interest in pushing his society's ideology—particularly gender ideology—to its limits goes beyond his culture's focus on the meaning of differences between the sexes, allowing his fiction to reveal implications of gender that otherwise go unexamined; this extremism also tends to disclose the meaning of ideology for individual psychology to a degree that the more conventional discourse of the seventeenth and eighteenth centuries does not.

Richard Allestree, in his immensely influential *Ladies Calling* (1673), declares the universality and necessity of distinctions between men and women:

All Ages and Nations have made som distinction between masculine and feminine Vertues, Nature having not only given a distinction as to the beauties of their outward form, but also in their very mold and constitution implanted peculiar aptnesses and proprieties of mind, which accordingly vary the mesure of decency; that being comely for the one Sex, which often is not (at least in the same degree) for the other.[9]

Allestree makes clear that both bodies and minds are inextricably bound by sexual difference; "outward form" ensures and enforces differences in the "very mold and constitution" of the mind. Violating those distinctions, in body *or* mind, thus violates Nature and disrupts the proper interaction of the sexes, as a 1738 article in *The Gentleman's Magazine* also warns:

The Distinction in each Sex of the inward Qualities of the Mind, and the outward Form of the Body, is the Ground and Foundation of their mutual Love and Affection: So that when either Man or Woman deviates from what is more peculiar to their own Sex, and approaches in any Thing too near the other, they must consequently become less amiable and pleasing to one another, the farther they have departed from their respective Qualities and Characters.[10]

Anxiety about maintaining distinctions is figured in terms of coming too near the other sex, which is equated with straying too far "from their respective Qualities and Characters." To approach in one sense is to deviate in the other; a woman who resembles men repels men, a man who resembles women repels women. Thus, both sexes detest the mixing of their own qualities with the qualities of the other, and that loathing guards "natural" desire from unnatural deviation.[11] Both sexes must maintain the position, inward qualities, and outward form given by nature, or nature itself is disordered. Even (or especially) the rakish writers strive to control or eradicate deviation; although they may not be bound by decency, they too believe that relations between the sexes depend on a stable system of sexual difference. By focusing on the body, however, the rakish writer reveals the fundamental disparity between desire for union and desire for difference. François Bruys speaks of intercourse as Nature's "Sport . . . in *dividing* us only to *join* us the closer again":

Men and Women separately considered, we may say, are but *imperfect* Creatures, and as it were only half of one another. The human Species is divided into *two* Sexes, and is not properly perfect, but in the Union of *both*. Nature has conferred on each Sex distinct Graces and Charms to allure the other, and by this reciprocal Communication of particular *Beauties*, consists the beautiful Order of *Nature*.[12]

While Allestree seems at least potentially interested in the independent qualities of each sex, the author of the 1738 article and Bruys both portray gender differences primarily as enticements in the service of heterosexual union. But the emphasis on "mutual Love and Affection" or "Union" undermines and colors the requirement for distinctions; union implies the loss or submergence of the distinctions on which it is grounded. This paradox informs both physical and metaphysical discourses on gender, and it is a paradox that *Clarissa* repeatedly engages, most notably through the character of Lovelace.[13]

Allestree, Bruys, and the journalist all imply they will divide their attention between the two sexes, but in fact the passages I have cited all appear in texts that "dissect" the *female* sex alone. Analyzing gender characteristically means to analyze women. The difference between men and women is the difference in women;

the fascination with sex is the fascination with what is so often called in the eighteenth century "The Sex." Although male "effeminacy" and degeneracy are attacked in the eighteenth century, sometimes with loathing and violence, even those attacks are often grounded in the sense that men are taking inferior habits from inferior beings. For example, Ned Ward, describing the "*Sodomitical* Wretches . . . who call themselves the *Mollies*," says they "are so far degenerated from all masculine Deportment, or manly Exercises, that they rather fancy themselves Women, imitating all the little Vanities that Custom has reconcil'd to the Female Sex . . . and to mimick all Manner of Effeminacy, that ever has fallen within their several Observations; not omitting the Indecencies of lewd Women."[14] Men sink to women's level, but women who take on male vices sink to the state of animals: as Allestree says, "Nothing human [is] so much beast as a drunken woman."[15] Examinations of masculinity tend, in this period, to be reflexes of examinations of femininity. But the ideological centrality of union, and thus, in particular, the focus on men's need of women, repeatedly subverts the attempt to maintain the division between the sexes and subverts as well the commonly held belief that masculinity can operate independently of femininity—that it can be the unexamined norm from which femininity deviates—or that it can be untainted by femininity. Thus, although Richardson's first two novels focus on their heroines, *Clarissa* becomes an analysis of masculinity through its analysis of femininity. As we will see in *Sir Charles Grandison*, when Richardson tries to represent masculinity directly in the portrait of the "good man," the disabling of feminine mediation actually tends to cut the reader off from the central character, if not from the entire novel.

Bruys' enthusiasm for the union of the sexes in intercourse, and the ideological problems that union creates, are repeated and embodied in another union of the sexes of interest to the eighteenth century—the hermaphrodite.[16] In *A Dissertation on Hermaphrodites* (1750), George Arnaud describes the disturbances of identity, particularly gender identity, that occur in a marriage of hermaphrodites:

But if divines are at a loss to decide under what kind they should rank the capacity of a subject, in whom they find the two sexes, how much more must they be so, when chance joins together in marriage two perfect hermaphrodites! This case is, indeed rare, yet it happened towards the middle of the last century in the kingdom of Valentia: two young persons were married, and very soon after they were both in the state of pregnant women; they were prosecuted as guilty of the most abominable crime; but Laurence Matthieu, a physician [changed to "a lawyer" in the corrigenda][17]as prudent as knowing, who was consulted on their score, at the moment they were carrying to the place of execution, in order to be burnt alive, decided in their favour, the church having given them the Power to be joined together, and to make but one body and one flesh.[18]

The two hermaphrodites, mirror images of doubleness, take the conventional models of union and "mutual Love and Affection" to their logical limits. This couple is in danger of execution for twice embodying deviation and performing perversion; their double, mirroring bodies are redoubled by pregnancy. Matthieu saves the two (four?) by reducing them to one; he punningly asserts that they simply literalize the doctrine that husband and wife are one flesh. The story is thus at once utterly outlandish—pure fantasy— and central; it portrays deviant bodies simultaneously as cursed and as incarnations of sacramental union.

The tales of hermaphrodites frequently carry messages about desire as well as about gender and sex; it is when love and, most notably, marriage occur that hermaphrodites come under the public gaze.[19] Arnaud's story of two hermaphrodites marrying and impregnating each other not only exposes a superfluity of sex organs, it allows a mystified and displaced view of same-sex desire. Masked by the doubled heterosexual union that the double pregnancy implies are the figures of two men in love with each other, or two women in love.

The hermaphrodite and other figures of myth and fantasy incorporate and materialize the contradictory desires that psychoanalysis sees at the heart of sexuality. Lawrence Kubie, for example, argues that the wish for "magical bodily change" is present to some degree in all sexual activity, and that sexual activity always offers the fantasy of gender transformation.[20] Although sexual intercourse seems to promise the experience of a radical difference between the sexes, Kubie suggests that fantasies of being both sexes may counteract or cancel the "evidence" of the senses. This argument implies that the enforcement of differences between the sexes will always be undermined by desire for sexual union; further, the artificial enforcement of difference as a constituent aspect of desire may always be in danger of collapsing under the pressure of identification with the desired one. These tensions between identification and desire necessarily complicate the model of "natural" heterosexuality.

The implications of these duplicitous or contradictory desires—manifested in Lovelace's wish both to identify with and to possess women—permeate the text of *Clarissa*. With its correspondences between a pair of women and a pair of men, its mirroring repetition of scenes from the perspective of heroine and hero, the form of the novel replicates and reinforces the concern with the construction of gender and the performance of sexuality. Attention to gender and sexuality emerges in discourse and action, and through the representation of the interaction of male and female bodies and masculine and feminine minds. Yet *Clarissa*, even more than *Pamela*, presents distinctions between the sexes as shadowed and disrupted by differences *within* each sex, as well as by the fundamental paradoxes of gender identity and sexuality.

Clarissa and Lovelace do not simply represent femininity and masculinity—each is seen as extraordinary in relation to others of his or her own gender. For both of them and for the novel that contains them, gender is a central category; each character defines himself or herself and the other in terms of gender and in terms of sexual difference. Lovelace initially seems convinced that he is not confined but liberated by gender, although because his sexual union with Clarissa comes to carry all the freight of his project, that project depends, in some sense, on Clarissa as representative of her sex; further, in the course of the novel Lovelace's definition of himself as a gendered and sexed being becomes bound absolutely to Clarissa. Thus, despite the opposition and the difference between them, masculinity is shown to be inextricable from femininity. Clarissa sees herself as confined and bound by the fact she is female, but ultimately she works free of Lovelace, of her body, and of her sex. The price for this transformation, however, is death.

The novel seems inexorably, tragically propelled toward the death and transfiguration of its heroine; the world represented in *Clarissa* cannot incorporate her as a living body and must expel and memorialize her. The Gordian knot of gender relations is not untied but cut. Alongside this teleological aspect of the novel, however, exists a mode of investigation and discovery that derives from Lovelace's obsessive, reiterative trials of femininity—his trials of Clarissa.

Lovelace, throughout the novel, tries to claim for himself a privileged position with respect to women—one that combines external and internal knowledge. At some moments Lovelace's knowledge of women seems to come from the great store he has accumulated in his career as a seducer of women, but in the passage quoted at the beginning of this chapter he claims an even closer relation to female history. It is as if his progress from bashful to bold were equivalent to an evolution from female to male, and so, therefore, his bashful past makes him privy to female secrets. He believes he can exploit this identification with women in order to control them. Self-knowledge can partly replace and cover over actual information about women for Lovelace; if he himself has "a great deal of the soul of a woman," he has only to look within to obtain complete insight. Thus Lovelace deploys his identification with women in order to compete with them as interpreters of their own actions, a strategy familiar from Richardson's descriptions of his own authorship.

Lovelace's progress from female to male, from bashful to bold, has, in his view, been interrupted or partially reversed by his contact with Clarissa. She has induced a state of double sex—a kind of hermaphrodism—in him, reawakening the original innocence lurking within or behind his bold persona, an innocence that has, paradoxically, created his secret knowledge of women and allowed him to prey on them. As if by mimetic contagion, Clarissa's modesty recreates bashfulness in him, which in turn produces both the power to "know" women and impotence in dealing with Clarissa herself. Lovelace implies that only by courting the danger of impotence and by being inquisitor into female experience does he gain his valuable insight.

Lovelace underscores his insight by invoking the metamorphic figure of Tiresias. Tiresias acquires the position of judge and expert witness in the Olympian argument about men's and women's relative enjoyment of sexual intercourse, because of knowledge gained in his metamorphoses from male to female and back again.[21] His metamorphoses serve to explain why Tiresias is the prophet to consult about sexual pleasure, but the circumstances of his transformations imply another set of meanings as well.[22] When Jove and Juno call on Tiresias as the only person capable of comparing sexual pleasure, they require him to speak for all men and all women on the basis of individual experience. His personal, and double, experience of sex is itself mirrored in the reason for his change of sex; Tiresias becomes a woman, and then a man again, because he twice sees two serpents coupling. The voyeur of and dual participant in sexual acts, he is inside, outside, and on both sides of sexual intercourse and, more generally, of gender itself. In his single person he represents multiple and conflicting desires. The power of this myth comes perhaps from Tiresias's ability *simultaneously* to embody double desires while preserving an integrated, single, and ultimately male body. Having been both male and female, observer and participant in the act of intercourse, he incorporates transformation without diminishing his present masculinity and heterosexuality.[23]

Calling on his memory of sexual intercourse when he was a woman, Tiresias settles a paradigmatic quarrel about female sexual pleasure—in woman's favor, but not, so to speak, in favor of the woman: Juno loses her wager with Jove. It turns out, according to Tiresias, the one who should know, that women derive greater pleasure from sex than do men. But Juno could think that all the evidence she has (from the myths we all know) about Jove's exploits indicates that Jove at least and, by analogy, all men enjoy sex more than she (and enjoy more sex than she). Infuriated by the latest information about her own sexuality from an authoritative outside source, she blinds the bearer of the bad news. Juno's rage may be exacerbated by her realization that she does not even have the privilege of being the only woman on the scene; Tiresias, as ex-woman, has usurped her position by his ability to speak for women without the disability of speaking (only) as a woman. Juno is hardly necessary in this man-to-man joke about female sexuality, except as the vestigial figure of the victim. Jove consoles Tiresias by giving him prophetic insight; thus, in another instance of overdetermination in the tale, Tiresias not only gains knowledge from crossing the lines of gender, he also receives a special supplement to perception, an extra potency to redress a symbolic castration. Both in the origin of his changes of sex (the scenes of serpents coupling) and in the story of Juno's reason for blinding him, Tiresias's viewing of sexual intercourse "causes" his paradoxical blindness and insight. His voyeurism is both punished and rewarded. Seeing the forbidden sets the voyeur outside sexual activity—viewing it—but in a privileged position with respect to it.

Voyeur and sequentially double-sexed, Tiresias, as Lovelace claims to do, speaks from the experiences of both men and women. He has observed women, and feels he has, in the past, experienced what it is to be a woman, and so speaks with the authority of one who can compare. To speak from the standpoint of the woman-in-the-man, however, may also render the woman redundant.[24] If a man can incorporate both sexes in himself, having transcended the limitations of femininity but recalling its lessons, he may need not women, only the idea of woman. Tiresias and Lovelace use knowledge of femininity in order to exclude women's voices and women's bodies from consideration. Identification with women and knowledge of femininity thus may turn into weapons against women.

Dangers (for women and for men) similar to those created by Lovelace's Tiresian perceptions of femininity are explored in the memoirs of Herculine / Abel Barbin, a French hermaphrodite of the nineteenth century:

> As the result of an exceptional situation, on which I do not pride myself, I, who am called a man, have been granted the intimate, deep understanding of all the facets, all the secrets of a woman's character. I can read her heart like an open book. I could count every beat of it. In a word, I have the secret of her strength and the measure of her weakness, and so I would make a detestable husband for that reason. I also feel that all my joys would be poisoned in marriage and that I would cruelly abuse, perhaps, the immense advantage that would be mine, an advantage that would turn against me.[25]

Herculine/Abel dramatically predicts dire results from the union of a woman and a hermaphrodite—in this case, one who, like Tiresias, claims feminine knowledge for a (now) male self. Although he disclaims pride in his knowledge, his sense of the "immense advantage" he has acquired signals an understanding of the relations between men and women as adversarial. Herculine/Abel's insider's knowledge of women seems to have left few traces of empathy; his plangent account focuses almost entirely on *him*self. He warns of the destructive potential of a man who has been a woman, echoing to a remarkable degree Lovelace's misogynist conviction that femininity is constituted by a secrecy that, once exploded, destroys the power of women—a view also maintained by Mr. B and many of the readers of *Pamela*. He also echoes Richardson's eroticized description of the hearts "open before me" in his letter-writing youth. Once a man acquires knowledge of "the secrets of a woman's character" all women are presumed to lose their power over him. Herculine/Abel, Tiresias, and Lovelace all assume that the experience of being a woman—or being like a woman—allows them to understand, triumph over, and elide the particularity of women's experience. But knowledge of the female heart seems to be a dangerous, double-edged weapon; Herculine/Abel vividly imagines the destruction he could wreak on himself and his wife. The specter of same-sex desire hovers over this scenario, as it does over all the tales of hermaphrodites; although medical and legal questions about assigning a sex and a gender to an ambiguous body tend to take up the foreground, the machinery of taboo also operates in the background, set in motion by the fear of "deviant" desires.

Herculine/Abel's sense of the cruel abuse of which a man-woman would be capable in marriage is borne out by Lovelace's abuse of Clarissa and other women; like Lovelace, Herculine/Abel seems to see the possibilities of sadistic pleasure in the "immense advantage" while recognizing, as Lovelace does not, that the advantage could double back on him—"turn against" him—if he used it in the service of desire. Crossing the boundaries of gender endangers if it is a double cross; using the knowledge gained through identification with women to control or possess women will subject the man to punishment, as is clear in the mythological example of Tiresias.

Herculine/Abel imagines the misery of too great knowledge that can result from crossing boundaries, but the other person—the woman—may also refuse to be known and may not be as easily read as Herculine/Abel and Lovelace believe. Lovelace's attempt to incorporate Clarissa, to assimilate her to the idea of woman that he has developed, and thereby make her redundant, a simulacrum of the heroines of his rakish tales, meets with massive physical and psychic resistance from Clarissa. One of the leitmotifs of the novel involves the confrontation of Lovelace's theories of women—based on his self-assured identification with women and on his repetitive seductions—with the actual experience of dealing with Clarissa. Clarissa counters Lovelace's idea of woman, powerfully differentiating herself from other women, as well as from the interpretation he tries to impose on her from without and within, an interpretation that attempts to smooth away any individuality she might claim. Her exemplarity—here, *for* her sex rather than *of* it—not only disrupts Lovelace's placement of her in the categories of sexual victim and sexual property but also, to some extent, problematizes the naturalness of those categories for women. Richardson, who shares the privileged position of Herculine/Abel and Lovelace with respect to women, distinguishes himself from them by the purity of his motives and by his freedom from desire for the woman he represents: identification without desire. But Richardson too is implicated in the construction of the categories his novel relies on. The trials to which Clarissa is subjected exhibit her exemplarity; Richardson—and the reader—reaps the moral and aesthetic advantages of her suffering. Demonstrating Clarissa's exemplarity requires an almost endless probing and uncovering of the female body and mind. We participate in Clarissa's suffering not only from the inside, from the position of identification and empathy we gain from her letters, but, perhaps less willingly or more guiltily, from the viewpoint of the person causing that suffering; inevitably, we are subject to the pleasure of the spectator too.

Lovelace admits that he finds sadistic pleasure in his trials of Clarissa, but he locates the origin of sadism in women, forging yet another ambiguous link of his own being to femininity. Temporarily abdicating his power in order to shift blame, he makes himself a mimic of women in the process of controlling them: "I am half-sorry to say, *that I find a pleasure in playing the Tyrant over what I love.* Call it an ungenerous pleasure, if thou wilt: Softer hearts than mine know it. The women to a woman know it, and *shew* it too, whenever they are trusted with power. And why should it be thought strange, that I, who love them so dearly, and study them so much, should catch the infection of them?" (V: 115) (789–90). He makes his tyranny resemble a venereal disease caught through making love to an infected body. The imitation he describes in this passage is rendered physical in an earlier discussion of female investment in feline violence:

I once made a charming little savage severely repent the delight she took in seeing her tabby favourite make cruel sport with a pretty sleek bead-eyed mouse, before she devoured it. Egad, my Love, said I to myself, as I sat meditating the scene, I am determined to lie in wait for a fit opportunity to try how *thou* wilt like to be tost over *my* head, and be caught again: How *thou* wilt like to be patted from me, and pulled to me. . . . And after all was over between my girl and me, I reminded her of the incident to which my resolution was owing. (IV: 17)[26]

Lovelace elides cat and woman in this justification for sexual sadism—he claims only to imitate the woman's actions, but his mimicry of her as a voyeur of violence seems to be born at the same moment as her pleasure rather than being a later, moralizing comment on it. When he sits "meditating the scene," his pleasure replicates and exceeds her pleasure. He makes the "little savage" responsible for his punishment of her, but the sexual, *physical* pleasure for himself he derives from this scene of sadistic voyeurism clearly alerts us to the ulterior motives for his claims of reciprocity, imitation, and resemblance. Lovelace repeatedly produces these instances of his resemblance to and imitation of women, but without acknowledging the danger that he himself could become either the tool or the victim of those he imitates. This threat not only appears with respect to women he seduces but also surfaces in Belford's accusations, and his occasional self-accusations, that he is a tool of James Harlowe, of Mrs. Sinclair and the whores; he even paranoiacally imagines that Clarissa's sufferings at the hands of the Harlowes are simply part of a plot to turn him into a husband.

He seems happy to allow women the credit for originating some of his strategies; allowing them power demonstrates his omnipotence when he triumphs over them. But to imitate women blurs the line that separates him from them. Although Lovelace wants to play with this boundary by reproducing feminine wiles, his play also unleashes the possibility that he will be transformed or taken over by a woman whose powers exceed his. Lovelace sees just this danger when he warns Belford that "to tell me of my acquisition in [Clarissa], and that she, with all her excellencies, will be *mine* in full property, is a mistake—It cannot be so—For shall I not be *hers*; and *not my own?*" (V: 14) (734). Union with Clarissa poses the danger that she might triumph over him, so that he becomes the possessed rather than the possessor. Lovelace's belief in an unproblematic sexual union depends absolutely on an unacknowledged hierarchy. Clarissa repeatedly challenges Lovelace's right to superior status and ownership of her by refusing to accept the validity of a hierarchy based on gender; she instead insists on a moral basis for actions.

Lovelace tries to overcome his fears of union with Clarissa by invoking an almost superstitious belief in marriage as an all-powerful weapon possessed by men: "Should I even make the grand attempt, and fail, and should she hate me for it, her hatred can be but temporary. She has already incurred the censure of the world. She must therefore chuse to be mine, for the sake of soldering up her Reputation in the eye of that impudent world" (IV: 55) (575). Lovelace persistently represents the female body as susceptible to his powers to reintegrate and transform; through the gift of marriage he can solder Clarissa up, erasing his own marking of her. The instrument that ruptures also heals the wound, a process that gives him ownership of her sexed body.[27] After the rape he again declares that marriage can transform actions and bodies. By turning the two into "one flesh," marriage will also presumably retroactively turn rape into legitimate intercourse: "And then, can there be so much harm done, if it can be so easily repaired by a few magical words; as I, Robert, take thee, Clarissa; and I, Clarissa, take thee, Robert, with the rest of the for-better and for-worse Legerdemain, which will hocus pocus all the wrongs, the crying wrongs, that I have done to Miss Harlowe, into acts of kindness and benevolence to Mrs. Lovelace?" (VI: 230).[28] This cynical trivialization of marriage as trickery— with its implied denial of the seriousness of rape—only partly conceals the belief that the ceremony has genuine power to transform. After Lovelace has raped Clarissa, he tries again to integrate her body in his, even at the expense of self-wounding: "If you will be mine, your injuries will be injuries done to myself" (V: 340) (909). Lovelace's proposal essentially seeks to convert one kind of injury—Clarissa's physical and psychic suffering in the rape—into another, the social and economic "loss" a man suffers when he marries a woman who is not a virgin. This equation depends on the doctrine that husband and wife are one flesh, and on its legal equivalent, the concept of the "feme covert" (which submerges a woman's identity in that of her husband).[29] But Lovelace's offer to assume Clarissa's injuries through marriage constitutes not only a strategy for erasing or redefining her body but also an attempt to change his; to marry Clarissa would allow Lovelace to play at being victim as well as perpetrator of the rape, both in imagination and in fact.

Lovelace appears to deploy his identification with and knowledge of women to gain power over them; to himself and his correspondent he represents his fascination with femininity as entirely subservient to his desire for conquest, revenge, and pleasure. But in basing his quest for power on identification and knowledge, Lovelace reveals his own dependence on and ensnarement in the feminine. If the surrounding culture offered a more stable and absolute distinction between the sexes, and if Lovelace could detach himself from her, he might simply be able to conquer and expel Clarissa. But because of the instability of sexual difference and because of Lovelace's various reasons for investment in Clarissa, he finds himself unable to disengage. Union in sexual intercourse or marriage implies both the desire to conquer and the wish to be dissolved in another.

જી

Lovelace's effort to gain power over Clarissa by incorporating femininity in himself alternates with attempts to reduce the ambiguity and the shiftiness of femininity, through either violent action or imaginative redefinition. Ultimately, these strategies seem to resolve into attempts to uncover the masculine within the feminine. When Clarissa repels or defeats Lovelace's fantasies—when she fails to respond to his desire—Lovelace often manipulates appearances, or the meaning he attaches to appearances, to try to achieve his ends.[30] Lovelace's characteristic deployment of disguise uses and recasts the association between women and disguise current in the period. Lovelace turns this association against Clarissa in two ways: he tries to remake her by giving her new

names, new clothes, a new identity; and he accuses her of the
"feminine" faults of disguise and subterfuge. These associations
between women and disguise are not simply external impositions,
as my discussion of similar issues in *Pamela* shows; even Clarissa
herself feels called upon to defend her sex against accusations of
dissembling:

Miss Biddulph's answer to a copy of verses from a gentleman, reproaching our Sex as acting in disguise, is not a bad one, altho' *you* [Anna
Howe] perhaps may think it too acknowleging for the female character.

> Ungen'rous Sex!—To scorn us, if we're *kind*
>   And yet upbraid us, if we seem *severe*!
> Do *You*, t'encourage us to tell our mind,
>   Yourselves put off disguise, and be sincere.
> *You* talk of Coquetry!—Your own false hearts
> *Compel* our Sex to act dissembling parts. (I: 11) (44)

This passage "acknowledges" feminine dissembling while locating
its origin in masculine manipulation; the verses describe the two
sexes locked in a reciprocating refusal to unmask, and are themselves part of a (literary) exchange. By citing the verses, Clarissa
enters into the exchange but detaches herself from the circuit of
reciprocal disguise; she reproduces the description of the dissembling parts played by "our Sex" while distancing herself. As in
Pamela's invocation of duplicity, the problem of disguise is thus
circulated in the text without being conclusively attached to the
heroine.

Through intense observation or sexual intercourse Lovelace
imagines that he can strip off the disguise he associates with
women; by flattening femaleness to a single meaning, he will be
able to subjugate women, reduce them to mere bodies, or make
them echo his desires. He will force women to acknowledge their
bodies, to acknowledge desires that the developing ideology of
femininity tries to deny, repress, or erase—and those desires will
turn out to be identical with his. But in returning to the attempt
to cause women to mirror his desires, he may also invest them with
the power he wants to keep for himself.

The battles between Lovelace and Clarissa over the definition of her body and self are figured by him in terms of deceptive surfaces that must be removed. Lovelace repeatedly tries to arrive at a kernel or attain an endpoint to his quest through both physical and mental stripping and penetration, but neither the rape nor any other action achieves final knowledge of mind or body. By conceiving of the rape as a conclusive unveiling of the body, Lovelace sets himself up for failure; the body itself cannot be fully detached from the conflicting fantasies and meanings that constitute it or from its function as an "outward Form" signifying "inward Qualities of the Mind."

Lovelace tries to read Clarissa's body in terms that deny the possibility of mystery to her or that expose her mystery as falsification and disguise. Before he has raped Clarissa, he represents the relation between surface and depths in her "person" as if the appearance she offers him exists primarily as a disguise beneath which he will find what he has always found in women. In his description, her body becomes a covering she assumes to conceal her "identicalness" with other women, an identicalness that he celebrates for what he can make of it and mocks for what it lacks. But of course once the body becomes a covering there are no further physical "depths" to uncover.

Lovelace reflects complacently on the paradoxical lack of difference between women that makes even Clarissa herself, the most extraordinary of women, like all other women: "—And sometimes do I qualify my ardent aspirations after even this very fine creature, by this reflection:—That the most charming woman on earth, were she an Empress, can excel the meanest, in the customary visibles only—Such is the equality of the dispensation, to the Prince and the Peasant, in this prime gift, WOMAN" (III: 221) (493). Lovelace asserts that women's similarity creates solidarity among men; the women themselves fall to secondary importance. This purportedly democratic and homosocial impulse appears again in a letter to his servant/spy Joseph Leman, in which he defends himself against an earlier accusation of rape and locates his pleasure in his own cleverness rather than in "sensuality":

The affair of Miss Betterton was a youthful frolick. I love dearly to exercise my invention. I do assure you, Joseph, that I have ever had more pleasure in my Contrivances, than in the End of them. I am no sensual man; but a man of spirit—One woman is like another—*You understand me, Joseph*. In Coursing all the sport is made by the winding Hare. A barn-door Chick is better eating. . . . Miss Betterton was but a Tradesman's daughter. (III: 228)[31]

Lovelace employs the woman he has "seduced" (i.e., raped) to bridge the class barrier that separates him from Joseph Leman while reasserting his class difference from the woman herself; women's similarity produces this assertion of equality among men, an assertion cynically calculated only to enable the next seduction/rape. Women are available to all men, no matter what rank the woman holds, because their lack of difference places all women on the same plane, lower than any man; thus a peasant may possess an empress. But this purportedly democratic impulse peels back to reveal another structure important in *Clarissa*: Lovelace's reiterative fantasies of successful competition with other men for women.[32]

Lovelace locates lack of difference among women in the body, refusing at this point to construe female identity in any other way. If Clarissa can be transformed into an interchangeable, exchangeable function, the threat of what might lie behind what he calls the "customary visibles" can be contained. That is, Lovelace equates woman here with her genitals—the customary *in*visible he does not name but assumes to be at the root of Clarissa's lack of difference from all other women. At this juncture Lovelace conceives of his project as a simple one: He wants to strip off the disguises that cause Clarissa to *appear* different from all other women, and he imagines that, by revealing to her and to himself her lack of difference, he will destroy her power over him. He will reveal that she is not unique (not the phallic woman?) and that therefore no basis exists for her claims of superiority to and difference from other women; he will see nothing he has not seen before, or, rather, he will see again the nothing that he has seen in other women.[33]

But the moment of her demystification, deflation, and exposure constantly recedes out of his grasp, and Lovelace must begin again to define Clarissa and redefine *himself* in relation to Clarissa so that he can continue after each setback she deals him. Instead of freeing him from her, his encounters with her threaten to expose or alter him. In a displaced expression of the effect he wishes to have on her, he offers his own body and soul up to be remade, imprinted with her image: "Darkness, light; Light, darkness; by my Soul!—Just as you please to have it. . . . Take me, take me to yourself; Mould me as you please; I am wax in your hands; Give me your own impression; and seal me for ever yours" (III: 139).[34] This extravagant, "feminine" self-definition refigures his body as malleable, receptive, changeable—all the things he wants Clarissa to be, but she is not.

Lovelace's redefinitions frequently involve a continued struggle with the meaning of the body and the meaning of gender, and each attempt to define her body has implications for his. For example, Lovelace locates within Clarissa the contest that seems to the reader to be going on between them for possession of her body. He presents Clarissa as herself possessed by a foreign power and too "feminine" to endure the invasion: "Yet her charming Body is not equally organized. The unequal partners pull two ways; and the divinity within her tears her silken frame. But had the same soul informed a masculine body, never would there have been a truer hero" (IV: 204) (647). The battle within Clarissa's body belongs more to Lovelace's wish to define and limit her power than to Clarissa herself. But that description of a hymeneal rupture from within betrays Lovelace's ambivalent desire for a shadowy masculine presence, a "truer hero" who would be a more appropriate adversary than is the Clarissa who inhabits a woman's body. This oblique fantasy of a masculinized Clarissa, who would either have to shed her present body or hollow it out, betokens a returning anxiety about what her body represents to him. The wish to make Clarissa as double as he is himself repeats the strategy of making her like him, but also thereby subverts his project of reducing her to the body; if she has a masculine soul in a feminine body, she may be the inverse of him (a feminine soul in a masculine body), but the power of her soul has been underscored.[35] Lovelace seems unable to accept the body's femininity; he uneasily remakes it in his own image (or remakes his own image) in order to define its power over him, needing to find in her body some version of himself or his sex. The strategy of feminizing himself to gain imaginative access to Clarissa is thus mirrored in the attempt to masculinize her, but the splitting and the duplication set in motion by these redefinitions seem finally to spin out of control.

The attempt to contain both sexes in one body reappears in a fantasy that recalls Mr. B's attempt to rape Pamela while he is dressed as a woman. Lovelace is propelled into this imaginary scene by his sense that the desirability of women impinges on his consciousness even at worship. The fantasy concerns crossing gender boundaries that seem to have been created so that they can be crossed:

But, now I think of it, what if our governors should appoint Churches for the *Women* only, and others for the *Men*? . . .

There are already male and female Dedications of Churches.

St. Swithin's, St. Stephen's, St. Thomas's, St. George's, and so forth, might be appropriated to the men; and the Santa Katharina's, Santa Anna's, Santa Maria's, Santa Margaretta's for the women.

Yet, were it so, and life to be the forfeiture of being found at the female Churches, I believe that I, like a second Clodius, should change my dress, to come at my Portia or Pompeia, tho' one the Daughter of a Cato, the other the Wife of a Caesar. (III: 64–65) (419–20)[36]

The gendered churches simply function to create another taboo for Lovelace to violate, another location for enforcing and transgressing difference. The very arbitrariness of the fantasy gestures toward the arbitrary nature of other boundaries. This idle fantasy of dressing as a woman, though detached from the plot, not only resonates with Lovelace's other boundary crossings, it also shows him clothing and disguising his own body in order to "come at" the body of the woman. The link of clothing and body reappears when Lovelace further attempts to claim Clarissa's behavior—and

her body—as his own production through representations of the
female body as itself a kind of clothing. In his plotting mode, he
confidently predicts to his confidant Belford that "the moment the
rough covering that my teazing behaviour has thrown over her affections is quite removed, I doubt not to find all silk and silver at
bottom, all soft, bright, and charming" (IV: 216).[37] By appropriating to himself even her rejections of him—depicting those rejections as a rough covering created by his behavior—he reasserts
the power to remove the covering by simply ceasing to tease. He
stages a strip-show for himself; through his possession of the covering, he gains possession of the "silk and silver" within. Finally
describing what might lie beneath, Lovelace engages in some pres-
tidigitation; a convenient slippage occurs between covering and
body, for the silk and silver that he finds "at bottom" closely recall
the "silken frame" of his reference to her body when he imagined
her with a masculine soul. The fact that the last layer is silk and
silver suggests that both covering and covered are in some sense
fabric—or fabrications. Even the language of revelation confuses
surface and interior, blocking imaginative access to any conclusive
knowledge. This unstable system of reference, in which the inside
becomes indistinguishable from the outside, has its own unstable
analogy in Lovelace's overt wish to invest in Clarissa's actual clothing. He explains to Belford his reasons for wanting to give Clarissa
clothes: "One, the real pleasure I should have in the accommo-
dating of the haughty maid; and to think there was something
near her, and upon her, that I could call *mine*: The other, in order
to abate her severity, and humble her a little" (III: 121) (449). He
believes dressing her will give him access to the body that has been
itself depicted as a species of clothing, and that may therefore become a kind of object or property; to have something that is his
"upon her" seems to be the first step toward possession of her—
a possession he perceives as demeaning to her. But his easy progress inward is imaginary, its aim rendered ambiguous by the constitutive confusion between body and clothing: The point at
which success would be achieved retreats inexorably out of sight.

Lovelace's incessant reformations of the meaning to be assigned

Clarissa do not result in a conclusive uncovering of the female body. Identification and uncertainty constantly intervene to disrupt his efforts to objectify, label, and dismiss Clarissa. Even in a fable of reciprocal exhibition Lovelace seems impelled initially to supply a male body to stand in for Clarissa, covertly undermining his aims by reformulating the struggle between them as a scene of masculine competition: "Thou remembrest the contention between the Sun and the North-wind, in the Fable; which should first make an honest Traveller throw off his cloak" (IV: 204) (647). The north wind begins by "puffing away most vehemently" but only succeeds in causing the traveler to "wrap his surtout the closer about him." When the sun's turn comes,

> he so played upon the Traveller with his beams, that he made him first unbutton, and then throw it quite off. . . . The victor-god then laughed outright . . . and pursued his radiant course, shining upon, and warming and cherishing a thousand new objects, as he danced along. . . . I, in like manner, will discard all my boisterous inventions; And if I can oblige my sweet Traveller to throw aside, *but for one moment*, the cloak of her rigid virtue, I shall have nothing to do, but, like the Sun, to bless new objects with my rays. But my chosen hours of conversation and repose, after all my peregrinations, will be devoted to my goddess. (IV: 205) (647)

Lovelace here provides a wishful scenario of mutual display: He "discards" his boisterous inventions—she/he in response throws aside the cloak of her rigid virtue / the rigid cloak of her virtue. But Lovelace slides past the implications of that "*one moment*" in which her virtue becomes a surface that peels off, focusing instead on his own display, which in turn will release him for further, repetitive exhibitions. That single, slightly represented glance into what appears under the cloak leaves him, as he says, "nothing to do" but to continue on his way as glorious, engendering force, graciously willing to devote himself to Clarissa in his moments of repose. Clarissa's covering of virtue, in all its supposed rigidity, produces in Lovelace an equivalent, mirroring rigidity; he is fixed, *unable* to "bless new objects" in his persona as phallic sun until she releases him by changing—by ceasing to represent fixity. But

Lovelace fails to imagine what would be revealed by the removal of her "cloak"; only a threatening "nothing" remains.

Lovelace more than once tries to convert the spectacular effect that Clarissa has on him into a source of pleasure and self-exhibition. In order to see Clarissa after she escapes to Hampstead, Lovelace engages in one of his characteristic disguises; when he appears at the place she has been staying he is a gouty "antiquated beau." Lovelace eventually throws off his disguise in reaction to her overwhelming presence. Clarissa "opened the door, and blazed upon me, as it were, in a flood of light, like what one might imagine would strike a man, who, born blind, had by some propitious power been blessed with his sight, all at once, in a meridian Sun" (V: 83) (772).[38] It is she who embodies the sun; she both blinds and illuminates. Lovelace claims he is "forced" to reveal himself, but it is easy to see him as competing with her:

I saw it was impossible to conceal myself longer from her, any more than (from the violent impulses of my passion) to forbear manifesting myself. I unbuttoned therefore my cape, I pulled off my flapt slouched hat; I threw open my great coat and, like the devil in Milton [an odd comparison tho'!]

> I started up in my own form divine,
> Touch'd by the beam of her celestial eye,
> More potent than Ithuriel's spear!
> (V: 83; brackets in original) (772)[39]

Lovelace describes himself as engaged in actions almost identical to those he projects onto Clarissa as the traveler in his fable of the sun and the traveler quoted above. His purportedly "forced" self-revelation, which combines involuntary erection with willful striptease, figures as a reciprocating response to Clarissa's blaze, matched by her celestial, superpotent eye. In line with other Lovelacean revelations of Clarissa's covert possession of masculinity, her body and her eye appear phallic and engendering, but what they are assumed to engender is himself. Lovelace at once finds a scene of masculine competition in their opposition, and he paradoxically creates himself as an offspring of the contest.

Lovelace depicts Clarissa's blaze and her eye as focused on his own divine, Satanic body, but this passage does demonstrate a shift in representation from that earlier fable; that is, she is now the sun, not he. Clarissa resurrects this figure when she calls on a vengeful eye to destroy Lovelace:

Now, said she, that thou *darest* to call the occasion *slight* and *accidental* [Lovelace's false fire, which was to have led to her rape], and that I am happily out of thy vile hands, and out of a house I have reason to believe *as* vile, traitor and wretch that thou art, I will venture to cast an eye upon thee—And O that it were in my power, in mercy to my Sex, to look thee first into shame and remorse, and then into death! (V: 89) (775)

In the intensely echoic structure of the novel, Clarissa redirects against Lovelace his fantasies about her. Lovelace imagines an eye that invests him with potency while it threatens; Clarissa imagines one that shrivels and kills. But Clarissa invokes the "eye of the basilisk" out of frustration with her lack of power, not as a prop to desire; she has no hope of realizing her fantasy, although it could be argued that her curse does come to pass. Her more characteristic representation of herself, a representation that again echoes Lovelace's version of her, is as "wrapped" in her innocence, barricaded behind the "mantle" of her integrity.

Clarissa's resistance assumes for Lovelace the form of an elaborated, seductive surface, designed to entrap and defeat him. When he cannot elicit reciprocal exhibitions from her, when he is balked in his attempts to demonstrate that their bodies are equivalent and made for each other, he accuses her of a hypocritical effort to increase her body's value by refusing to share it or make it easily available. Lovelace complains that, even when they hover on the brink of marriage, Clarissa still "makes every inch of her person . . . sacred" (IV: 333) (705). She will not cede the smallest outpost—not a breast, not a lip. Lovelace views the female body as susceptible to a kind of imaginative dismemberment and conquest while Clarissa seeks to retain a sense of herself as an inalienable whole.[40] Lovelace attributes her assertion of the inviolability of margins to an artful attempt to heighten his response. He flamboyantly accuses her of manipulation of appearances: "She has read, no doubt, of the Art of the Eastern Monarchs, who sequester themselves from the eyes of their subjects, in order to excite their adoration, when, upon some solemn occasions, they think fit to appear in public" (IV: 333) (705–6). These exotic tyrants conceal nothing of value, but acquire value through concealment, and in their secrecy they contrast with the phallic, openly exhibitionist figures—such as the sun—that Lovelace employs to describe himself. He asserts that Clarissa's power derives from her refusal to expose her body and thus depends at once on mystification and adornment, and on the imaginative desires of those—himself, for example—who watch her:

> But let me ask thee, Belford, whether (on these solemn occasions [that is, the rare appearances of the Eastern monarchs]) the preceding cavalcade; here a great officer, and there a great minister, with their Satellites, and glaring equipages; do not prepare the eyes of the wondering beholders, by degrees, to bear the blaze of Canopy'd Majesty (what tho' but an ugly old man perhaps himself? yet) glittering in the collected riches of his vast Empire?
>
> And should not my Beloved, for her own sake, descend by *degrees*, from *Goddess-hood* into *Humanity*? (IV: 333–34) (706)

The ugly old man lurking behind the blaze and glitter of empire is a strange figure for the woman who mesmerizes Lovelace. His attack on Clarissa for imperially, craftily withholding her presence reveals the propelling hope (or fear) that she too, beneath that blaze, is equivalently lacking (or equivalently possessed of what Lovelace has)—"but an ugly old man perhaps" herself? The ultimate devaluation in the move from empress to emperor to "ugly old man" itself reverberates throughout the text: When Lovelace imagines what lies behind Clarissa's mysterious, impenetrable surfaces, he can only see or imagine in terms of a distorted mirror image. In fact, he frequently characterizes himself as an Eastern monarch or a competitor with Eastern monarchs.[41]

The Eastern monarch thus condenses in a single figure Lovelace's imperial designs on women and his anxieties about the mys-

teries contained in Clarissa's body. But by using this figure to cast
doubt on the power and meaning of Clarissa, Lovelace ambiguously invests her with his own potency and with his own impotence in relation to her. Like his comparison of himself with bashful women, this analysis of Clarissa's mystery asserts his difference
from her while acknowledging her power over him.

Lovelace tries to counter his awe of Clarissa's power and her
impenetrability by reinvesting himself with imperial power and
by reasserting that he, not she, possesses the body that should be
viewed as the all-important spectacle. These strategies emerge in
the odd fantasy of a trial for kidnapping and rape that embellishes
the later editions of *Clarissa*.[42] Lovelace, while playing games of
cat and mouse with Clarissa before the rape, decides that Anna
Howe, Mrs. Howe, and "the officious prancer Hickman" deserve
punishment for opposing him and interfering with his plans for
Clarissa. Anna, in particular, bears the brunt of Lovelace's sadism
in this imaginary escapade. Throughout the novel Lovelace uses
Anna to mediate his relations with Clarissa, and he also employs
her to substitute for Clarissa or to displace certain of his responses
to Clarissa. In his attempt to locate the genesis of his sadism in
women, and at the same time link himself to Clarissa, for example, he likens Anna's behavior to his own, claiming that she is his
double as well as Clarissa's. He asserts her masculinity most explicitly during Clarissa's escape to Hampstead, when he tells the
gullible women about Miss Howe: "I represented her [Anna] to
be an arrogant creature, revengeful, artful, enterprising, and one
who, had she been a Man, would have sworn and cursed, and com-
mitted Rapes, and played the devil, as far I knew [*and I have no
doubt of it, Jack*]" (V: 135; brackets in original) (801). His early
scheme for raping Anna offers another way to double his enjoyment of his projected triumph over Clarissa and to build up his
revenge against her as a masculine competitor. But the fantasy of
raping Anna quickly fades in comparison to the attractive fantasy
of being put on trial for the rape and kidnapping.[43]

The trial seems to represent a chance to focus all eyes on his own spectacular presence, but it also signals the extent to which Lovelace's fantasies of power are inextricable from the power he locates in women. Initially the trial seems to provide Lovelace the pleasure of appropriating female sexuality for his own ends:

Would not a brave fellow chuse to appear in court to such an arraignment, confronting women who would do credit to his attempt? The country is more merciful in *these* cases, than in *any others*: I should therefore like to put myself upon my country.[44]

Let me indulge a few reflections upon what thou mayst think the *worst* that *can* happen. . . . How bravely shall we enter a court, *I* at the head of you, dressed out each man, as if to his wedding-appearance!— You are sure of all the women, old and young, of your side.—What brave fellows!—What fine gentlemen!—There goes a charming handsome man!—meaning me, to be sure!—Who could find in their hearts to hang such a gentleman as that! whispers one Lady. . . . While another disbelieves that any woman could *fairly* swear against me. All will croud after *me*. (IV: 256–57)

The criminal trial celebrates Lovelace's phallic potency, and rape becomes the prelude to the (more satisfying) seduction of an audience. In this parody of a wedding, the women are displayed as objects of desire who exist primarily to enhance Lovelace's status:

But then comes the triumph of triumphs, that will make the accused look up, while the accusers are covered with confusion.

Make room there!—Stand by!—Give back!—One receiving a rap, another an elbow, half a score a push apiece!

Enter the slow-moving, hooded-faced, down-looking Plaintiffs.

And first the Widow, with a sorrowful countenance, tho' half-veil'd, pitying her Daughter more than herself. The people, the women especially, who on this occasion will be five-sixths of the spectators, reproaching her—You'd have the conscience, would you, to have five such brave gentlemen as these hanged for you know not what?

Next comes the poor maid—who perhaps had been ravished twenty times before; and had not appeared now, but for company-sake. . . .

But every eye dwells upon Miss [Anna Howe]!—See, see, the handsome gentleman bows to her!

To the very ground, to be sure, I shall bow; and kiss my hand.

See her confusion! See! she turns from him!—Ay! that's because it is in open court, cries an arch one!—While others admire her.—Ay! that's a girl worth venturing one's neck for! (IV: 257–58)

Lovelace speaks in female voices to "reveal" the hypocrisy the female victims conceal behind their veils and sorrowful countenances, and produces an entire phantasmal community to endorse his self-exhibition. This courtroom saturnalia allows Lovelace to expose the "truth" behind women's performances and to exhibit himself as the prized object of female competition. The imaginary women who speak for the silenced victims are speaking the desire that Lovelace believes he can uncover in the resistant bodies of Anna and Clarissa.

Lovelace collects in himself the desires of all the members of the court and of the audience: "Then we shall be praised—Even the Judges, and the whole crouded Bench, will acquit us in their hearts; and every single man wish he had been me!—The women, all the time, disclaiming prosecution, were the case to be their own. To be sure, Belford, the sufferers cannot put half so good a face upon the matter as we" (IV: 258). In this complex fantasy Lovelace's satisfaction arises from a spectacle of multiplied and projected identification; he does not simply produce a narrative of himself acting for the applause of onlookers or for his own satisfaction, but instead refracts and augments his pleasure via the imagined pleasure of the audience. In a neat circuit of overdetermined desire, he imagines the male onlookers imagining themselves him, and the females imagining themselves raped by him; thus, like Tiresias, he incorporates all possible positions and genders in himself while eradicating the victims.

Lovelace's play with the implications of spectacle develops a scene of triumph out of a scene of punishment. But in Lovelace's account of the procession he—the triumphant figure who has condensed all sexual pleasure in his own body—gradually diminishes into the prop of a spectacle that centers on him while requiring nothing of him except his presence. He is hollowed out by the audience he conjures up. He takes over the position of the silenced victims of the rape, whose existence had been obscured by the focus on him:

Let me tell thee, Jack, I see not why . . . we should not be as much elated in our march . . . as others may be upon the most *mob-attracting* occasion. . . . Suppose . . . the *grandest* parade that can be supposed, a Coronation—For, in all these, do not the royal guard, the heroic trained-bands, the pendent, clinging throngs of spectators, with their waving heads rolling to-and-fro from house-tops to house-bottoms and street-ways, as I have above described, make the principal part of the Raree-show? (IV: 259)[45]

While casting a cynical eye on the effect of royal stage-managing and simultaneously justifying his pride, Lovelace makes the "hero" of the spectacle (and thus, by analogy, himself) dwindle into a shell produced by (or subjected to) the mob: "And let me ask thee, If thou dost not think, that either the Mayor, the Embassador, or the General, would not make very pitiful figures on their Gala's, did not the trumpets and tabrets call together the Canaille to gaze at them?" (IV: 259). This diminished figure of the hero at the center of a crowd, invested with power only by the noise and the gaze of that crowd, recalls Lovelace's deflationary comparison of Clarissa with the Eastern monarchs. Lovelace's displacement onto the gazing crowd of the power he has just gathered from them parallels his claim that Clarissa's power resides only in the accretions of surface and secrecy that attract the eye of the gazer. His denial to her of uniqueness and his assertion that she is rendered powerless by his greater power thus collapse into a covert, complex identification of his situation with hers.

Lovelace works to construct images and interpretations of Clarissa, and particularly of Clarissa's body, that will counter his own fears, that will compete with her constructions of herself, and that will further his plots by making her available psychically and physically to him. This part of his project involves him repeatedly in the comparison of Clarissa to other women and to general ideas about femininity, comparisons that profoundly implicate the novel's author.

Lovelace initially tries to devalue Clarissa and strip her of her individuality, though her admirers celebrate her for uniqueness and exemplarity. But Lovelace's efforts to reduce Clarissa to what he construes as the lowest common denominator of femininity depend in part on his perception of her uniqueness—in fact, his fear or hope that she might be unique among women propels him to put her on trial. Richardson tries explicitly to deny that Clarissa's exemplarity detaches her from her sex or removes her from the human sphere; he admonishes the reader in his 1751 introduction that Clarissa is not "impeccable"—not an angel—and asserts that Lovelace sees her as angelic because his "*heart* was so corrupt, that he could hardly believe human nature capable of the purity, which . . . shone out in *hers*" (I: vii). Seeing Clarissa as angelic—a saint, not a woman—allows Lovelace to avoid altering his perception of women, as Richardson recognizes. But Richardson's own emphasis on Clarissa's double function as an embodiment of femininity and a pattern for women shares with Lovelace's alternating impulses to debase and exalt her the tendency to disconnect the female self from the female body and further to separate virtuous femininity from vicious. Clarissa's exemplarity, despite Richardson's denials, depends as much on her difference from other women as on the characteristics she shares with them, and that exemplarity also relies on her eventual departure from the body that threatens to deny her difference.

Belford's rhapsodic assertions of Clarissa's divinity and sexlessness, for example, do not seem too distant from the view Richardson tries to endorse:

I am ready to regret that such an angel of a woman should even marry. She is in my eye all mind: And were she to meet with a man all mind likewise, why should the charming qualities she is mistress of, be endangered? Why should such an angel be plunged so low as into the vulgar offices of domestic life? Were she mine, I should hardly wish to see her a Mother, unless there were a kind of moral certainty, that Minds like hers could be propagated. For why, in short, should not the work of Bodies be left to *mere* Bodies? (IV: 11) (555)

Belford tries to save Clarissa's mind from the clog of her female (reproductive) body, which in his view can only endanger and diminish her. Pregnancy and maternity would intrusively literalize the physicality against which he tries to defend her. He hopes for a kind of "propagation" that would bypass the body. Belford's dichotomy of body and mind has its acknowledged basis in the belief that there are two species of women: those who are all body, and those who, like Clarissa, are all mind. This dichotomy, although it is put into the mouth of a rake, prefigures Clarissa's disembodiment in the course of the novel, and calls to mind the contrast of Clarissa's angelic nature with the diabolical physicality of the whores. It seems to be part of a process that leaves Clarissa's body precisely nowhere.

Belford's distress at the idea Clarissa might descend to domestic offices and to motherhood counters and echoes Lovelace's hope that he has impregnated Clarissa in the rape. He writes to Belford that "it would be the pride of my life to prove, in this charming Frost-piece, the Triumph of Nature over Principle, and to have a young Lovelace by such an angel" (VII: 14) (1147). Belford and Lovelace, for opposing reasons, construe pregnancy as an acknowledgment of the body, even as an acknowledgment of desire. According to beliefs still prevalent in the mid-eighteenth century, Clarissa's pregnancy could have signified enjoyment of the rape, as conception was presumed to require female orgasm.[46] Both Lovelace and the Harlowes watch intently for evidence of the betraying sign.

Clarissa's body, however, thwarts Lovelace's attempt to mark it; she refuses to respond appropriately to his penetration of her, nor will she acknowledge that her body has been the agent of self-betrayal, at least of the kind he wants. This resistance baffles and frustrates him: "At times, I cannot help regretting, that I ever attempted her; since not *one power either of Body or Soul* could be moved in my favour; and since, to use the expression of the philosopher, on a much graver occasion, There is no difference to be found between the skull of king Philip and that of another man" (V: 295) (885). Lovelace blames Clarissa's intractable body and soul for the pleasure and triumph he misses in the rape, but her immovability is not the ultimate cause for his failure. The rape was supposed to demonstrate conclusively a whole raft of contradictory hopes, fears, and desires; it was originally to function as an endpoint to Lovelace's quest, to liberate him for future action, to force Clarissa to acknowledge her body's desire for him, and to reveal as deluded her belief (and his fear) that she was somehow different from other women. But the lack of (genital) difference between Clarissa and all other women, represented here in the reference to dead men's skulls, ceases to be a cause for celebration; it now creates a gnawing dissatisfaction. Raping Clarissa has not allowed him to locate the kernel of her being, nor has he reduced her to her body.[47] The rape leaves Lovelace in the impossible position of seeing Clarissa as totally different from all other women, yet absolutely indistinguishable from them.[48] The rape has, in a sense, no ontological status.

The question of what sort of being Clarissa has, and what relation body and mind have in her, becomes crucial to Lovelace and the novel. Richardson's solution to the problem—Clarissa's death and beatification—is not one that can satisfy Lovelace on the physical plane, and it also causes Richardson himself considerable unease.[49] Although Belford wants to save Clarissa from the body, Lovelace wants to deny her anything but a body, at least before the rape: "We have held, that women have no Souls: I am a very Turk in this point, and willing to believe they have not. And if so, to whom shall I be accountable for what I do to them? Nay, if Souls they have, as there is no Sex in Ethereals, nor *need* of any, what plea can a Lady hold of injuries done her in her Lady-*State*, when there is an end of her Lady-*ship*?" (IV: 330) (704). For all its sophistry and misogyny, Lovelace's reasoning seems similar to the words of the converted Belford, when he is a spectator at Clarissa's deathbed: "How many opportunities must thou [Lovelace] have had of admiring her inestimable worth, yet couldst have thy senses so much absorbed in the WOMAN in her charming person, as to be blind to the ANGEL that shines out in such full glory in her mind!" (VII: 299) (1299). "Woman" and "angel" oppose and merge as definitions for Clarissa. Lovelace, in despair at the inexorable approach she is making to death, curses himself for failing to recognize her difference and casts that difference as defeminization: "Curse upon my *contriving genius*! Curse upon my *intriguing head*, and upon my *seconding-heart*!—To sport with the fame, with the honour, with the *life*, of such an angel of a woman!—O my damn'd incredulity! That, believing her to *be* a woman, I must hope to *find* her a woman! On my incredulity that there could be such virtue (virtue for *virtue's* sake) in the Sex, founded I my hope of succeeding with her" (VII: 400) (1344). Lovelace, unable to believe that a "woman" could die from rape, seems to arrive temporarily (and paradoxically) at the position that she is not a member of the sex to which the rape has established she (physically) belongs. (And presumably she must be an angel, since the other possibility would be that she is a man.) She becomes mystically different and the same, both in his perception and in her own representation of herself. Clarissa prepares to wed death and God, not Lovelace, and she declares that "never Bride was so ready as I am. My wedding garments are bought" (VII: 373) (1339).[50] Neither she nor her author denies her transcendence of the body; she leaves it behind because it has brought her danger and destruction, and because, apparently, angel and woman cannot coexist successfully in a living, female body—or at least they cannot in this society.

Lovelace's attempt to know Clarissa's baffling body enmeshes him in problems and contradictions that the novel itself cannot work free of, partly because the novel faithfully reproduces—but cannot solve—ideological problems in the construction of femininity. Clarissa at once fits into the category of (extraordinary) woman and also transcends it, leaving the meaning of the category itself ambiguous. Richardson wants to assert that Clarissa's heroism can be emulated—that she is an exemplary woman, but not free of human faults—and to show that she is angelic, a saint whose being cannot be confined to the body. Richardson's solution is to show that Clarissa's virtue finally conquers Lovelace's doubts about women, and to suggest that the world is unable to recognize and reward such virtue.[51] But when the focus broadens to include characters other than Clarissa, these quasi-religious solutions to the double bind seem incomplete and contradictory. While Lovelace's belief in the validity and strength of his own interpretation of femininity may blind him to Clarissa's *non-physical* difference, he is also working from his previous experience of women as duplicitous, an interpretation that Richardson, uncomfortably, to some degree allows; by pointing up Clarissa's glorious uniqueness through the contrasting depiction of Arabella Harlowe, Mrs. Sinclair, and the whores, Richardson gives partial (if unacknowledged) support to Lovelace's view of women. Although Lovelace refuses to admit the possibility of true virtue in women, his failure to recognize the distinction between Clarissa and the other women is not merely perverse. It is possible to see in Lovelace the representative of an old order confronting a new ideology: His rakish belief (or fantasy) that every woman is at heart a rake collides with Richardson's deployment of the cult of true womanhood. But Richardson's novel has feet in both camps (or characters in both worlds); despite its wholehearted support of Clarissa's exemplarity, and the defeat through her of Lovelace's cynical system, suspicions about women's duplicity and lustfulness retain sufficient influence—have sufficient force—to impel Richardson to create secondary female characters who collectively represent all the stereotypical faults of women.[52]

The strains of reconciling the stereotyped representation of the other women in the novel with the representation of Clarissa reside not only in Lovelace's response to Clarissa and his construction of her, but in Richardson's own equivocal differentiation of Clarissa from all other women, even Anna Howe. Lovelace's sense of heroic endeavor requires that Clarissa be an adequate opponent—different, powerful—so that his triumph over her is not a foregone conclusion (as it would be and has been in the cases of other women), but at the same moment he works to define her as powerless and not-different, a version of other women in a new guise. As we have seen, that contradiction is often "settled" by Lovelace's search for a lurking masculinity in Clarissa; if Clarissa is really more like him, her power and her resistance are less extraordinary. This quest in turn mirrors his own appropriation of femininity. The corollary of this pervasive psychological unease with the categories of gender can be seen also in Clarissa's initial inability to understand the bad women in the novel.[53] In her attempts to comprehend the viciousness of women like Arabella Harlowe, Mrs. Sinclair, and the whores—without altering her definition of femininity—Clarissa, and even Lovelace at times, tends to interpret their actions in terms of masculinity; she describes, for example, Mrs. Sinclair's "worse than masculine violence" in the rape (VI: 174) (1011). By substituting masculinity as the standard against which she judges the women, however, Clarissa duplicates in another register Lovelace's intermittent, covert attribution of masculinity to her. Definitions based on gender begin to seem less and less stable, more and more inadequate; "natural" qualities and appropriate behavior in both sexes are so restricted that it is necessary to label whole ranges of activities as disruptive, deviant, or violations of boundaries.

Lovelace's misogyny allows him to misread Clarissa's essential sincerity and honesty, but his discounted representation of her and Anna as his female equivalents, equally duplicitous, equally disguised, is displaced by Richardson onto the other women in the novel. That is, however wrong Lovelace is shown to be about Clarissa and Anna, he is proven right about many of the other women. Lovelace, in other words, if he is to go on the evidence of his past successes and present company, does not err in assuming that women craftily exchange virginity for marriage, nor is he wrong to believe that there may be something behind or beneath the coverings women affect, both physically and metaphorically. *Pamela*, of course, confronts these problems directly; the heroine "disguises" herself and gains a husband by maintaining her virginity. In his second novel Richardson removes Clarissa from the taint of the earthly reward Pamela receives; *Clarissa* casts the exchange of virginity for marriage in a sordid light by telling the story of the whore Sally Martin's failed attempt to lure Lovelace into marriage;[54] and he identifies disguise and duplicity as wicked traits belonging to Lovelace and the bad women—although, as Margaret Doody remarks, "it is rather shocking to find how much of the disguise theme emerges through [Clarissa]."[55] By detaching from Clarissa some of Pamela's problematic attributes, Richardson tries to ensure an unequivocal response to this heroine. But in doing so he privileges her "good" femininity and anathematizes many of the other women. And the sporadic attempts to assimilate women's evil to "masculinity" or to locate their corruption in men's acts reverberate uneasily with the patterns of Lovelace's cooptive cross-gender identification; the basis for moral distinctions between the sexes becomes hopelessly confused.

First Arabella, then Mrs. Sinclair and the whores serve as antitypes of Clarissa, but they sometimes also become parodies or imitations of her, compounding the problems of resemblance and distinction that absorb Lovelace. Even Clarissa is taken in by the whores who dress up as Lovelace's relatives, and Lovelace succumbs briefly to Sally Martin's performance as Clarissa when the real Clarissa has escaped him for the last time. Although Lovelace justifies his trials of Clarissa by claiming a need to distinguish the false feminine from the real, the novel itself also evinces a genuine concern with the issue. Lovelace's response to Sally Martin's mimicry exposes the scope of the problem of interpreting women:

Come said she [Sally], what will you give me, and I'll be virtuous for a quarter of an hour, and mimic your Clarissa to the life? . . . The little devil was not to be balked; but fell a crying, sobbing, praying, begging, exclaiming, fainting, that I never saw my lovely girl so well aped. Indeed I was almost taken in; for I could have fancied I had her before me once more.

O this Sex! this artful Sex! There's no minding them. At first, indeed, their grief and their concern may be real: But give way to the hurricane, and it will soon die away in soft murmurs, trilling upon your ears like the notes of a well-tuned viol. And, by Sally, one sees, that Art will generally so well supply the place of Nature, that you shall not easily know the difference. Miss Clarissa Harlowe indeed is the only woman in the world I believe that can say, in the words of her favourite Job (for I can quote a text as well as she), *But it is not so with me.* (VII: 145–46) (1217)

Sally's imitation of Clarissa raises troubling issues for Lovelace. In this performance, Clarissa's essence is reduced to a series of hysterical gestures that seem theatrical and faintly ludicrous. Through some combination of self-deception, wishful thinking, and Sally's acting powers, Lovelace momentarily convinces himself of the performance's validity. He then produces a plangent discourse on feminine adaptability, finally focusing on Clarissa's exemplarity and her immunity from the taint of "the sex" in an effort to escape the disturbing possibility that Clarissa, as member of "the sex," partakes of its ambiguous qualities. If Sally could "be" Clarissa, is Lovelace not overvaluing the actual Clarissa? If Sally can be Clarissa, is it not possible that Clarissa might be Sally, and that he has been fooled—despite the evidence of her heartbroken response to the rape—into thinking her different? This latter formulation is, of course, the double expression of a fear and a wish; he has wanted to turn Clarissa into Sally, but he also fears that there is no difference between them, as the evidence of his senses tells him. If there is no difference between Clarissa and the whores, Clarissa cannot be *transformed* into one of them because she already resembles them. And if there is no possibility of transformation, he has no power to transform; *he* makes no difference, has made no impression on the world of women.

Sally's performance thus explicitly confounds, however briefly, one of *Clarissa*'s secondary lines of demarcation—the line separating the virtuous woman from the whore. This line is most fiercely drawn in the genre picture of Mrs. Sinclair's death. After describing the nightmarish physicality of the whores who appear in dishabille around Mrs. Sinclair's deathbed, Belford portentously declaims, "I admire, and next to adore a truly virtuous and elegant woman: For to me it is evident, that as a neat and clean woman must be an angel of a creature, so a sluttish one is the impurest animal in nature" (VIII: 52) (1388). Lovelace's obsessive trials of Clarissa's virtue are only one aspect of the desire to fix the boundaries between good women and bad women; Lovelace wants to prove that there are no virtuous women, and Richardson to prove that there are heroic, implacable women of virtue. These overt projects to some extent mask and confuse the more pervasive—and more difficult—project of defining sexual difference. Mrs. Sinclair and the whores slide disconcertingly from being women to being animals, or men, unsettling the gender categories and showing glimpses of monstrous bodies. Even though subdividing women into whores and saints may allow Richardson to recirculate and scapegoat negative feminine qualities in the service of exalting the pure woman, the danger remains that the outcast group may taint the exalted one because of ineradicable resemblances between them and her.

Lovelace's increasingly uneasy reliance on Mrs. Sinclair and her accomplices in his pursuit of Clarissa—as illustrated by his response to Sally's performance—is another facet of the same investment in femininity that characterizes his relation to Clarissa herself. By ruling over Mrs. Sinclair and the women of "the house," Lovelace seeks to discover the relation of vicious femininity to virtuous, and the relation of both to masculinity. But in some sense Lovelace gets too close to the women and they get too close to him. He hopes to enlarge his power by appropriating theirs, but in using them to supplement and endorse his own authority he recreates the same problems of dispersal and self-diminution implicit in his other efforts to mediate his desires through possession of and identification with an admiring audience.

Lovelace's real (not phantasmic) female audience seems more likely to supplant him than to supplement or applaud his power. Over and over Lovelace, Belford, Anna, and Clarissa insist that women lost to virtue *exceed* men in wickedness. Lovelace's equivocal celebration of Mrs. Sinclair after her participation in the rape shows the strength of his superstitious belief in women's excess: "Mrs. Sinclair is a true heroine, and, I think, shames us all. And she is a *woman* too! Thou'lt say, The best things corrupted become the worst. But this is certain, that whatever the Sex set their hearts upon, they make thorough work of it. And hence it is, that a mischief which would end in simple robbery among men rogues, becomes murder if a woman be in it" (V: 314) (896).[56] Lovelace here endorses Mrs. Sinclair's heroism primarily to berate himself for his own inadequacy. He uses the unnaturalness and extremism liberated in female violence to goad himself to a particularly male violence, though he retains his belief in his own sex's prior claim to power and strength. But the sense that the rape is underwritten by the women's desire to bring Clarissa to their own level troubles Lovelace deeply. Their demonic investment in Clarissa's fall— "*You owe us such a Lady*" (III: 283) (522)—disturbs Lovelace with the implication that they may be capable of usurping his power and of draining away his potency—and that *his* penis has become *their* instrument, not his own:

And *here* from Below, from BELOW indeed! from these *women*! I am so goaded on—

Yet 'tis poor too, to think myself a machine in the hands of such wretches.—I am *no* machine.—Lovelace, thou art base to thyself, but to *suppose* thyself a machine. (IV: 226) (658)

These doubts about his masculine primacy, and the frantic reassertion to himself of his independent power, recall both his fantasy of Clarissa as the Eastern monarch and his own diminution and displacement from the position of triumphant rapist.

In another sign of his displacement from the center of the scene, Lovelace also becomes disturbed by the notion that the whores' desire to humiliate Clarissa supersedes and even replaces their desire for him, although he tries to claim credit for having made them diabolical:

After all, what devils may one make of the Sex! To what a height of— What shall I call it?—must those of it be arrived, who once loved a man with so much distinction, as both Polly and Sally loved me; and yet can have got so much above the pangs of jealousy . . . and promote a Competitorship in his love, and make their supreme delight consist in re-

ducing others to their level!—For thou canst not imagine, how even
Sally Martin rejoiced last night in the thought that the Lady's hour was
approaching. (V: 4) (729)[57]

The women's power over him, consolidated by their involvement
with the rape, is underscored by his continued, unwilling dependence on their company: "But I will go down to these women—
and perhaps suffer myself to be laughed at by them" (VI: 45)
(940). His dread that they will deflate him does not stop him from
being drawn to their claims of identity with Clarissa (which coexist with the suggestion of their identity with him, even to the
extent of their desiring her rather than him) and to their claims
that they can uncover Clarissa's similarity to them and train her
to be like them. This formulation exposes the contradiction in
their assertion, for if Clarissa is already like them, why should she
need training? Lovelace doubts their assertion of identity—their
own investment in dragging Clarissa to their level is too obvious—but he continues to listen because he wants to believe what
they tell him:

Devil fetch them, they pretend to know their own Sex. Sally was a
woman well educated—Polly also—Both have read—Both have sense—
Of parentage not mean—Once modest both—Still they say had been
modest, but for me—Not entirely indelicate *now*; tho' too little nice for
my *personal* intimacy, loth as they both are to have me think so.—The
old one, too, a woman of family, tho' thus (from bad inclination, as well
as at first from low circumstances) miserably sunk:—And hence they all
pretend to remember what *once* they were; and vouch for the inclinations
and hypocrisy of the whole Sex; and wish for nothing so ardently, as that
I will leave the perverse Lady to their management, while I am gone to
Berkshire; undertaking absolutely for her humility and passiveness on
my return; and continually boasting of the many perverse creatures
whom they have obliged to draw in their traces. (VI: 45) (940)

The whores' dubious claims of identity with Clarissa and knowledge of the truth about the "hypocrisy of the whole Sex" sound
suspiciously like Lovelace's assertions that his former bashfulness
makes his understanding of women a variety of self-knowledge.
Their boasts of conquests also echo—sourly—Lovelace's vaunting

about the bodies of women he has seduced. The whores' boasts provoke Lovelace in part because the women threaten to succeed in conquering Clarissa (which he failed to do), but also because the emptiness of his own boasts of conquest suggest that their knowledge of female nature is as inadequate as his when it comes to dealing with Clarissa. In short, their specious claims reveal the vacuity of his.

Mrs. Sinclair and the whores threaten to replace Lovelace as designer and executor of plots and conspiracies, turning him into their servant as well as their master—a "machine," as he puts it.[58] It becomes clear that his proposals for proceeding against Clarissa have been emptied of desire: "In this situation; the women ready to assist; and, if I proceeded not, as ready to ridicule me; what had I left me, but to pursue the concerted scheme . . . and to convince her [Clarissa], that I would not be upbraided as the most brutal of Ravishers for nothing?" (VI: 55) (946). These multiplied substitutions for a flagging or absent desire show the extent to which Lovelace's power has been usurped, first by his own dismal performance as rapist, and next by *all* the women, both those who threaten him with ridicule and the one who condemns him as "brutal ravisher." Because the rape on which he depended for so much has gained him nothing—not epistemological satisfaction concerning Clarissa or femininity, not Clarissa's acknowledgment of desire, not revenge, not sexual satisfaction, not her humiliation—he seems emptied, and thus particularly susceptible to the whores' taunts and to Clarissa's reemergent power.

One of Lovelace's "concerted schemes" to humble Clarissa after the rape—a scheme pursued without desire—is transformed by Clarissa into a scene of "innocence . . . triumphant: Villainy . . . debased" (VI: 64) (951), as Lovelace reports in a moment of self-disgust mediated by the watching whores. In this scene, Clarissa repossesses her body essentially by offering to replay the rape as a symbolic self-penetration, or a kind of displacement upward; in a paradoxical step toward complete reintegration she represents as her own the power he has imagined only *his* body holds.

Clarissa announces to Mrs. Sinclair and the whores that she is unmarried, threatening the "vile women" with ruin. When Lovelace tries to advance on Clarissa, he reports,

> she turned to me; "Stop where thou art, O vilest and most abandoned of men!—Stop where thou art!—Nor, with that determined face, offer to touch me, if thou wouldst not that I should be a corpse at thy feet!"
>
> To my astonishment, she held forth a penknife in her hand, the point to her own bosom, grasping resolutely the whole handle, so that there was no offering to take it from her.
>
> "I offer not mischief to any-body but myself. You, Sir, and ye, women, are safe from every violence of mine." (VI: 62–63) (950)

When Lovelace approaches her again, she makes ready to stab herself until he retreats, his "heart pierced, as with an hundred daggers!" (VI: 65) (951), and her life is saved. Lovelace's use of the language of piercing—directed at himself—replicates Clarissa's turning of the phallic knife on herself.

Clarissa wrests the power to create spectacles from Lovelace at the moment she grasps the penknife.[59] The balance of power seems to shift conclusively away from Lovelace; rather than his hoped-for scene of phallic display—with the woman he has raped silently endorsing his triumphant masculinity, a female audience desiring him, and a male audience wishing to be him—he suffers the whores' mockery, and he suffers the raped Clarissa's usurpation of his phallic centrality. It is his body, not hers, that is hollowed out, invaded by the opposite sex, and remade.

Lovelace's defeat in *Clarissa* has been construed as showing the self-limiting nature of his chameleonism. Arthur Lindley, for example, sees Lovelace as doomed by "his protean character, [his] lack of a stable self."[60] According to Gillian Beer, Lovelace's "passion for disguise makes of him an existential hero constantly fashioning and refashioning himself, while at the same time he reveals the pathological extent of his ontological uncertainty . . . by his dread of 'acting out of character,' that is, by ceasing to be a Rake."[61] Yet this view of Lovelace as a man compelled to follow out the deadly implications of his roles, to the erosion of his self, does not fit with the details of his use of self-transformation. Lovelace seems to be defeated less by the lack of a stable self than by irreconcilable desires, particularly the wish simultaneously to capture and to replace women. His libertine's obsession with all details of femininity seems clearly to be a manifestation of these desires; the secondary tales of seduction in *Clarissa* constitute a repetitive attempt to catalog, define, and thereby exorcise the female threat that Lovelace as Tiresias wants to defuse by incorporating femininity in himself. Clarissa, however, cannot be exorcised; she definitively gets under his skin, not he under hers. Even violence against her does not dispel her power over him.

Lovelace's policy has always been to consort only with virgins; having deflowered and impregnated women whom only he has marked, he can dismiss them as devoid of mystery. But his compulsive movement to the "next" woman—justified by Lovelace as revenge upon the sex from which his "Quality Jilt" came—indicates that his penetration and explosion of the mystery of woman remains incomplete; he has yet to quiet what impels him. Clarissa arrests Lovelace's progress through the bodies of women because she refuses to embody his fantasies about women, and refuses to repeat sexual acts; she will not be a whore, and she is not a mother. All Lovelace's other women have entered into a compact with him, a compact in which they assent to the power of his desires, participate in those desires, and allow the repetition of sexual acts. They then expire in childbirth or turn into whores, becoming in either case knowable and fixed—easy to discard—while Lovelace himself remains fluid, mysterious, and metamorphic, although still unsatisfied. His self is not "precarious" before the rape, as Eagleton says,[62] although it is apparently metamorphic; instead he has imagined he had the power not to be defined, or at least to shift definitions at will, a power destroyed by the rape.

Before the rape Lovelace has the potential to be defined and to define himself in several ways, but after the rape he is, for Clarissa, a rapist. Terry Eagleton believes that the rape is a disaster for Lovelace because in it the female body becomes absolutely real: "In raping Clarissa [Lovelace] unmasks not the 'nothing' of her 'castration,' but a rather more subversive absence: the reality of the woman's body, a body which resists all representation and remains stubbornly recalcitrant to his fictions."[63] As well as invoking the Lacanian "real," Eagleton seems to echo Luce Irigaray's celebration of the feminine as that which is outside representation and that which undermines representation. But it is arguable that what Richardson produces is a shift, not a refusal. In fact, it is the rape that allows Clarissa's removal from the site of sexual activity; her body ceases, in some way, to be the body of a woman and begins to belong to another sphere of identity. Leo Braudy sees Clarissa adopting "Gulliver's method, separating her personal identity from the contamination of body in search of a definition of character based on inner principles and order. Both consider the body to be a weak defense against the necessary incursions of the world."[64] As she becomes the exemplar to her sex, those sexual differences that have been the grounds for Lovelace's play with gender become increasingly mystified. The paradox is not so much Clarissa's as Richardson's; in his effort to remove Clarissa from the taint of being a fallible woman he comes to endorse Lovelace's intermittent assertion that she is not a woman but an angel, a being without sex. The sharp distinction drawn between Clarissa and all other women in the book places her in a category both inside and outside femininity. Clarissa escapes the body and escapes the rape.

Because Clarissa refuses his definition of her and closes herself against his identification with her, Lovelace cannot move on to the next woman; Clarissa is still unassimilated to the category of woman, and he cannot yet fully believe she is an angel. He attempts repetitions of the rape and indulges in fantasies of little Lovelaces to comfort himself, trying anything that will cause this affair to repeat other affairs, and that will allow him to recover his Tiresian mobility. It is not so much that Lovelace fears acting out of character as that he has limited his field of activity, disastrously, to Clarissa; if she does not play, he cannot act at all. Clarissa arrests Lovelace's ability to recreate himself by using the bodies of women, and she cuts off his easy faith that he can understand and appropriate femininity. The rape, and Clarissa's response to it, conspire to force the recognition of Lovelace, not Clarissa, as separate, defined, fixed, *not* protean—and the recognition of masculinity, not femininity, as limited and univalent.

The sign of the absolute inefficacy of Lovelace's transformations, although not their cessation, comes in an elaborate plot to rape or seduce Clarissa a second time. He needs to make good the dissatisfactions of what would now be the first of two rapes; he hopes that a supplementary seduction might also redefine the original rape as a seduction. This fresh act of intercourse, he imagines, will allow him to effect some sort of compact with Clarissa, or even force her retroactive acknowledgment of desire for him. It will have the magically reintegrative power that he has imagined for marriage. Repeating the rape seems for Lovelace to be the only chance to gain possession of the first rape and of Clarissa. He sees that relying on the women of the brothel seriously undermined the (first) rape, but his fantasy of the second rape compulsively repeats that element of female complicity, as if rape is not possible for him without accomplices. In some sense these women seem to be necessary representatives of his desire to change into a woman in the sexual act, or perhaps strange representatives of the homosexual (lesbian?) component of his desire. It is this desire that Judith Wilt, however flamboyantly, responds to in her assertion that Mrs. Sinclair and the whores, not Lovelace, rape Clarissa. Lovelace requires the presence of these women as voyeurs, perhaps to ratify the rape and perhaps in order to stand in for him as voyeur. The cast of characters changes between the first rape and the second, but the fantasied assault takes place in a bed already warmed by a pair of women. And it is this fantasied scene, rather than the rape itself, that reproduces most closely the gender transformations in the attempted rape of Pamela.

The fantasy of the second rape casts an odd light on Lovelace's desires. Lovelace seems here to require a rich and shifting sense of his own gender and identity, and to demand that Clarissa remain purely and stereotypically female—to be a stable, unchanging ground—as well as utterly passive. But the scene focuses on his body, his transformations, not on her body or her desirability.

Lovelace wants to regain his mastery over metamorphoses, particularly in order to be the sole agent of transformations; he wishes
to possess Clarissa without being possessed by her.

Lovelace presents his fantasy of the second rape, which is also
its elaborated plan, as if it were a dream. He employs an unchar-
acteristically leaden irony to make clear to Belford that this is a
dream mostly in the sense that it is something he has dreamed up.
His description of the wished-for event bristles with "me-
thoughts" and melodramatic language. With delight he ventril-
oquizes the female participants inveighing against him as the
"*plotting villain*" and "*unchained* Beelzebub" (VI: 12) (922). In the
fantasy, Clarissa is supposed to have escaped, with Dorcas's help,
to the house of a virtuous dowager: "But, by some quick transition, and strange metamorphosis, which dreams do not usually
account for, methought, all of a sudden, this matronly Lady was
turned into the famous Mother H herself; and, being an old acquaintance of Mother Sinclair, was prevailed upon to assist in my
plot upon the young Lady" (VI: 12) (922). This shabby invocation
of metamorphosis revives Lovelace's pretense or belief that to
change the names of his cohorts gives him transformative powers.
But a residue of magical change does linger, although it has been
given initially into the hands of the women: The madam disguised
as a dowager deforms maternity, and Mother H, as the double of
her acquaintance Mother Sinclair, prepares to repeat the scene of
Clarissa's rape as controlled fantasy: "Then, methought, followed
a strange Scene; for, Mother H. longing to hear more of the young
Lady's Story, and night being come, besought her to accept of a
place in her own bed, in order to have all the talk to themselves.
For, methought, two young Nieces of hers had broken in upon
them in the middle of the dismal tale" (VI: 12) (922). This scene,
in which one rape is to be the subject of conversation at the performance of the next, shows Lovelace as the dreamer-voyeur, privy
to a female scene of female secrets. Lovelace imagines himself as
the central but absent figure in the scene of feminine intercourse,
and contemplates his mastery of the bonds of female commiser-
ation and solidarity, fictional bonds he has created in order to have
the imagined pleasure of destroying:

Accordingly going early to bed, and the sad story being resumed, with as great earnestness on one side as attention on the other, before the young Lady had gone far in it, Mother H. methought, was taken with a fit of the Colic; and her tortures encreasing, was obliged to rise to get a cordial she used to find specific in this disorder, to which she was unhappily subject.

Having thus risen, and stept to her closet, methought she let fall the wax taper in her return; and then [O metamorphosis still stranger than the former! What unaccountable things are Dreams!] coming to bed again in the dark, the young Lady, to her infinite astonishment, grief, and surprize, found Mother H. turned into a young person of the other Sex: And altho' Lovelace was the *abhorred of her Soul*, yet, fearing it was some *other* person, it was a matter of some consolation to her, when she found it was no other than himself, and that she had been still the bedfellow of but *one* and the *same* man. (VI: 12–13; brackets in original) (922)

Lovelace gloats over his own entrance, which occurs, so to speak, between brackets. His desire to be all participants at once communicates itself through his excited sentences, especially at the generative moment when identities and genders dissolve. The intoxicating moment in which Lovelace imagines Clarissa discovering Mother H "turned into a young person of the other Sex" is the quintessential moment of magical bodily change, but it is familiarity—repetition and sameness—that is presumed to be a comfort to Clarissa. The moment of actual intercourse is, by contrast, anticlimactic; Lovelace treats it, in fact, cavalierly:

A strange promiscuous huddle of adventures followed; Scenes perpetually shifting; now nothing heard from the Lady, but sighs, groans, exclamations, faintings, dyings—From the gentleman, but vows, promises, protestations, *disclaimers of purposes pursued*; and all the gentle and ungentle pressures of the Lover's warfare.

Then, as quick as thought (for Dreams thou knowest confine not themselves to the Rules of the Drama), ensued Recoveries, Lyings-in, Christenings, the smiling Boy, amply, even in *her own* opinion, rewarding the suffering Mother. (VI: 13) (922)

Lovelace does not seem interested in imagining fully the success of his plot; as he has said earlier, "More truly delightful to me the seduction-progress than the crowning act: For that's a vapour, a bubble!" (IV: 139) (616). The crucial moment for him may be not the rape but the moment of transformation and recognition—when he most powerfully explores the possibility of combining in himself male and female in sexual union. Clarissa's presence is only vestigially necessary. That transformation should have occurred in the original rape, and did not. In a perverse extension of this fantastic plot, Lovelace imagines having seduced Anna Howe; Lovelace's two offspring—Anna's daughter and Clarissa's son—will "in order to consolidate their mammas friendships (for neither have Dreams regard to *consanguinity*), intermarry; change Names by Act of Parliament, to enjoy my Estate" (VI: 13) (922). Incest succeeds metamorphosis as Lovelace's method of incorporating in himself and under his name all sexual activity connected with Clarissa's body; he extends his authority even more definitively through the lines of patriarchal inheritance. This incestuous lineage, which he sees as entirely his, although it is farcically enough portrayed, conveys the absoluteness of Lovelace's need to be master of all transactions, as well as his wish to elbow Clarissa aside. It is when Clarissa most threatens his authority by evading what he sees as the necessary consequence of rape—whoredom, maternity, or death—that this scenario of multiplied reassertion occurs. Clarissa's recently acquired (sexual) knowledge, which manifests itself, tellingly, in her total distrust of women, deflates Lovelace's "dream," with its promiscuous employment of metamorphoses:

What shall I say now!—I, who but a few hours ago had such faith in dreams, and had proposed out of hand to begin my treatise of *Dreams sleeping* and *Dreams waking*, and was pleasing myself with the dialoguings between the old matronly Lady, and the young Lady; and with the two metamorphoses (absolutely assured that every-thing would happen as my dream chalked it out); shall never more depend on those flying follies, those illusions of a fancy depraved, and run mad. (VI: 18) (925)

Lovelace distances himself from the failed plot, but the signs are now clear that he is no longer "master of metamorphoses" but perhaps a servant, caught in his own desires for transformation.

After Clarissa has rehearsed for the first time in her own words the full details of the events leading up to the rape, Anna Howe responds with an extravagant explanation of Lovelace's power to alter himself and of the barrier Clarissa erects to his ability to transform events and persons:

I never had any faith in the Stories that go current among country Girls, of Spectres, Familiars, and Demons; yet I see not any other way to account for this wretch's successful villainy, and for his means of working-up his specious delusions, but by supposing (if he be not the Devil himself) that he has a Familiar constantly at his elbow. Sometimes it seems to me, that this Familiar assumes the shape of that solemn villain Tomlinson: Sometimes that of the execrable Sinclair, as he calls her: Sometimes it is permitted to take that of Lady Betty Lawrance—But, when it would assume the angelic shape and mien of my beloved friend, see what a bloated figure it made! (VI: 179–80) (1014–15)

Ironically, and now belatedly, Anna accords Lovelace the honor of being the "master of metamorphoses." But the ubiquitous familiar of her imagination differs from the metamorphic figure of Lovelace's dream, because each of the "shapes" taken by "the familiar" can now be traced to its creator and stripped of its disguise; Lovelace's inability to create a convincing double for the inimitable Clarissa signals the limit of his previously limitless power. The exposure of Lovelace's creatures spells the dismantling of Lovelace's structure of deceit. Anna and Clarissa, by defining those about Lovelace as his creatures, as transformations of his being, paradoxically begin to contract the range of alterations left him. Once Lovelace's creatures are linked with him, he can no longer impersonate them undiscovered, and once he has been stripped of his assistant villains, his metamorphoses begin to lose their conviction and scope. The exposure of the links joining him to his accomplices exposes him too.

Lovelace is increasingly blocked by Clarissa's resistance and refusal, as well as by his own transgressive, contradictory desires. Richardson's representation of the Pyrrhic victory that Clarissa obtains seems designed to celebrate the death of Lovelace's rakish, libertine philosophy at the hands of a conception of femininity

that was still struggling for ascendancy. But the history of the
reception of *Clarissa* makes clear that the attractions of the rake
were anything but dead, and in a different register, it is also clear
that Richardson has no delusions about the pressures that require
Clarissa's death to secure the purity of her reputation. Lovelace's
attempt at incorporating the body of Clarissa in his own body,
perhaps because of its close resemblance to the daring undertaking
of Richardson himself in his novels, seems bound to fail, perhaps
in part to expiate Richardson's guilt at the resemblance or even to
deny it.[65] Although the novel seems to represent the failure of a
conventional rape, it is clear that the way the plot—Lovelace's
plot—goes wrong is not conventional. Lovelace claims at several
moments to be responsible for Clarissa's glory; without his trials
of her, hers would have remained an obscure, domestic life. Lovelace's boasts damn him, but they also seem to speak for Richardson
himself, who imagined these scenes of suffering for the greater
glory of Clarissa and of woman.[66] My focus on Lovelace's moments
of fantasy points up the moments when the resemblance between
Lovelace and Richardson as plotters becomes strongest.

Lovelace's motivation for his attack on Clarissa is not simply
sexual in the restricted sense; his desires cut to the heart of gender,
and his failure to satisfy his desires looks as if it may redefine gender conclusively by disallowing the belief that he can know more
about women than women know about themselves. By removing
Clarissa from the field of sexual difference and baffling Lovelace,
Richardson defeats Lovelace's imperial claims to understand every-
thing about women. Lovelace is excluded where Richardson goes;
Clarissa's heroic pathos makes her a figure of religious transcendence, inaccessible to her rapist, but not to her author.

තිළ

Clarissa's removal from the field of sexual difference and her
(problematic) transcendence of the body are not ultimately conclusive; Lovelace continues his refusal to acknowledge any transformation, even the transformation of death, and Clarissa herself
tries to ensure the integrity and representational qualities of her

body after her death. Although her body has become an encumbrance to her, her preparations of it for deathbed and coffin have the aura of an artistic self-memorialization that parallels her careful preparation of the text of *Clarissa*: She transcends her body, but she retains its use as a representation of herself. Before she dies, Lovelace makes his last attempts to possess her by trying to replace her self-memorialization with his own representations of her. Although he is now at one remove from her, only able to view her through the mediation of Belford's letters, he reconstructs her on the stage of his imagination, continuing his assumption of power over her and continuing his claim of superior knowledge of her character and being:

> How the dear creature's character rises in every line of thy Letters! But it is owing to the uncommon occasions she has met with that she blazes out upon us with such a meridian lustre! How, but for these occasions, could her noble sentiments, her prudent consideration, her forgiving spirit, her exalted benevolence, and her equanimity in view of the most shocking prospects (which set her in a light so superior to all her Sex, and even to the philosophers of antiquity) have been manifested? (VII: 318) (1309)

Lovelace audaciously claims to be the author of Clarissa's "blaze" because he has provided the "uncommon occasions" for her display of greatness. He justifies rape, immurement, and psychological torture by the results—his model seems to be lives of the saints (as written by the persecutors). But this saint's life appears to illustrate not so much the glory of God as the effectiveness of Lovelace in exposing Clarissa's own glory. While Lovelace speaks as a convert to belief in Clarissa's uniqueness, he also underscores his place as the artist and creator of the setting that allows her to shine forth—thus usurping not only God, but Richardson. His words also recall that earlier account of the spectacular effect Clarissa has on him at Hampstead, where she "blazed upon me, as it were in a flood of light, like what one might imagine would strike a man, who, born blind, had by some propitious power been blessed with his sight, all at once, in a meridian Sun" (V: 83) (772). On that occasion Lovelace celebrates her phallic force by claiming that it engenders him; here he celebrates her blaze by claiming he engendered it. He has shifted from the fetishization of her body to a fetishization of her "character," the being represented in writing, but the verbal echoes between the two passages suggest that the memory of her body as fetish object continues to propel Lovelace.

Clarissa's flight from the dangers of sexual display might be said to find its successful conclusion in her death. But, in fact, her continuing presence—as author of her will and even as contributing author and editor of *Clarissa*—keeps the problem of the meaning of her body actively before the reader: "But the occasion of my death not admitting of doubt, I will not, on any account, that it [her body] be opened; and it is my desire, that it shall not be touched but by those of my own Sex. . . . It is my desire that I may not be unnecessarily exposed to the view of any-body; except any of my relations should vouchsafe, for the last time, to look upon me" (VIII: 97–98) (1413). Her attention to the sex of her body after she will have relinquished it even returns her to a tentative faith—seriously damaged by Mrs. Sinclair insofar as she sees her as a woman—in her own sex, and to the expression, at least, of a faith in her family. The subterranean associations of this passage equate the gaze of observers outside her family with the touch of men and, as becomes clear when she continues, with Lovelace's rape of her:

And I could wish, if it might be avoided without making ill-will between Mr. Lovelace and my Executor, that the former might not be permitted to see my corpse. But if, as he is a man very uncontroulable, and as I am Nobody's, he insist upon viewing *her dead* whom he ONCE before saw in a manner dead, let his gay curiosity be gratified. Let him behold, and triumph over the wretched Remains of one who has been made a victim to his barbarous perfidy: But let some good person, as by my desire, give him a paper, whilst he is viewing the ghastly spectacle, containing these few words only: "Gay, cruel heart! behold here the Remains of the once ruined, yet now happy, Clarissa Harlowe!—See what thou thyself must quickly be;—and REPENT!—" (VIII: 98) (1413)

The reconstitution of the female body as inviolable and immune to the pressures of invasion and definition takes place at the expense of life. Clarissa is a corpse, speaking of sexual scandal in writing—her body itself a *memento mori*.

Lovelace claims the corpse, frantically insisting on his right to possess her heart and her body despite her absence from them. He plans, in his madness, to have her opened and embalmed, "to preserve the Charmer from decay" (VIII: 44) (1383). He asserts that her heart is his: "her *heart*, to which I have such unquestionable pretensions, in which once I had so large a share, and which I will prize above my own, I *will* have. I will keep it in spirits. It shall never be out of my sight" (VIII: 44) (1384). Lovelace's transfer of his attentions from her genitals to her heart is part of the shift from sex to sentiment that the novel accomplishes.

Beyond this attempt to possess (and dismember) her body, he also protests his ability to speak for her: "Altho' her Will may in some respects cross mine, yet I expect to be observed. I will be the interpreter of hers" (VIII: 46) (1385). This ownership is clearly identified as deriving from their "marriage"; he names her as Clarissa Lovelace and declares that his rights in her have precedence over the rights of her family. This dark parody of marriage presents them as "one flesh," one person—Lovelace—even in her absolute absence.

In a final allegorization of the meaning of the rape, Lovelace goes even further to fetishize and to erase Clarissa. He returns for a last time to the attempt to define the female body in relation to himself. His narrative of the struggle between Clarissa and Lovelace figures Clarissa as a miser and Lovelace as a thief—a thief, as he has said earlier, of his own joys:

Suppose *A*, a Miser, had hid a parcel of gold in a *secret place*, in order to keep it there, till he could lend it out at extravagant interest.

Suppose *B* in such great want of this treasure, as to be unable to *live without it*.

And suppose *A*, the *Miser*, has such an opinion of *B*, the *Wanter*, that he would rather lend it to him, than to any mortal living; but yet, though he has *no other* use in the world for it, insists upon very unconscionable terms.

B would gladly pay *common* interest for it; but would be undone (in *his own* opinion, at least, and that is every-thing to him) if he complied with the Miser's terms; since he would be sure to be soon thrown into *gaol* for the debt, and made a *prisoner for life*. Wherefore guessing (being an arch, penetrating fellow) where the *sweet hoard* lies, he *searches* for it, when the Miser is in a *profound sleep*, finds it, and runs away with it.

B, in this case, can be only a *Thief*, that's plain, Jack. . . . Suppose this same miserly *A*, on awaking, and searching for, and finding his treasure gone, takes it so much to heart, that he starves himself;

Who but himself is to blame for that?—Would either Equity, Law, or Conscience, hang *B* for a Murder? (VIII: 144–45) (1438)

Lovelace recasts Clarissa's rape and death as a competition between men over gold; in this last-ditch attempt to make Clarissa responsible for both rape and death he again must elide the femininity that defines, both for her and for him, the basis of the battle between them. Although he aims to expose Clarissa's overvaluation of her physical integrity, his allegorizing fails to solve his problems. By representing the rape as a theft of gold—Clarissa the greedy, miserly owner; Lovelace the daring thief—he seeks to separate Clarissa from her body, to make her virginity a possession that can be removed from her and owned by another. Although this conception of virginity as property has a long history, explored, for example, in *Pamela*, Lovelace's allegory defamiliarizes and discredits it. The allegory tries to detach the part of Clarissa that can be raped—her femaleness—and represent it both as a thing ("a parcel of gold") and as a space (the "secret place"), though the body that remains to protect this treasure becomes male. (Thus Lovelace seems to resume his search for a masculine competitor in lieu of Clarissa.) But when Lovelace moves from static equivalences (Clarissa = miser; Lovelace = "the wanter"; marriage = life imprisonment) to the narration of the rape, the problem of defining what the rape *does* resurfaces: What is it that Lovelace "runs away with"? The allegory depends on the conventional formula that he has taken her virginity, the virginity that can be lost but not gained; Lovelace does not become a virgin or the possessor of Clarissa's virginity. His "ownership" of other virginities, other maidenheads, has been founded on the women's desire for him, their impregnation by him, and, frequently, their death in childbirth. These other women have, in one way or another, ceased to be who they were. Clarissa's death is a rejection of all these possibilities; by not defining her self as a body disintegrated by the rape or as one whose essence is possessed by another, by not acquiescing in her commodification, Clarissa engages in a self-transformation that arrests change. Richardson's radicalism emerges in the refusal to define the female body as Lovelace does: something that can be dismembered. But the radical or revolutionary implications of Clarissa's stand are muted by the paradox that Clarissa's metamorphosis is into a state of changelessness.

As the transformations of Lovelace and Clarissa show, metamorphosis occurs in both the service and the avoidance of desire; at times it represents the presence of desire, at times it results from transgressing boundaries set on the expression of sexuality. In Ovid's tales of magical change, metamorphosis seems to result from desire—Narcissus becomes a flower because he desires himself to no avail—but metamorphosis, in a mysterious and less linear logic, seems also to be the aim and the essence of sexual desire. If desire causes metamorphosis at the same moment that metamorphosis is the aim of desire, tales of transformation will necessarily exhibit doubled or dreamlike forms of narration to account for the doubled, contradictory presence of desire.[67]

In Ovid, the transformations motivated by sexuality initially seem to be governed or justified by the usual narrative laws of cause and effect; they are extraordinary events issuing from events ordinary enough in themselves, fantastic extensions of a rational order. But this rational basis is disrupted from within by the conflicting causes and aims of metamorphosis. On the face of it, for instance, Daphne asks her father to turn her into a tree so that she can remain inviolate.[68] Her desire to remain a virgin "causes" her transformation, and the agent of her transformation is her father's ability to transform. But the urgency of Phoebus' desire for her also "causes" the metamorphosis. Daphne and Apollo's twin desires, conflicting and equivalent, are arrested, stabilized, and perhaps solved by her metamorphosis. Her transformation functions as a stay against a different transformation; she remains a virgin by being encased in a form to which the concept of virginity does not apply. As a result of Daphne's transformation, Phoebus' rapacious physical desire itself changes into the impulse to memorialize and appropriate; Phoebus turns Daphne-as-Laurel into a memento of his love as well as a representation of himself—the laurel is "his" tree.[69]

A virgin's shrinking from sexual knowledge has sufficient power, although only with paternal assistance, to thwart lust by means of a conclusive transformation. But this dream of a virgin's strength can also be read as the story of male—paternal and divine—collusion. Phoebus forces her to take refuge in an altered form, and her father helps. Clarissa's own transformation into a progressively more spiritual being, and then into the emblem of saintly death, shows a similar ambivalence about the power of physical virginity, the place of lust, and the collusion of the father.[70] Richardson makes considerable claims for the ability of spiritual virginity to transform and illuminate, but not only do those claims appear in the context of an insistently sexualized world—even perhaps require that world for their effect—they also rest on the assumption that a transformation to preserve virginity requires death; in Clarissa's case as in Daphne's, this is death at the hands of the lover and the father. Daphne's afterlife as a tree and Clarissa's afterlife as an angel (and text) may not be equal, but they are equivalent. Both metamorphoses, apparently flights from the desires of others, testify to the enduring strength of desire.

Lovelace's own Tiresian, protean self-transformations in pursuit of his desires both match and fail to live up to the alteration performed in Clarissa's radiant death. Although Lovelace has figured his trials of Clarissa in terms of the removal of her disguise and concealment, the novel tracks down Lovelace himself, revealing to Clarissa *his* disguises and concealments. Lovelace's sense that the secrets of women, once known, will destroy their power comes to restrict him, not her. The rape ends Lovelace's transformations in two ways: Most obviously, once Lovelace is a rapist, Clarissa is no longer in doubt about his meaning or about the meaning of masculinity.[71] So, in that sense, Lovelace, not Clarissa, is stripped and revealed (to her) by the rape. On a banal level, the rape may prove that he has a penis and she does not, but he fails to make that difference meaningful. Terry Eagleton has argued that the rape tries to uncover Clarissa's "lack" or her "castration," but instead finds the "real." But if we assume, as my argument does, that Lovelace wants to find himself as *both* masculine and feminine in her, the lack she reveals is his inability to incorporate her body in his, and his inability to define femininity as his own, wholly subsidiary fantasy.

The bodies that have been at issue in *Clarissa* are sealed by death—and writing—but the meaning to be attached to them remains unsettled and ultimately inconclusive. The barrage of models and concepts that Lovelace deploys to understand, shape, and conquer the idea of woman through Clarissa fails to create a definitive interpretation of femininity, in part because the construction and constitution of Lovelace's own sex and gender are bound to femininity by identification and incorporation on the one hand, and difference, opposition, and union on the other. Lovelace's attempt to use identification and incorporation to pursue a temporary and easily disowned coupling reveals the blockage that the confrontation between incompatible modes of conceptualizing gender and sexuality can produce. Richardson, himself deeply implicated in Lovelace's identification with femininity, defines Clarissa—and, with her, femininity—as absolutely different, apparently expelling and anathematizing Lovelace's predatory identification—but Clarissa's difference wavers between being personal and a product of her sex. Lovelace's identification across the supposedly impassible boundary between the sexes destabilizes both gender difference and masculinity; although Lovelace is expelled—consigned to hell—his incorporative desires leave their mark not only on the model of masculinity, but on Clarissa and on femininity. The removal of Clarissa from the taint of Lovelace's identification leaves her nowhere to go but to heaven—or into the memorial text of *Clarissa*.

"The Good Man, Alas!":
The History of Sir Charles Grandison and the Triumph of Masculinity

Sir Charles Grandison, the novel that was written to supply the portrait of the "good man"—to match Richardson's virtuous women and to redeem masculinity from the rakes he had represented—has seemed, to many readers, to be lacking at the core.[1] The central purpose and, even more, the central character fail to elicit from Richardson and the reader the moral, intellectual, and imaginative excitement found in *Pamela* and *Clarissa*.[2] Richardson himself recognized that a transposition of qualities and gender was required for him to write the "good man"; he felt his talents lay in producing good women—and bad men: "I own that a good woman is my favourite character. . . . I can do twenty agreeable things for her, none of which would appear in a striking light in a man. Softness of heart, gentleness of manners, tears, beauty, will allow of pathetic scenes in the story of one, which cannot have place in that of the other. Philanthropy, humanity is all he can properly rise to."[3] Even readers sympathetic to the novel have found Sir Charles's "philanthropy and humanity" inadequate food for the imagination; a frequent critical strategy is to deplore the oppressive dreariness of the hero and then proceed with relief to the "female pleasures" present in the lively and expressive heroines.[4] But because the glacial presence of Sir Charles is, in part, predicated on the exposure, repression, and denial of "female pleasures," in this chapter I would like to explore the interdependence of the masculine and feminine in *Grandison*, and to read the fates of the good women and the bad men who must give way to Sir Charles Grandison.

Grandison is the literary heir to *Clarissa*, not only in the sense that it works as reparation for the earlier novel, but also because Sir Charles Grandison himself is the offspring of a "rake" and an "angel" who bear strong resemblances to Lovelace and Clarissa. His mother's fate points up the tragic results of marrying a rake— the very fate some of Richardson's correspondents had suggested for Clarissa when they pressed for her marriage to Lovelace. Not only does Charles's virtuous mother suffer moral torments in life, but she also dies because of a duel: Frightened by injuries her husband receives, she sickens and expires; witty, charming Sir Thomas survives to torture his daughters, keep mistresses, and banish his son from the kingdom so Charles will not witness his degradation. (Sir Thomas finally dies, appropriately, in the midst of negotiations for a new teenaged mistress.) This filiation also serves as sign of the transfer of (literary) power and imagination from the constellation good woman / bad man to the good man: Because Lovelace and Clarissa are dead, Sir Charles Grandison can live.

But, of course, they are not dead, only transformed. Although *Grandison* seems at times to deny or repress signs of the patterns of gender transformations and sexual disruption that appear in *Pamela* and *Clarissa*, those patterns do reappear, but in new forms, often displaced or reoriented. In this novel Richardson attempts to create a new social contract, a community ruled over by a benevolent, perfect lawgiver, Sir Charles Grandison. What would elsewhere in Richardson's work tend to belong to the individual psyche becomes in this novel community property.[5] This transition to a relentlessly social view of character, prefigured by the latter half of *Pamela* and by *Pamela*, Part 2, inflicts losses that have, for many readers, proved fatal to interest. The novelist's utopian vision, which looks in particular to harmonious and virtuous relations between the sexes, is created out of the same imaginative materials and the same strategies that Richardson used to produce a tragic view of gender in *Clarissa*. Voyeurism is drained of its secrecy and transformed into exposure and exhibition. The duplicity that haunts the feminine in *Pamela* is rendered as the literal doubleness of the hero's relation to the two heroines of the novel. Anxieties about masculinity are distanced from the hero, but his phallic power and his rigidity are endorsed at the expense of others; many of the men around him die, are emasculated, or are reduced to feeble gratitude by his inexorable force. Sadism here becomes the property of the virtuous; torture serves reform and revelation, not sexual menace. Feminine power is scapegoated and redirected to underwrite the hero and the community. The novel inverts and reverses many of the strategies that inform the investigation of gender in *Pamela* and *Clarissa* without entirely discarding those strategies. And ultimately, in the collision of old methods and evolving ideals, the undertow created by the old tactics and materials—and what they represent—is too strong for those new ideals, particularly the new ideals of masculinity.

Perhaps partly because Sir Charles is much less directly accessible to the reader or to the other characters than are Pamela, Clarissa, and Lovelace, the sexual politics of *Grandison* are paradoxically both more openly displayed and more explicitly displaced from the body and mind of the hero. The triumph of virtuous masculinity takes place through Sir Charles and because of Sir Charles, but he himself does not, to all appearances, engage in battle. In the absence of the rich psychic lives of Lovelace and Clarissa, *Grandison* forces us to read signs; unable to know Sir Charles from within, we infer him from the bodies and minds of others. The accretion of interpretation and praise around Sir Charles *creates* Sir Charles as hero, just as the love for him professed by women creates him as lover.

Grandison begins with an apparent misdirection that indicates the problems with gender that will continue to trouble the book throughout: In a novel whose subject is the "good man," Sir Charles himself does not appear until the reader has come to know Harriet Byron. A witty and vivacious young woman, Harriet

promises at first to be the (sole) heroine, but her energy will be
severely dissipated by her desire for the apparently unattainable
hero, and her position in the fiction will be compromised as well
by the later appearance of a supplementary heroine, Clementina
della Porretta. Our response to Sir Charles is predicated on Harriet's desire for him and gratitude to him. Later more women (and
men) will smooth his path to us, interpret for him, and evidence
his attractions. Richardson conceived of this delay in the appearance of the hero as strategic preparation (or as a kind of foreplay):
"But who is the good man that you think you see at a little distance?—In truth he has not peeped out yet. He must not appear
till, as at a royal cavalcade, the drums, trumpets, fifes and tabrets,
and many a fine fellow, have preceded him, and set the spectators
agog, as I may call it. Then must he be seen to enter with an eclat;
while the mob shall be ready to cry out huzza, boys!"[6] This letter
to Lady Bradshaigh disconcertingly recalls Lovelace's meditations
on the relations between usurping crowd and diminished hero (see
Chapter 2, pp. 80–81). And indeed, the comparison between Sir
Charles and Lovelace is more far-reaching than it may initially appear, for Sir Charles's effect and power, like those of Lovelace, do
reside largely in the "drums and trumpets" of his laudatory spectators in the novel as well as outside it, and the impact is more
stultifying and ominous for all—including the good man himself—than perhaps Richardson would be prepared to admit. Lovelace's anxiety about the phallic properties of the figure at the center of the parade may indirectly inform the life of this hero, too.

The delay in the appearance of Sir Charles allows Richardson
to recapitulate in miniature some of the motifs of *Pamela* and *Clarissa*, and in general to focus on the inner workings of the virtuous
woman under pressure from bad (or vapid) men. But perhaps because of the teleology of this part of the novel—all roads lead to
Sir Charles—Harriet Byron's suitors seem, for the most part,
crude and pale imitations of Lovelace. Preparing the way for the
hero involves the representation of some inadequate examples of
masculinity; these men allow the heroine to define her relation to
men while still free of love's transforming (or humiliating) effects.

Harriet's sensitivity to male oppression recalls the situations of Clarissa and Pamela, but, at least initially, her responses to men—like the analysis of women—appear as part of a more social, less personal investigation of the nature of gender and the sexed body than occurs in *Pamela* and *Clarissa*.[7] For example, Harriet's anger at her rakish suitor, Greville, leads her to generalize about male subterfuge in terms that recall Clarissa's revulsion against men's deceit, but that lack the powerful sources of Clarissa's anxiety:

O these dissemblers! The hyaena, my dear, was a *male* devourer. The men in malice, and to extenuate their own guilt, made the creature a *female*. And yet there may be male and female of this species of monsters. But as women have more to lose with regard to reputation than men, the male hyaena must be infinitely the more dangerous creature of the two; since he will come to us, even into our very houses, fawning, cringing, weeping, licking our hands; while the den of the female is by the highway-side, and wretched youths must enter into it, to put it in her power to devour them. (1.24)

The flare-up of outrage seems both excessive and slightly impersonal in context—she is more annoyed with Greville than genuinely frightened of him. This complaint is followed by the equally impersonal, didactic claim that, despite the evidence of Clarissa, detecting and defending against such monstrous creatures are not difficult—and are the moral responsibility of women: "It is not difficult, my dear, to find out these men, were we earnest to detect them. Their chief strength lies in our weakness. . . . We should not prove the justice of their ridicule by our own indiscretions. But the traitor is within us. If we guard against ourselves, we may bid defiance to all the arts of man" (1.24). Although the descriptions of male and female hyaenas tip the balance of blame against men, the second passage suggests that it is the woman who contains treacherous desire, which Harriet pictures both as an alien intruder and as an aspect of the self. The second passage recalls conduct-book admonitions, echoing too the warnings implied by Clarissa's story and explicitly spoken by Lovelace. Harriet's successive attacks on masculine license and feminine self-betrayal expose the interdependence of the two, but her words also show signs of equivocation, a doubleness in the voice; the description of men as hyaenas exhibits a certain lurid energy and imaginative engagement, but the warning to women seems to point out the direction *Grandison* will follow, and to carry with it the weight of a cultural admonition. This novel, in fact, proposes to free women from the need to repress desires (the traitor within) by creating a "good man" to counteract the hyaenas. A woman who falls in love with Sir Charles need not—should not—deny her desire. Richardson thus adumbrates the warnings to women of male perfidy he has produced elsewhere, but then seeks to deny their universality, presenting Sir Charles as the glorious flower of masculinity and the ultimate reward for women.

The interval before the entrance of Sir Charles Grandison, and thus before masculinity can be redeemed, depicts a fictional world in which the meaning of gender distinctions is contested. These distinctions are explored in terms of the difference between men and women and of differences within each sex. The first part of the novel has as a governing image the looking glass, symbol of unity and difference; Harriet initially uses the mirror to reflect various versions of herself, to play with possibilities of representation, and to create and interpret herself and others. The mirror signifies the male narcissism of Sir Hargrave Pollexfen, Harriet's most determined and violent suitor, but it is also used by Harriet to satirize and parody the usurping and devouring men she encounters, and as a figure for writing. The mirror allows Harriet to attack masculine aggression while distancing herself from the attack; with the mediation of the mirror, she can claim merely to represent, not judge. As in her attack on hyaenas, by using the mirror Harriet appropriates the prop of an ancient "truth" about women—that they are vain and fall in love with themselves when they look in mirrors—to indict and mock male vanity.[8] Harriet's appropriation of the mirror as a tool of representation becomes progressively more daring and active:

Sir Hargrave, the whole time of dinner, received advantage from the su-
percilious looks and behaviour of Mr. Walden; who seemed, on every-
thing the Baronet said, (and he was seldom silent) half to despise him;
for he made at times so many different mouths of contempt, that I
thought it was impossible for the *same* features to express them. I have
been making mouths in the glass for several minutes, to try to recover
some of Mr. Walden's, in order to describe them to you, Lucy; but I
cannot for my life so distort my face as to enable me to give you a notion
of one of them. (1.46)

Harriet uses the mirror to try to reproduce on her own face the
ludicrous expressions on the face of a man; she uses a mirror to
make herself a mirror, in a sense. Like many mirrors, she gives
back an image that defamiliarizes and transforms the original. She
also performs a kind of witty masquerade, assuming the distorting
expressions of male authority, and exposing them as hideous and
laughable because of their unsuitability to the female face. She
frees the picture of the woman looking in a mirror from its associations with female vanity, and uses it to produce a derisive representation of a man.

Mr. Walden, the pedant she mocks, predictably sees women
as nothing more than featureless conduits for male genius, magnifying mirrors: "You have thrown out some extraordinary things
for a *lady*, and especially for so young a lady. From *you* we expect
the opinions of your worthy Grandfather, as well as your own notions" (1.52).[9] Walden's condescending remarks to Harriet appear
during a long debate over female education that also covers the
battle between the ancients and the moderns; not only the subject
of conversation but the representation of the scene and its characters continue the extensive interrogation of gender roles and of
desire. For example, among the audience is the "masculine" Miss
Barnevelt, whose enthusiasm for Harriet's cogent but modest re-
buttal of Walden domesticates same-sex desire and, at the same
time, reasserts the bodily basis of femininity. Miss Barnevelt attests to the universal appeal of Harriet, and her presence discreetly
marks the outer limits of Harriet's possible transformations of
gender roles: "She [Miss Barnevelt] profess'd that I was able to

bring *her own sex* into reputation with her. Wisdom, as I call it, said she, notwithstanding what you have modestly alleged to depreciate your own, proceeding thro' teeth of ivory, and lips of coral, give a grace to every word. And then clasping one of her mannish arms round me, she kissed my cheek" (1.57). In writing of this occurrence, Harriet again resorts to the mirror to aid her composition of text and body, to slip away from "inappropriate" desire, and to produce a further twist in her masquerade: "Just here, Lucy, I laid down my pen, and stept to the glass, to see whether I could not please myself with a wise frown or two; at least with a solemnity of countenance, that, occasionally, I might dash with it my childishness of look; which certainly encouraged this freedom of Miss Barnevelt. But I could not please myself. My muscles have never been used to any-thing but smiling" (1.58). These physical parodies and performances in the mirror support and move toward written forms of masking: Harriet creates a letter from Miss Barnevelt (to whom she gives "a brother *man* to write to, not a woman," to emphasize further Miss Barnevelt's violation of her gender role), ventriloquizing Miss Barnevelt's desire "that I had been a man for [Harriet's] sake" (1.69). This slightly vertiginous moment repeats as comedy those moments of cross-gender identification so prevalent in *Clarissa*; Richardson, writing as a woman, writes as another woman wishing she were a man for love of her self. But here the crossing of gender seems externally imposed and almost devoid of psychic energy, as well as free of plot significance. Miss Barnevelt's desire is figured as masculine because it is directed at a woman (and perhaps because desire is itself understood to be masculine) and because Miss Barnevelt, though female, assumes "mannish" airs and habits. Miss Barnevelt's open, cheerful violation of her prescribed gender role seems to be a dead end; her desire does not stand in for the desire of a powerful male in the fiction, as does that expressed by Mrs. Jewkes, for example. Miss Barnevelt attests to Harriet's attractions and allows Harriet scope for her wit. In her satirical letter, Harriet freely crosses gender lines to depict her own desirability while disowning the effects of that crossing.

Harriet also guys Mr. Walden's condescension: She has him echo Lord Chesterfield's notorious remark that "women are but children of a larger growth," calling women "but domestic animals of a superior order. Even ignorance . . . is pretty in a woman" (1.70).[10] Misogyny is deflated by the woman's masquerade; reading those remarks over a female signature frames and makes them doubly ludicrous, despite the fact they hardly differ from current commonplaces about the female sex. Both the written and the physical reflections Harriet engages in have the power to disrupt the smooth operations of sexual difference by displacement and doubling. Miss Barnevelt, as rogue element in the dichotomy of the sexes, also helps to unsettle gender roles; Harriet equally mocks her own sex—here appearing in masculine guise—and the other sex, thus keeping her position unfixed.

But the mirror resumes its monitory force as sign of feminine transgression in the course of Harriet's abduction by Sir Hargrave Pollexfen, and the novel begins to restrict feminine play and transgression. Harriet has been carried off in the aftermath of a masquerade ball—through a logical slide on which the novel actively insists, the abduction occurs *because* of the masquerade—and the specter of feminine transgression is conjured up in the fraught association of a mirror and a masquerade costume. During a violent scene between Sir Hargrave and Harriet, she glimpses herself in the mirror: "I arose, and as the candle stood near the glass, I saw in it my vile figure, in this abominable habit, to which till then, I had paid little attention. O how I scorned myself!" (1.161). Sir Hargrave has just exploded in misogynist accusation: "Miss Byron, said he, you are a *woman*; a *true woman*—And held up his hand, clench'd. . . . Miss Byron, proceeded he, after a pause, you are the most consummate hypocrite that I ever knew in my life" (1.161). "Woman" and "hypocrite" are synonymous terms of abuse. When Harriet sees in the mirror the outward and visible sign of "woman"/"hypocrite," she takes those meanings on herself. The mirror does not penetrate disguise or promote self-knowledge—Harriet is not a hypocrite, nor is she guilty of disguise—but the representation she sees in the mirror traps her as surely as if she were both hypocrite and disguised. The mirror returns her to the state in which femininity is constructed out of the interaction of hyaenas without and treachery within; she loses her command over representation, and the mirror signals that loss.

Richardson's equivocal use of the mirror to endorse and subvert feminine self-regard appears also during one of the stormy trials of Clarissa. Clarissa is being pressed by the Harlowes on behalf of the loathsome Solmes: "I had put myself by this time into great disorder. . . . I sat down fanning myself (as it happened, against the glass) and I could perceive my colour go and come; and being sick to the very heart, and apprehensive of fainting, I rung. . . . I heard my Brother pronounce the words, Art! Female Art! to Solmes" (II:198) (308). Clarissa's perception of her emotions has split; she experiences her disorder but also watches it in the mirror. Her fluctuating color should authenticate her suffering, but a crude alternative reading—"Female Art!"—also exists within the scene. Clarissa's reading of herself in the mirror does not support James Harlowe's interpretation, just as Harriet's distaste for her reflection does not support Sir Hargrave's interpretation, but the mirror does inscribe a division in these women, a division that leaves them prey to self-disgust and vulnerable to attack.

Harriet's masquerade costume—she is dressed as an "Arcadian princess"—marks her transgression even in her own eyes while Sir Hargrave Pollexfen manipulates the sartorial codes to "prove" her guilt. When Sir Charles Grandison happens on the unfolding abduction, Sir Hargrave reveals Harriet's dress to tell against her: "The vile wretch said, he had only secured a runaway wife, eloped to, and intending to elope from, a masquerade, to her adulterer [Horrid!]: He put aside the cloak, and appealed to my dress" (1.166; brackets in original). Sir Hargrave virtually has her in a straitjacket, having tied a handkerchief over her head, muffled her in the capuchin cloak, and captured her hands. As she reports, "Except that now-and-then my struggling head gave me a little opening, I was blinded" (1.163). The masquerade costume metaphorically exposes her, and Sir Hargrave and the enveloping capuchin literally immobilize her and deprive her of the use of her senses.[11]

Harriet loads herself with blame, seeing the masquerade costume later in a metaphorical mirror, lamenting "my presumptuous folly, in going dress'd out, like the fantastic wretch I appeared to be, at a vile, a foolish masquerade.—How often, throughout the several stages of my distress, and even in my deliverance, did I turn my eye *to* myself, and *from* myself, with the disgust that made a part, and that not a light one, of my punishment!" (1.168). Sorrowful self-examination and self-division replace parody of others, and female error, however innocent, puts an end to Harriet's detached analysis of appearances. But Richardson has, in a sense, altered the direction of Harriet's earlier declaration that, for women, "the traitor is within." In the case of Harriet's masquerade costume, the traitor seems to reside in the clothing, which symbolizes the vanity and the transgression of which she herself seems free; the masquerade costume endangers her, allowing Sir Hargrave to capture her and almost to rape her. No traitor actually lurks in Harriet's bosom, although treachery surrounds her; the "traitors" are external, in the persons of the double-agent servant, William Wilson, and the Awberry women, who refuse to save her from Sir Hargrave. The dress of the Arcadian princess, which she submissively puts on, represents feminine vanity and danger; it both does and does not adhere to her.[12] But the guilt Harriet feels at attending the masquerade is endorsed by Sir Charles and by the novel; the weight of the costume is too great to fling off entirely. Harriet has to pay for her free mockery of men—her other masquerade—just as, later, Sir Charles's independent, witty sister, Charlotte, must be "matronized" and domesticated to pay for her energetic mockery of her husband. Masquerade and mirror are recovered as aspects of the warnings to women against vanity and transgression.

The masquerade and the abduction engender a kind of fall for Harriet. Her control of the mirror, as we have seen, is lost; the mirror now reflects shame, not power, and the novel belongs to her rescuer, Sir Charles Grandison. Sir Charles's defeat of Sir Hargrave and, by extension, of the swarm of Harriet's suitors appears in the foreground, but Harriet endures a certain loss at the advent of Sir Charles too; from being a manipulator of representations, she becomes the patient recorder of male glory. Her satire and parody subside, handed over to the other outrageous woman, Charlotte Grandison (who will herself be subdued). Sir Charles's heroic entrance reorients the analysis of gender produced in the novel; masculinity triumphs through Sir Charles's systematic consolidation of power over men, and Harriet Byron's flexible and exuberant deployment of female power gives way to the dictates of love and male authority.

ϡ

The consolidation and celebration of masculinity in the person of Sir Charles Grandison—the transfer of power I have been mapping—begins with payment from a man as well as from a woman: male tribute in the form of (symbolic) castration, and the use of a woman as object of exchange, join to strengthen Sir Charles's position in relation to the other characters in the novel. Sir Charles's defeat of Sir Hargrave involves a literal transfer of goods in combination with a symbolic act of emasculation; through superior strength, Sir Charles wounds Sir Hargrave and carries off Harriet. After asking Harriet if she will put herself in his protection, Sir Charles proceeds to break Sir Hargrave on a wheel, in a scene that is meticulously described by the hero himself:

"I opened the chariot-door. Sir Hargrave made a pass at me. Take that, and be damn'd to you, for your insolence, scoundrel! said he.

"I was aware of his thrust, and put it by; but his sword a little raked my shoulder.

"My sword was in my hand; but undrawn.

" . . . I seized him by the collar before he could recover himself from the pass he had made at me; and with a jerk, and a kind of twist, laid him under the hind-wheel of his chariot.

"I wrench'd his sword from him, and snapp'd it, and flung the two pieces over my head.

" . . . Sir Hargrave's mouth and face were very bloody. I believe I might have hurt him with the pommel of my sword.

"One of his legs, in his sprawling, had got between the spokes of his chariot-wheel. I thought that was a fortunate circumstance for preventing further mischief." (1.140–41)

Sir Charles diffuses his own agency so that we receive the distinct impression that Sir Hargrave has caused his own injuries, adding further to the sense that Sir Charles embodies providential retribution. The defeat of Sir Hargrave, however, has a more complicated and contradictory life in the novel than this brisk description would suggest.

Sir Charles tells his audience that the encounter with Sir Hargrave has been reported as "nothing in the world . . . but two young rakes in their chariots-and-six, one robbing the other of a lady" (1.142–43). This cynical reaction points in several directions: Richardson seems at once to acknowledge the banality of the rescue as a plot element while showing the gap between the report and the truth; and he presents the callousness and the misogyny of the surrounding world to highlight, in contrast, Sir Charles's virtuous care for women. But Grandison partly undermines this contrast by echoing the perception of women as possessions that can be stolen; he flatteringly remarks that Sir Hargrave "might well give out that he was robbed; to lose such a prize as Miss Byron, and his sword besides" (1.143). Later he asks Mrs. Reeves, "How can we well blame the man who would turn thief for so rich a treasure?" (1.148). "Trafficking in women" thus does not belong solely to cynical misogynists or rakes, and the invocation of that model puts Harriet in her place as an object of exchange—although the exchange at first seems to go wrong.[13]

Grandison is represented as too moral to participate in an overt competition with another man over a woman (and too superior to need to compete), or too high-minded even to recognize the implications with respect to woman or man of a competition. In fact, Grandison's refusal of the homosocial bond his action ought to forge with his opponent nearly unhinges Sir Hargrave, who pursues Grandison with demands that he acknowledge the tie he created by his encounter over Harriet. Harriet struggles to deny her own entrapment in the teleology that requires Sir Charles to acquire her; since Sir Charles seems to fail to recognize that the two are fated to fall in love, Harriet feels humiliated at her own subscription to the romance imperative. The secret source of Grandison's baffling lack of interest in Harriet Byron ultimately crystallizes into another triangle, this one involving Sir Charles and two women—Harriet and Clementina della Porretta—and apparently untouched by male homosociality until we discover the place of Clementina's brother in Sir Charles's relation to her.

Although the narrative moves to focus on the relationship between Harriet and Sir Charles, Sir Hargrave Pollexfen does not vanish after Sir Charles "disposes" of him. He does, however, seem to be reduced to a fairly limited meaning and function. If he has not endured literal castration in his initial encounter with Grandison, he has experienced physical injuries and a symbolic emasculation that have links to other, more explicit wounds in the world of the novel. The specter of castration appears repeatedly in *Sir Charles Grandison*; both Jeronymo della Porretta (the brother of the second heroine, Clementina) and Mr. Merceda, Sir Hargrave's rakish associate, suffer "groin" injuries that punish them for acts of sexual aggression. Sir Hargrave's injuries are the only ones Sir Charles inflicts; in fact, Sir Charles rescues both Jeronymo and Merceda (along with Sir Hargrave) from those who want to wound them, but his presence at all three scenes-of-the-crime signals the continuity of his involvement. I will return to an examination of those wounds, after a look at Sir Hargrave.

Sir Hargrave, in the aftermath of Harriet's rescue, stages two more scenes in his quest to regain his masculinity (to recover his sword) and to escape or overturn the effects of his injuries. He attempts to replay as a less lopsided duel Sir Charles's disarming of him; at the same time, however, he competes with Harriet for the position of most wounded by the abduction/rescue, apparently aiming to gain possession of her as recompense for his losses. He seems uncertain whether he should play the man or the woman. In response to Sir Hargrave's overtures, Sir Charles displays his heroism by resisting the restrictive code that defines both manliness and honor in terms of dueling.[14] Richardson's didactic purpose—itself partly an expiation for the duel at the end of *Clarissa*—comes under conflicting pressures, as a number of readers from the eighteenth century on have remarked. Sir Charles can resist duels, but he always does so from a position of physical as well as moral superiority. We are left in no doubt that he would win any duel.[15] His authority is too great to be diminished; in a gesture of absolute phallic superiority he takes the pistols Sir Hargrave has offered, discharges them out the window, and then refuses any reciprocal display in response to Sir Hargrave's increasingly hysterical gestures: "Sir Hargrave threw open his coat and waistcoat, and drew; and seemed, by his motions, to insist upon Sir Charles's drawing likewise. Sir Charles had his sword in one hand; but it was undrawn: the other was stuck in his side: his frock was open" (1.253). Sir Charles need not prove his authority over Sir Hargrave, partly because Sir Hargrave has already been conclusively unmanned and infantilized: "Sir Hargrave even sobbed . . . like a child.—D—n my heart, said he, in broken sentences—And must I thus put up—And must I be thus overcome?" (1.252). The initial stages of Richardson's redefinition of masculinity in *Grandison* require a violent and direct defeat of masculine violence. But although the hero is involved in this defeat, he consistently defuses and denies the compulsion it requires. The burden of castrating others never settles on Sir Charles, although he frequently is associated with it. He does not inflict castration, but, like the Freudian/Lacanian father, he presides over the threat of its performance.[16]

Sir Hargrave focuses his obsession with defeat on the marks left on his face; he returns to those marks over and over, presenting them not as the outward signs of internal suffering, but as the source of suffering itself. As wounds to his sense of narcissistic wholeness, these marks both diminish him and represent his loss. Sir Hargrave attempts to trade on them in his doomed but unabated campaign to win Harriet: "He had a *right*, he said, to see me [writes Harriet]: He was a sufferer for my sake. They saw, he told them, that he was not the man he had *been*" (1.269).[17] When he is allowed to see Harriet, he compares his visible facial wounds with her invisible suffering: "*I* have forgiven worse injuries, point-ing to his mouth" (1.269). Since he never inflicted the rape that was the threat behind his abduction of Harriet, his "disfigured" mouth takes priority in his mind. The comparison of his mouth with her genitals seems quite clear, if unspoken. Sir Hargrave at-tempts to appropriate, on behalf of the marks on his face, the sym-pathy and pathos that would have attached to Harriet's body had she been raped. This abbreviated competition recalls the much more extensive explorations of similar themes in *Clarissa*, when Lovelace claims that the injuries *he* has sustained from the rape are far greater than any suffered by Clarissa herself. Of course, Sir Hargrave's efforts to put himself in the place of the wounded woman (who can be displaced in this case because, paradoxically, she has not been wounded) conflict with his attempts to convince Sir Charles, his competitor, and himself that he is still whole and fully masculine.

Sir Hargrave's narcissistic pleasure in himself gives way to the perception of lack. Now he refuses to look in the mirror: "Curse me, if I can bear to look at myself in the glass!" (1.254). Harriet reports that he is "mortified with the damage done to a face, that he used to take pleasure to see reflected in the glass (never once looking into either of those in the parlour he was in, all the time he staid)" (1.288). Before the abduction, Harriet disapprovingly presented a vignette of Sir Hargrave's "feminine" vanity: "He for-gets not to pay his respects to himself at every glass; yet does it with seeming consciousness, as if he would hide a vanity too ap-parent to be concealed" (1.45). The disfiguring of his countenance even takes priority over the loss of Harriet; in fact, his desire for Harriet is now coded as the desire for a substitute or restitution for the loss or lack he cannot face in the mirror. The mirror signals loss, just as it did for Harriet.

A contemporary account of the imagined consequences for criminals of literal castration helps to illuminate Sir Hargrave's wounds as well as the other wounds in the novel. In 1750 a correspondent of *The Gentleman's Magazine* addresses the problem of criminals' pleasure in displaying themselves, even at their executions, and proposes castration, rather than hanging, as a punishment for "capital" crimes—in a sense literalizing Freud's equation of decapitation and castration:

I am serious in proposing *castration* for the men, whenever they commit a crime that by the present laws would entitle them to the gallows. Intemperate lust is the most frequent cause of such crimes, and what more adequate punishment?

 . . . Many of these wretches are more anxious about the safety of their bodies, than either the fatal catastrophe itself, or the misery that may succeed it.—Their bodies are themselves. The body relishes pleasure and enjoyment, and is the only object of their concern.

[In castration, the correspondent sees] A kind of *ignominy* too, that subjects them to the highest contempt of those very creatures who have principally contributed to their ruin.

Should a capital C be marked on each cheek, their contemptible, infamous circumstance would be known to every one they meet: Yet they would still be capable of labour, and in a condition of benefitting society both by it and by example.[18]

The writer's dream is to make the criminal body absolutely (and literally) readable, and to make it completely undesirable to the real criminals, women—"those very creatures who have principally contributed to their ruin"; even castration is apparently inadequate to the task, so the mark of castration must also be imposed. In *Grandison*, it seems that the mark may be the primary bearer of meaning; what has happened to the body is sometimes secondary.

Sir Hargrave's punishment, which suggests castration while not quite being it, perfectly fits his crime, which threatened but did not perform rape. Sir Hargrave can be seen as a de-authorized version of Lovelace: in Margaret Doody's words, he is "from the beginning, a light and foolish character, who is, unlike Lovelace, incapable of bringing events to any serious catastrophe."[19] To put it in other terms, he lacks the equipment for rape.[20] But, more important, the novel has no investment in Harriet's being raped;

it does, however, have an interest in the threat of rape. Yet if, as Doody suggests, that threat is unconvincing because of Sir Hargrave's insubstantiality, why does it appear at all? Although the threat of rape can be explained in terms of Richardson's revision of *Clarissa*, and its prevention can be seen as a return to the comic mode of *Pamela*, the averted rape in *Grandison* performs an important part in the novel's structure as well as in its analysis of gender. Sir Hargrave, it seems, stands in for Harriet Byron; his violent "castration" and *his* loss of the mirror's pleasure stand in for her displacement from the center of the novel, serving to remind the reader and Harriet herself that, at least in this text, Sir Charles has exclusive rights to power. In more explicitly psychoanalytic terms, it could be said that Sir Hargrave's emasculation discreetly signifies Harriet's inability to possess the phallus.

Sir Charles's entrance into the novel effects a double transfer of power, although the change in balance it signals might also be figured as a shift of power in a triangle: Sir Hargrave (who also represents the swarm of Harriet's suitors) gives way to Sir Charles as the standard of masculinity, and Sir Charles takes over from Harriet the position of central character. Sir Charles usurps the narrative power and energy raised by the contention between the other two. He could be said to share the limelight with Harriet, but that is probably not the experience a reader has of the novel. The disabling of Sir Hargrave, to some extent, mirrors the disabling of Harriet; Sir Hargrave and Harriet are both disarmed, shown their inadequacy, their lack, by Sir Charles. Harriet can eventually regain a position and a self through Sir Charles, but Sir Hargrave cannot. Sir Charles—the man who never draws his sword—is created in part by the diminishment of the other men in the novel, as well as by the submission of women to their desire for him.

The later reiteration of the theme of castration, in two separate examples, suggests its broad significance for Richardson's project of creating the "good man."[21] Sir Hargrave only reenters the novel to endure a second near-castration. Sir Hargrave and his friend, Mr. Merceda, are rescued by Sir Charles and his physician friend,

Mr. Lowther, outside Paris on Mont Martre. The rakes have been guilty of "a vile attempt . . . on a Lady's honour at Abbeville"; the Lady's husband and brothers are the men in pursuit. Charlotte Grandison, now Lady G, describes the event, but the provenance of this description, ultimately directed to Harriet Byron, is extraordinarily complicated: Charlotte first receives a visit from a friend of Mr. Lowther's, who brings a letter from Lowther; then another friend, Mr. Beauchamp, is with Charlotte and borrows the letter; Mr. Beauchamp then consults the servant of Sir Hargrave who was present at the event, and writes a letter to Dr. Bartlett, Sir Charles's friend and mentor. Finally, from that letter, Charlotte makes an "abstract" for Harriet and at the end apologizes for its length: "I thought to have shortened it more than I have done. I wish I have not made my abstract confused, in several material places: But I have not time to clear it up" (2.433). Neither the rescuer nor the victims can speak directly to us about this event; it seems to need multiple layers of wrapping before Charlotte and Harriet can touch it. Narrative unease seems *de rigueur* for discussions of castration. Charlotte's squeamishness about representing the event, however, contrasts sharply with her open enthusiasm for the (missed) chance to emasculate rakes: "And let me add, that had the relations of the injured Lady completed their intended vengeance on those two Libertines (A very proper punishment, I ween, for all Libertines), it might have helped them to pass the rest of their lives with great tranquillity; and honest girls might, for any contrivances of theirs, have passed to and from *masquerades* without molestation" (2.431). Charlotte's reference to the masquerade here foregrounds the connection between this episode and Sir Hargrave's averted rape of Harriet. The symbolic castration Sir Hargrave suffered in the aftermath of that episode is, by this, brought nearer to actual execution, but still withheld or avoided. Although Sir Hargrave is a target, the text focuses on Mr. Merceda's injuries. Richardson's insistence on the threat of castration for sexual aggression is matched only by his apparent reluctance to impose it unambiguously.

The text lingers on the details of the wounds in a way that

suggests the power of the image lies in the combination of the threat and its being averted:

[Mr. Merceda] had, besides, two or three gashes, which, but for his struggles, would have been but one. (2.433)

[Merceda] has, it seems, a wound in his thigh, which, in the delirium he was thrown into by the fracture, was not duly attended to; and which, but for his *valiant* struggles against the knife which gave the wound, was designed for still greater mischief. (2.433)[22]

Richardson keeps the sword hanging over him; he neither recovers nor succumbs entirely.

Charlotte's reference to the masquerade has disturbing effects; though she offers a "feminist"-utopian vision of a world of emasculated rakes, that fantasy has troubling implications for women as well as men. As Charlotte ends her "abstract," she reverts to a consideration of the masquerade: "As you, my dear, always turn pale when the word *Masquerade* is mentioned; so, I warrant, will ABBEVILLE [the site of the attempt on the woman] be a word of terror to these wretches, as long as they live" (2.433). The notion that women could only be safe if libertines were to be castrated reveals a deeply pessimistic view of male sexuality (except for Sir Charles's) and of the realistic prospect for female safety. Perhaps the darkness and hopelessness in that view help explain the covert stab at Harriet. When Charlotte equates Harriet's terrors at the word "masquerade" with the terrors "Abbeville" will represent for Merceda and Sir Hargrave, she returns to the belief, obliquely expressed by Sir Charles, that Harriet's trip to the masquerade is a transgression that requires—and has caused—punishment. As the men courted castration, so she herself made rape likely. Sir Charles advised against legal restitution because Harriet's reputation would suffer, saying, "Masquerades . . . are not creditable places for young women to be known to be *insulted* at them" (1.143). The equation may again signal the correspondence between Harriet's loss at the masquerade and castration.[23]

The other instance of near-castration, again arrested by Sir Charles, who again happens on the scene, plays a pivotal role in the plot, recasting or prefiguring recurrent elements of love and violence; through his rescue of his Italian friend, Jeronymo della Porretta, from a revenger's knife, Sir Charles finds himself teaching English to Jeronymo's sister, Clementina, who falls in love with him. Strong similarities appear in the stories of the rescue of Harriet and the introduction to Clementina. Female desire and Sir Charles's authority emerge against the background of male injury; Sir Charles is again ambiguously connected to the threat of castration, and once again, in the initial unfolding of the tale, the detailing of the injuries underlines the dangers to male wholeness. Once again, too, there is a belated apology for dwelling on disgusting wounds, this time in a report from Sir Charles to Harriet:

[Jeronymo] had one [wound] in his hip-joint, that disabled him from helping himself, and which I found beyond my skill to do any-thing with; only endeavouring . . . to stop its bleeding. . . . His wounds proved not mortal; *but he never will be the man he was*: Partly from his having been unskilfully treated by this his first surgeon; and partly from his own impatience, and the difficulty of curing the wound in his hip-joint. Excuse this particularity, madam. The subject requires it. (2.121; emphasis added)

Jeronymo and Sir Charles, former friends, were estranged before this lucky rescue because Sir Charles had reproached Jeronymo for his immorality with women, and warned him against his mistress. Another lover of that mistress hires the men who attack Jeronymo in the wilds of the Cremonese. Thus, Jeronymo's punishment, like that of Sir Hargrave and Mr. Merceda, fits the crime of sexual transgression. Yet Sir Charles's agency in the punishment may create a sense of unease about the hero's status in the fiction as well as his power. (Does he have only to condemn an action for punishment to ensue?) Grandison's ambiguous responsibility for the castration/rescue-from-castration of his fellow characters signals his quasi-authorial standing in the novel. Sir Charles warns Jeronymo against his behavior, but averts the punishment—perhaps. He speaks the threat, but has nothing to do with its performance; he just happens on the scene. Grandison's connection to authority and authorship, which is figured through the castration of his fellow characters, stands as a parallel to the link between Lovelace and the author. Although Lovelace's sexual violence emerges from the cross-gender identification he shares with his author, that violence, performed on the bodies of innocent women, is wholly disowned by Richardson; the sexual destruction performed on the bodies of men themselves guilty of compulsion in *Grandison*, in contrast, appears to have the approval of Richardson.

The exact location and implications of Jeronymo's wound remain somewhat vague, despite the "particularity" of the description. The descriptions of the wounds, Sir Charles's assertion that Jeronymo "never will be the man he was," and the recurring fevers confusingly suggest at once that castration has happened, that it continues to happen, and yet never quite occurs—it hovers but does not land.[24] Jeronymo's fluctuating fever also mimics the rise and fall of Clementina's disorder, in another link between masculine injury and female troubles, or, it may be, the partial displacement of masculine injury onto a woman's troubles—or vice versa.

The peculiar persistence of the motif of deferral, the contrast between great interest in describing the wounds and ominous vagueness about their effects, along with the contradictory nature of Sir Charles's presence in scenes of emasculation, evidence the disturbances in gender and sexuality that Richardson's production of the good man necessitates, as well as the cost to the author of such absolute authority inside the fiction. Margaret Doody describes from another vantage point the problems Richardson faced in writing about virtuous masculinity: "Richardson found it nearly impossible to present a *man* fully exercising the moral faculty. . . . Perhaps the author feared that a male character involved in complex moral processes might appear too introverted or oversubtle, lacking in straightforward masculine authority and appeal."[25] The danger of the loss of masculine authority—which is also, as Doody suggests but does not say, the fear of being feminized—haunts the hero and, by implication, haunts Richardson himself. Terry Eagleton, in his brief assault on *Grandison* in the postscript to *The Rape of Clarissa*, more explicitly pinpoints the ideological and gender problems of Richardson's attempt to create what he calls "a womanly man, for whom power and tenderness are fully compatible."²⁶ Eagleton claims that, partly because Sir Charles's virtue creates no danger for him, his chastity has no social or political ramifications, as does the chastity of Clarissa and Pamela.²⁷ This difference in impact of male and female chastity concerned Richardson himself. The troubles he faced in creating a chaste man are illustrated in a story Richardson tells Lady Bradshaigh:

Did I ever tell you, Madam, of the contention I had with Mr. [Colley] Cibber, about the character of a good man, which he undertook to draw, and to whom, at setting out, he gave a mistress, in order to shew the virtue of his hero in parting with her, when he had fixed upon a particular lady, to whom he made honourable addresses? a male-virgin, said he—ha, ha, ha, hah! when I made my objections to the mistress . . . and he laughed me quite out of countenance!²⁸

That laugh echoes in the careful composition of *Grandison*. Sir Charles's rigid masculine virtue—the closing-off of psychic exploration of cross-gender identification that informs Lovelace—can be seen as an effort to ward off a "womanliness" implied by his chastity. But the recurrence of castration in the novel, as well as the intermittent scapegoating of femininity, suggests that the consolidation of Sir Charles's masculine virtue and power exacts a price not only from the author but from the other characters of the novel, leaching their energy and hobbling the representation of the central character himself.

♍

Richardson seems both to accept the danger that Grandison could seem too feminine and to suggest that the violence against other men and women in the novel is necessary to solidify his position; both strategies are part of a large-scale and in some ways heroic attempt to redefine masculinity for his era. The "unconscious guilt" that Terry Eagleton speculates must have inhered in Richardson's creation of Lovelace is expiated in Sir Charles.²⁹ And the crucial interaction of that atonement with the attempt to redefine "the hero," a movement in which Richardson was deeply involved,[30] gives Sir Charles a social and cultural meaning that is complicated and perhaps undermined by his status as reparation for Richardson's guilt. While Sir Charles seems composed of qualities designed explicitly to be the very reverse of Lovelace's, he also bears a powerful family resemblance to that rake in his Grand Signor—like conquest of hecatombs of women; and, of course, by using Sir Charles to reverse and revise Lovelace, Richardson seems to keep the example of Lovelace alive in Sir Charles. And if Richardson explores and exploits the psychic meanings of his own cross-gender identification through Lovelace, he works to control and socialize those impulses through the creation of Sir Charles.

Sir Charles is a character who stands in opposition to the eighteenth century's acceptance of the sexual double standard, and who, in his own person, repudiates many of the conventions of masculine aggression. But Richardson's anxiously excessive praise of Sir Charles's unique splendor, as well as the ominous presence of castration around him, betrays the cultural (and literary) dangers that threaten the new man. The representation of Sir Charles bears the marks of Richardson's sometimes conflicting interests and, perhaps more significant, betrays a dark view of male sexuality that the novel denies, only to let it creep back—in the form of a rakish father responsible for the death of a saintly mother, for example, and in such moments as Charlotte's celebration of castration as solution to male aggression.

The representation of Sir Charles is also disturbed by problems in the hero's ambiguous relations to women and femininity; his angelic nature always seems in danger of being associated with femininity. His attacks on the surrounding culture sometimes appear intended to deflect attention from questions that might arise about his gender position:

I am not apt to run into grave declamations against the times: And yet . . . I cannot but think, that Englishmen are not what they were. A wretched effeminacy seems to prevail among them. Marriage itself is every day more and more out of fashion; and even virtuous women give not the institution so much of their countenance, as to discourage by their contempt the free-livers. A good woman, as *such*, has therefore but few chances for happiness in marriage. (2.10)

By attacking it, Sir Charles demonstrates that he does not suffer from "wretched effeminacy," but his beauty, for example, seems to encroach on female preserves: Harriet, in her first full description of his appearance, wonders enviously "what business a *man* has for such fine teeth, and so fine a mouth, as Sir Charles Grandison might boast of, were he vain" (1.181).

Richardson insists on the hypermasculinity and omnipotence of his protagonist at the same time he gives him some conventionally feminine attributes and shows him as intermittently cast into feminine positions. Richardson's attempt to transform gender roles through the creation of Sir Charles leads to problems partly because Richardson seems inclined to convert Grandison's associations with women and femininity into evidence of his masculine superiority. Although Lovelace's sexual aggression keeps his identification with women from appearing to threaten his masculinity, in *Grandison* Richardson is in the dangerous position of having to produce evidence of Sir Charles's phallic potency while emphasizing his chastity. Richardson supplies Sir Charles with attributes of masculinity that do not rely on explicitly sexual activity, but as Colley Cibber's helpless laughter at the idea of a "male-virgin" demonstrates, aristocratic masculinity divorced from a very particular notion of male sexuality is difficult to construct convincingly for an eighteenth-century literary audience. In order to be the new man—the new hero—Grandison must be sexually attractive, but it is clear that Richardson lacks a language—and perhaps the eighteenth century lacks a language—for masculine sexuality that does not rely on crude references to or hints of actual sexual experience or that derives from the kinds of physical description ordinarily coded as feminine.

If Sir Charles's beauty seems ambiguously sexed, so too does the quality of radiance attributed to him; it recalls both the blaze of Clarissa and the sun fantasies of Lovelace, themselves already in a complicated relation to ideas of gender. Even though Sir Charles's spectacular presence seems wholly beneficial, it actually has some troubling side-effects that arise from the questions about the gender of images attached to Sir Charles. Harriet not only feels at times overwhelmed and outshone by Sir Charles—"There is no living within the blazing glory of this man!" (1.384)—but she also fears that his superior embodiment of those very qualities for which women are known makes women themselves unnecessary and contemptible in his eyes: "Ah, my Lucy, one thing I am afraid of; and that is, that Sir Charles Grandison, politely as he behaves to us all, thinks us women in general very pitiable creatures" (1.373).[31] His glorious superiority usurps and lowers the self-esteem of women, gathering all erotic energy to himself, even to the point of disabling the proper desires of others, in a beneficent echo of the castrations that gather around him. Harriet reports (from secondhand information) the effect on his sisters of Sir Charles's return to England after their father's death: "But, do you wonder, that the sisters, whose minds were thus open'd and enlarged by the example of such a brother, blazing upon them all at once, as I may say, in manly goodness, on his return from abroad . . . should, on all occasions, break out into raptures, whenever they mention THEIR brother?—Well may Miss Grandison despise her lovers, when she thinks of him and of them at the same time" (1.373). Caroline has fallen in love before Charles returns, but Charlotte remains dissatisfied with all other men after she has seen her brother again. At times it seems that Sir Charles can only be made absolutely desirable and appropriately masculine by denying both desirability and masculinity to everyone else and by showing him as the only possible object of desire—even for his own sister. When Sir Charles finally does marry the long-suffering Harriet, hyperbolic comments suggest that other women's desires are conclusively thwarted:

Sister, said Kitty Holles, . . . we never, never, can think of marrying, after we have seen Sir Charles Grandison, and his behaviour. (3.239)

. . . As there is but *one* Sir Charles Grandison in the world, were his scheme of Protestant Nunneries put in execution, all the rest of womankind, who had seen him with distinction, might retire into cloisters. (3.396)

This jubilant celebration of Sir Charles seems intended to induce emulation among men and thus more marriages rather than the immurement of women, but the literal meaning of these statements differs too little from the characteristic mode of the novel's endorsement of Sir Charles to be entirely discounted.

Sir Charles, like Pamela and Clarissa, and like Harriet too, suffers from the conventionally female problem of troublesome, unwanted attentions from the other sex; in decided contrast to Pamela, Clarissa, and Harriet, however, Sir Charles possesses a mysterious knowledge of the opposite sex. He combines the (presumably passive) power of the desirable object with the power to penetrate the other. Sir Charles comes to resemble Lovelace in his vaunted knowledge of women, but Sir Charles, unlike Lovelace, encounters no heroic resisters, no Clarissas. There is no reason to repel this man's penetration.

Despite these indications that Richardson succumbed to the need to make his hero sexually knowing, he bristled at the requests of Lady Bradshaigh and other women that the good man be a "moderate rake." Richardson paraphrases Lady Bradshaigh: " 'The good man need only to assume the dress and address of the rake, and you will wager ten to four that he will be preferred to him.' " Richardson responds vehemently: "[The rake] must flatter, lie, laugh, sing, caper, be a monkey, and not a man. And can a good man put on these appearances? We have heard that the devil has transformed himself into an angel of light, to bring about his purposes; but never that an angel of light borrowed a coat and waistcoat of the devil, for any purpose whatever. And must the good man thus debase himself, to stand well with the fair sex?"[32] The language Richardson uses to resist the idea of the good man playing the rake—the devil borrowing the clothes of an angel of light—closely recalls Lovelace's Satanic disguise at the inn at Hampstead. While Richardson claims he only reluctantly interjected moments of moderate rakery in Grandison's character to placate "the fair sex," Sir Charles also demonstrates a deeper resemblance to rakes like Lovelace, notably in his immense power over women. As Carol Flynn observes, Sir Charles "realizes Lovelace's sexual fantasies as well as his dreams of conquest."[33] Grandison is supposed to arrive at his knowledge of and power over women through strictly honorable means, but Sir Charles's flashes of Lovelacean inside information about women create disorienting effects.

Sir Charles's sufferings from worthy—and unworthy—women, the price he has paid for the distinction and favor of women, seem to be part of the background for his deep knowledge of women. His wide experience of "the sex" both resembles Lovelace's knowledge of women and differs from it. In one example of Sir Charles's "moderate rakishness," he expatiates on the pleasures of courtship: "For my own sake, I would not, by a too early declaration, drive a Lady into reserves; since that would be to rob myself of those innocent freedoms, and of that complacency, to which an honourable Lover might think himself entitled; and which might help him [Don't be affrighted, Ladies!] to develop the plaits and folds of the female heart" (1.429; brackets in original). A muted version of Robert Lovelace's voice can be heard through Grandison's words. Grandison's hypothesized pleasure in delayed declarations also skates disturbingly close to his own actual treatment of Harriet; Sir Charles's impeccable reasons for not proposing to Harriet—his honorable obligation to Clementina della Porretta—allow him and the reader the (erotic) pleasure of seeing a virtuous woman in love but doubtful of the man's response. Harriet's distress produces Sir Charles's— and our—aesthetic and educational experience of feminine pathos, and gives Richardson his grounds for exploring, once again, the "plaits and folds of the female heart." Sir Charles possesses his knowledge of women in an oddly distanced way partly because Richardson seems anxious to present this penetration only from the outside. To show this man's knowledge of women from the inside would presumably involve Sir Charles in all the disturbing issues of cross-gender identification that characterize Lovelace. Because Richardson is intent on blocking and denying the dangerous traces of "effeminacy" in Sir Charles, these issues must be repressed or displaced. But they resurface, most prominently, in the distresses suffered by the heroines.

☙❧

The novel's exploration of femininity, especially of female suffering from thwarted desire, depends on the presence of Sir Charles, the universally desirable object, but Sir Charles himself (unlike Lovelace) does not take part in the investigation. His hands are clean. The exposure of female desire (which in this novel is normally desire for Sir Charles) is exemplified in the representation of the two heroines: Harriet Byron is brought to acknowledge her love for Sir Charles through a combination of bullying and self-betrayal, and Clementina della Porretta "speaks" her love through the derangement of body and mind.

The exposure of Harriet's feelings, which becomes a kind of group project, contains an implied threat of violation. Having escaped a potential rapist in Sir Hargrave, Harriet is attacked from several sides; she first fears that Sir Charles's "penetrating eye" will leave her without defense (2.118): "He had seen my regard for him thro' the thin veil that covered it; and began to be apprehensive (*generously* apprehensive) for the heart of the poor fool; and so has suffered Dr. Bartlett to transcribe the particulars of the story [of Clementina], that they may serve for a check to the over-forward passion of your Harriet" (2.161). Harriet fears being penetrated and then being rejected because of what is revealed. Sir Charles becomes "the sun darting into all the crooked and obscure corners of my heart" while Harriet "shrink[s] from his dazling eye" (3.132). The images of phallic sun and penetrating or engendering eyes are carried over from *Clarissa*, but rather than being distributed between hero and heroine, here they collect primarily around Sir Charles. But, in fact, revelation and penetration in this novel occur primarily through the agency of women (virtuous women, in contrast to Mrs. Sinclair and the whores in *Clarissa* and Mrs. Jewkes in *Pamela*), as if the implied violence of those acts had to be rigorously divorced from the hero.

Harriet's grandmother and aunt encourage her to "open [her] whole heart" to them, reminding her that "it is no disgrace to be in love with a worthy man. Love is a natural passion" (1.303). Her grandmother insists that, in any case, her disguises are so transparent that "every child in love-matters would find you out"

(1.304). Harriet repeats the lesson she has been taught: " 'If you love, be not ashamed to own it to *us*—The man is Sir Charles Grandison' " (1.309). In this context, penetration should cease to induce fear or anxiety. Falling in love with an impeccable man should free the woman from the need for concealment; a utopian candor between the sexes would result, were all men like Sir Charles.[34]

Richardson's equivocal interest in scenes of voyeuristic display, so evident in *Pamela*, in *Grandison* receives its final purging and redirection; the novel works relentlessly to expose all actions and desires to the light of day. Private thoughts become communal property, and exposure creates an admiring audience. Sir Charles embraces the shorthand-writer in the closet and accepts the presence of Father Marescotti at the keyhole. When Marescotti, Clementina's confessor, spies on Charles's conversation with the young Italian woman, Sir Charles tells him that "the man, who, in the greater actions of his life, thinks himself under the All-seeing Eye, will not be afraid of a fellow-creature's ear" (2.578). In a repudiation of the pervasive binary oppositions so often arrayed along the lines of gender, Sir Charles consistently denies any distinction between public and private, personal and social, or even inside and outside; thus, there appears to be little reason for disguise or concealment.

Harriet only communicates her feelings, however, as a result of a kind of trial. Sir Charles' sisters, Charlotte and Caroline, interrogate Harriet about her feelings for their brother in a scene of teasing that verges on torture. This trial has affinities with the trials of the heroines of *Pamela* and *Clarissa*, but, in keeping with the shift between those novels and *Grandison*, the heroine here is tried by a pair of women who are the virtuous agents of a virtuous man—a virtuous man whose interest in the heroine is, moreover, still in doubt. The aggression apparent in the scene thus does not seem to originate in a man, as occurs in the whores' assault on Clarissa or Mrs. Jewkes's attacks on Pamela; but neither is it clearly the property of Charlotte and Caroline. The difficulty of locating the source of the aggression adds to the scene's faintly

disturbing quality and makes Charlotte Grandison slightly ominous and threatening, somehow associated with a penetration that
is not ultimately hers to perform. In acknowledgment of this quality in Charlotte, there are comments elsewhere that, had she been
a man, like Anna Howe she would have been a daring rake.

Richardson's delight in enforcing exposure marks the scene. In
this respect it particularly resembles the trials in *Pamela* and *Clarissa*, although the context of virtuous femininity and the sense
that a social purpose is being fulfilled seem intended to redirect
any voyeuristic pleasure. Charlotte and Caroline (and the reader)
know the state of Harriet's emotions, so the examination becomes,
not a search for the truth, but the vehicle for Harriet's self-
exposure and for the ritual expulsion of feminine "disguise":

> [Charlotte and Caroline] entered my dressing-room arm in arm . . . they
> looked as if they had mischief in their hearts. . . . Punish her then,
> Charlotte, said Lady L [i.e., Caroline]. You have . . . been brought to
> speak out yourself; and so have acquired a kind of right to punish those
> who affect disguises to their best friends.
>
> Lord bless me, Ladies! And down I sat—What, what—I was going
> to say, *do you mean?* But stopt, and I felt my face glow. . . .
>
> She snatch'd [my handkerchief] out of my trembling hand, and put
> it round my neck—Why this *sudden* palpitation?—Ah! Harriet! Why
> won't you make confidents of your two sisters? Do you think we have
> not found you out before this?
>
> *Har*. Found me out! How found me out!—Dear Miss Grandison, you
> are the most alarming Lady that ever lived!—
>
> I stood up, trembling. (1.417–18)

This reads a little like a benign parody of one of the scenes in
which Mrs. Sinclair and the whores circle around Clarissa; and the
mockery of feminine weakness recalls (if mildly) Mr. B's and Lovelace's attacks on feminine hypocrisy, as well as Harriet's own encounter with Sir Hargrave. The sisters tease Harriet into tears:

> *Miss Gr*. Ay, Harriet, be sullen: Don't answer any questions at all.
> That's your only way, now. . . .
>
> *Har*. I won't be sullen, Ladies. Yet I am not pleased to be thus—
>
> *Miss Gr*. Then own yourself a woman, Harriet; and that, in some

certain instances, you have both affectation, and reserve. There are some
cases, my dear, in which it is impossible but a woman must be guilty of
affectation.

    Har. Well then, suppose I *am*. I never pretended to be clear of the
foibles which you impute to the Sex. I am weak, a very weak creature:
You see I am—

    And I put my hand in my pocket for my handkerchief.

    Miss Gr. Ay, weep, love. My sister has heard me say, that I never in
my life saw a girl so lovely in tears. (1.419)

The aesthetics of female suffering as well as the affectation of
women are directly endorsed by Charlotte, who stands in for the
community of viewers (or voyeurs). The framed comment about
Harriet's loveliness—framed by the assertion that it is a remark
made before—echoes the whores' mockery of Clarissa's distress
and Mr. B's taunts at Pamela's tears. (Mr. B tells Pamela: "O how
happy for you it is, that you can, at Will, thus make your speaking
Eyes overflow in this manner, without losing any of their Bril-
liancy! you have been told, I suppose, that you are most beautiful
in your Tears!" [p. 162].) After reducing Harriet to tears, the sisters return to the relentless forcing of her confidence (which she,
of course, is assumed to desire). The request for a reciprocal display, familiar as a prelude to sex in Lovelace's fantasies, here depends on an identification of one woman's concealment with another's: "Be not afraid to speak out, my dear, said Miss Grandison.
Assure yourself of my love; my true *sisterly* love. I once intended
to lead the way to the opening of your heart by the discovery of
my own, before my brother, as I hoped, could have found me
out—But nothing can be hid—" (1.420). The voluntary opening
of the heart to Harriet that Charlotte intended was forestalled by
Sir Charles's penetration; in the scene just before this one, Sir
Charles, through a public interrogation of Charlotte, has uncovered her affections for a disreputable lover. Thus Charlotte employs
on Harriet the same techniques of forced revelation to which Sir
Charles subjected her.

    Charlotte insists on the transparent readability of Harriet's
body—its availability for viewing and interpretation—claiming

that it is part of a kind of public discourse. Harriet's verbal confessions will only acknowledge what her body—that revealing female body—has already made clear: "If you would not be teazed, don't aim at reserves—But think you, that we could not see, on an hundred occasions, your heart at your eyes?—That we could not affix a proper meaning to those sudden throbs just here, patting my neck; those half-suppressed, but always involuntary sighs—[I sighed]—Ay, just such as that—(I was confounded)" (1.420–21; brackets in original). Harriet has become an animated illustration of repressed love, throbbing visibly and sighing audibly; confronted with her betraying body, she can only repeat the signs. But Charlotte, contrary to Harriet's fears and contrary to what we have been led to understand, suddenly asserts that only women (and the novel's readers) are privy to this delectable picture; the meaning of her body's signs and sighs *can*, in fact, be concealed from the object of Harriet's love—from whom, it has just been said, nothing can be hidden. Once the sisters have elicited Harriet's confession, they plan to assist her in keeping her secret from Sir Charles: "Nor would they wish that (Sir Charles) *should* suspect me. The best of men, they said, loved to have difficulties to conquer. Their brother, generous as he was, was a *man*" (1.423). The paradoxical simultaneous presence of the complete transparency attributed to Harriet (not to mention Sir Charles's ability to penetrate) and the claim that the sisters can keep her "secret" indicates that Richardson wants to eat his cake and have it too; secrets—secrets already known—are pried with difficulty and delight out of the female bosom; the woman is helpless under the pressure of love, but the man still has to (gets to) conquer the difficulties and conquer her. Richardson's ideological propensity for revelation and openness vies with his attraction to women's secrets as source of narrative and epistemological power.

Harriet's legibility—the legibility of her desire—engages the novel in a discourse that is necessarily problematic and contradictory. In Richardson's push toward the total revelation of a woman's secrets, he comes up against the powerful cultural definitions of women as constituted by secrecy, concealment, and duplicity—

the belief that women are made up of "plaits and folds." Ludmilla
Jordanova describes this conceptual connection between women
and secrecy: "Women's bodies, and by extension feminine attributes, cannot be treated as fully public, something dangerous
might happen, secrets be let out, if they were open to view. . . .
The secrecy associated with female bodies is sexual and linked to
the multiple associations between women and privacy."[35] The snag
that Richardson's text has run into is the snag of the female body.
Without some veiling or concealment, the female body will not
be a female body, available for penetration and opening only *in
private*. It is when the push to reveal Harriet gets too close to the
body that Richardson has to pull back, in order to reinstate Sir
Charles's masculine prerogatives. If Charlotte goes too far in exposing Harriet to public view, or Harriet goes too far in exposing
herself, Sir Charles will have no "difficulties to conquer," nothing
manly to do—and presumably then he will no longer be a man,
Harriet will no longer be a woman in the ways that count, and the
novel will be deprived of a subject.

Charlotte herself, the agent of this dangerous approach to public revelation, falls prey to the paradoxically public exposure of the
female body on the stage of private, familial sexuality; after being
bullied by her brother into marrying a foolish lord, Charlotte
fights a long guerrilla war with her intellectually negligible husband, but is ultimately entangled in the domestic world of submission, childbirth, and maternity. As Harriet says, when Charlotte gives birth, "Her past idle behaviour to him (her husband)
was but play. She will be matronized now. The *mother* must make
her a *wife*. She will doubly disgrace herself, if she loves her *child*,
and can make a jest of her *husband*" (3.388). Maternity consoli-
dates the bonds of matrimony; Charlotte herself calls the infant
"the cement between us" (3.404). In fact, it is in the course of an
erotically charged scene of breast-feeding and exposure that the
final rapprochement between Charlotte and her husband, Lord G,
occurs. Although Charlotte at first tries to hide from her husband
the sight of her body engaged in this maternal function—"an act
that confessed the mother, the *whole* mother!"—he happens on the

scene, like Actaeon on the goddess Diana, as she reports. Lord G is overcome with ecstasy: "Never, never, never, saw I so delightful a sight! Let me, let me, let me (every emphatic word repeated three times at least) behold again the dear sight. Let me see you clasp the precious gift . . . to that lovely bosom—The wretch (trembling however) pulled aside my handkerchief" (3.403). Her breasts, like the baby, no longer function simply as hidden or incorporated signs of sexuality or sexual intimacy, or as parts of Charlotte's own body; they instead become possessions of the half-private, half-public domestic sphere ruled over by the husband. This domestic sphere regulates and defuses the dangers of exposing the female body by displaying it in the service of the family and in a private space. This Diana does not set the dogs on Actaeon; she submits to him as her husband.

The exposure of the female body—and the female mind—seems qualitatively different from the display of male bodies and minds. The taint of force, of invasion, adheres to the opening out of women's bodies and minds. Richardson's other novels deployed rape, or the threat of rape, to reveal women; *Grandison* relies on madness, self-revelation, genteel torture, and gentle entrapment to induce revelation. But part of what propels Richardson is, I think, lost in the process of that new, socially grounded exposure. *Grandison* moves toward the celebration of openness, but something gets left behind. The loss or the refusal of a mystery, principally located in women, affects both author and reader. The sense that women in particular require some shield, some veil to elicit readers' involvement, appears obliquely in a complaint by Lady Mary Wortley Montagu about Harriet Byron; she can keep no secrets, Lady Mary objects, communicating "all she thinks to all the people she sees, without refflecting that in this Mortal state of Imperfection Fig leaves are as necessary for our Minds as our Bodies, and tis as indecent to shew all we think as all we have."[36]

Clementina della Porretta—who wants a veil but gets a strait-jacket instead—demonstrates the pain for women that can come with revelation, if their desires are thwarted or unanswered. But what Clementina is called on by the novel to reveal is as much the nature of man—*the* man, Sir Charles—as the nature of women, or her own desires.

Clementina appears in *Grandison* inside a frame; her story is initially produced to clear up mysterious lacunae in the relationship between Harriet Byron and Sir Charles. Clementina's story functions in particular as the answer to the question of why Sir Charles, the novel's hero, has not actively pursued Harriet, the novel's heroine. Clementina constitutes Sir Charles's "secret," just as Sir Charles has been Harriet's and also, it emerges, Clementina's. Harriet might be said to learn Clementina's story—which is Sir Charles's secret—as a double-edged reward for revealing her secret to the Grandison sisters; in a sense, she gains another woman's secret by giving up her own. Sir Charles's relationship with Clementina, which chronologically precedes his acquaintance with Harriet, is textually interwoven with it. Harriet reads the descriptions of Clementina's anguish and melancholy in the midst of her own struggles with apparently unrequited love, and she suffers for Clementina as well as for herself. Sir Charles conveys the story of Clementina delicately, partly through the mediation of his mentor, Dr. Bartlett, thereby leaving to another some of the celebration of his desirability. Clementina thus appears doubly framed, protected from direct view. She sometimes breaks out of the frame, asserting her primacy, but the novel ultimately returns her to her secondary, illustrative, supporting role.[37]

Although the relations among Sir Charles, Clementina, and Harriet are undeniably triangular, Richardson plays down that figuration in several ways: he creates barrier/conduits like Dr. Bartlett, and he adds duplicating characters like Olivia to draw off the energy and the threat of rivalry between women. These doublings and divisions are used, like identification, to explore and define the conflicts. Doubleness and division characterize Sir Charles preeminently, but Clementina is also divided by the war between her love for Sir Charles and her allegiance to the Catholic church, and her strength is being eaten away by her secret love. Harriet contends not only with her distress at Sir Charles's "divided heart," but with the split in herself that comes from her identification with Clementina, and with the conflict she endures from her belief that, in justice, Sir Charles should reward Clementina's suffering with the gift of himself. Just as the novel seems to revise voyeurism, opening out what is hidden to fix it firmly in the domestic sphere, so too does it reorient duplicity. Sir Charles's "double Love" in a sense hypostatizes duplicity; instead of a disruptive quality in an individual woman, we are presented with a man equivocally in love with two women, and the divided nature of Clementina recirculates doubleness in a different mode and direction.

Grandison meets Clementina della Porretta as a result of her brother's wounds. Those injuries lead to another: Clementina falls ill of lovesickness after Charles (not yet Sir Charles) becomes her tutor in the English language. Clementina's feelings are medicalized as well as placed in the context of her brother's sickness; because she is melancholy, her parents "consulted physicians, who all pronounced her malady to be Love" (2.126).[38] In the case of Clementina, Charles "causes" the disease—induces love in Clementina—and is brought in to cure its effects; in the case of Jeronymo, he warns of punishment and (perhaps) averts its execution. Clementina's malady, in fact, is not simply "Love"; a conflict splits her:

Her confessor, taking advantage of confessions extorted from her of regard for her tutor . . . had filled her tender mind with terrors, that had thus affected her head. . . . All that medicine could do, was tried: But her confessor . . . kept up her fears and terrors. He saw the favour her tutor was in with the whole family . . . and, betwixt her piety and her gratitude [to Charles for saving Jeronymo], had raised such a conflict as her tender nature could not bear. (2.128)

The standard eighteenth-century cure for lovesickness was marriage (i.e., sexual intercourse), but Clementina's family and Clementina herself are divided about whom she should marry: Grandison or the Count of Belvedere—or Christ. Clementina, a fervent Catholic, considers escaping the conflict between "piety" and love by becoming a nun. There is thus a social and religious context for this apparently internal ailment.

Clementina's conflict is doubled in Harriet's identificatory comments; Harriet's observations on Clementina appear in the interstices of the unfolding tale, marking out the lines of resemblance and difference between the two women who love Sir Charles. For example, Harriet notices that Sir Charles makes Clementina his "sister," just as he does her:

> Ah, Lucy! your Harriet is his *sister* too, you know! He has been *used* to this dialect, and to check the passions of us forward girls; and yet I have gone on confessing mine to the whole venerable circle, and have almost gloried in it to them. Have not also his sisters detected me? While the noble Clementina, as in that admirable passage cited by her,
>
> > ——*Never told her love,*
> > *But let concealment, like a worm i' th' bud,*
> > *Feed on her damask cheek.*——
>
> How do I admire her for her silence! But yet, had she been circumstanced as your Harriet was, would Clementina have been so *very* reserved? (2.157)

Harriet identifies and distinguishes, drawing up a "parallel between our two cases" in double columns. The two women take upon themselves—into their own bodies, psyches, and writing—the conflicts and desires that also have external causes.

Harriet's celebration of Clementina denies competition, focusing on internal conflict to the exclusion of any discord between the two women; Sir Charles is thus saved from close examination:

> Such a noble struggle did I never hear of, between Religion and Love. O Lucy! you will be delighted with Clementina: You will even, for a while, forget your Harriet; or, if you are just, will think of her but next after Clementina! Never did a young Lady do more honour to her sex, than is done it by Clementina! A flame, the most vehement, suppressed from motives of piety, till, poor Lady! it has devoured her intellects! (2.163)

Repression in the service of religion is elevated to heroism, and madness becomes a sign of female honor, the body consuming the mind to avert direct sexual expression. Clementina becomes an emblem of the battle of religion and love, but the siting of the battle in her self partially obscures the participation of other forces, other people, in her trauma. Most notably, it distracts us from Sir Charles's problematic "double Love."

Because *Grandison* moves toward exposure and revelation while producing situations of apparent concealment and doubleness, the category of duplicity, which seems to hover as a description of characters and events, has to be evaded or refuted. Doubleness and division are rigorously kept apart from duplicity; Sir Charles's apparently simultaneous love for two women must be seen to signal his superior sensibility, rather than double-dealing. Richardson has to work hard to maintain this distinction between division and duplicity, and he does so partly by burying and blurring the issue of Grandison's love; even before Charles meets Harriet, his affection for Clementina recedes constantly, covered by reticence and gentility, and is almost extinguished by his refusals to pressure Clementina, to violate her family's wishes, to change his religion, or to reject his country. Everyone, including Grandison, agrees that he must love Clementina out of gratitude, pity, and admiration, but direct expression of that love is markedly absent. The problem of the duplicity in a "double Love" is partly solved by making the first love impossible to pin down—or to pin on Sir Charles. And, further, the duplicity that might seem to adhere to the man's self-division is off-loaded onto the women. Harriet and Clementina *embody* Sir Charles's "double Love," so that it is not his and is not duplicitous. The overdetermination—there are too many different justifications and excuses for Sir Charles's love for two women—signals the excitement and the discomfort created for Richardson by the problem. When Lady Bradshaigh protests that "'it is impossible for a Man to be *equally* in Love with two *Angels* at the same time,'" in an incongruous shift of genders, Richardson sharply retorts that "the Apostle says, Woman was made for Man, not Man for Woman. It would be the greatest of

Indelicacies for a Woman to be thought to love two Men at the same time equally."[39] This rather confusing invocation of the double standard, which is followed by a teasing fantasy of Sir Charles's polygamous marriage to Clementina *and* Harriet, seems to suggest that splits or divisions in women are far more threatening than in men—and that polygamy is a natural state for virtuous men.[40] Richardson defuses the double love from his own position as author-father; he asks Lady Bradshaigh, "Is not Clementina my child as well as Harriet?"[41] In defending Sir Charles and his novel against accusations of indelicacy, Richardson represents himself—and, by implication, Sir Charles—as lover/author/father to two women. The congruence between Richardson and Sir Charles, developed in the scenes of castration, reappears in the narrative and romantic problem of "double Love." Authorial castration is matched by this overplus of desirable (and desiring) objects.

Richardson protests too much; he seems drawn to the representation of acts of apparent duplicity and to the pathos of women like Pamela and Clarissa who are accused of performance and hypocrisy—"Female Art!"—so that he can make himself and his readers privy to a truth about them that the world is too blind to see. But the suggestion that the "good man" is engaging in a duplicitous act by simultaneously courting two women creates a different set of difficulties, both in the airing of the suggestion (it is hardly an accusation) and in the dispelling of the doubts.

What Jocelyn Harris calls the "cold rectitude" of Sir Charles's response to Clementina, along with his deflection of Harriet's love, suggests again that Sir Charles is a character created around absence and deferral.[42] He is a kind of black hole, sucking up the energy of others, producing no light. He sometimes seems a placeholder for masculinity as much as he seems a person—as if the pressures of depicting virtuous masculinity leave nothing over for individual qualities. Some of the peculiarities in the presentation of Clementina derive from this heroic blankness. Clementina's demonstrative, illustrative suffering, built on allusions to figures such as Ophelia and Iphigenia, suggests that some textual excess is being worked off in her character. *Grandison* repeats and revises her appearances, showing us scenes that echo elements of other stories in the novel itself and of stories from outside the fiction. For example, Clementina's forced admission of love for Charles serves as a companion piece to Harriet's forced acknowledgment of love and indeed locates the love firmly in Clementina rather than in Charles. Clementina in her derangement takes over for Sir Charles, acting out with heightened gestures the emotions that he is assumed to feel, but to which we have no access. She seems to be a dumping ground for emotions and the perfect host for disease and excess.[43]

Clementina herself betrays an equivocal and shifting relation to those emotions; in one sense she tries—and fails—to conceal her love, but she also tries to fix the responsibility for her (as yet unacknowledged) state on the man who elicited her love. She dances around disclosure to Charles, worrying the question of what a modest woman can reveal: *"Open my mind*—What! whether I have any-thing to reveal or not?—Insinuating man! You had almost persuaded me to think I had a Secret that lay heavy at my heart: And when I began to look for it, to oblige you, I could not find it. . . . Pray, Sir, *tell* me, *invent* for me, a Secret that is fit for me to own" (2.152). Clementina attempts to counter the forces that mark her as the primary possessor of the disease of desire by trying to make Charles responsible for speaking her mind. Since he has disrupted her life by constituting her secret, she tries to make him tell her what the secret is. He, characteristically, refuses to express her desire, and he acknowledges no responsive desire. When Mrs. Beaumont takes over the interrogation, Clementina confesses what everyone already knows: "I can no longer resist you. I own, I own, that I have no heart but for Mr. Grandison. And now, as I don't doubt but my friends set you to find out the love-sick girl, how shall I, who cannot disown a secret you have so fairly, and without condition, come at, ever look them in the face?" (2.169). Now "lost to the joys of this life," having exposed a desire she believes shameful—shameful because self-exposure is itself, in a woman, an immodest activity irrespective of the thing revealed—she intends to cover herself with the veil of the convent

(2.172–73). The code of female modesty collides with the novel's investment in openness, causing Clementina to suffer shame and sickness; only another form of concealment offers her the hope of reintegrating the self. The loss of the secret—its transmission—represents to her a violation; worst of all, it is a violation of herself in which she has participated. She suffers a version of what Clarissa endures in the rape.

The medicalization of Clementina's desire creates an avenue for the exposure—the "letting"—of emotion, but it is a pathway fraught with danger and destruction for Clementina. Medicine justifies an apparently non-sexual invasion of the body, and in turn those invasive procedures allow the demonstration, through the body and through Clementina's speech, of both desire and anger. The doctors try to bleed Clementina in order to calm her, but she evades them:

She had felt the lancet; but did not bleed more than two or three drops.

O my mamma! And *you* would have run away from me too, would you!—You don't use to be cruel; and to leave me with these doctors— See! see! and she held out her lovely arm a little bloody, regarding nobody but her mother. . . . They did attempt to wound; but they could not obtain their cruel ends. . . . Dearest, dearest madam, don't let me be sacrificed. (2.190)

Having rendered her mother speechless, and having reopened Jeronymo's "unhealed wounds," Clementina speaks next to Charles: "Some-body is wrong: I won't say who.—But *you* will not let these doctors use me ill—Will you?—See here! shewing her bound-up arm to me—what they would have done!—See! They did get a drop or two; but no more" (2.191). The insistent call to her family and Charles to "See! see!" underlines Clementina's use of her body as spectacle. She displays fluids from inside herself, exposes the products of the female body, and ties her own plight to the other sexual injury in her family. She links tears with blood and turns men into women:[44]

Poor Jeronymo! My dearest brother! And have you not suffered enough from vile assassins? Poor dear brother!—and again stroked his cheek— How was I affected!

A fresh gush of tears broke from his eyes. . . .

See! see! Chevalier [Grandison], holding out her spread hand to me, Jeronymo weeps. . . . My hand—See! is wet with a brother's tears! . . . It is a grievous thing to see men weep! What ail they?—Yet I cannot weep—Have they softer hearts than mine?—Don't weep, Chevalier. . . . I would stroke your cheek too, if it would stop your tears. (2.192)

These tears, which ought to purify, instead by their link with Clementina's violently obtained blood, and by their analogy with Jeronymo's (genital) suffering, become charged with accusation against Charles himself.[45] From erotic pathos, the scene develops a sharper edge; Clementina is calling Charles to task for her suffering:

And do *you* wish it too, Chevalier? [asks Clementina]—Do *you* wish to see me wounded?—To see my heart bleeding at my arm, I warrant. Say, can *you* be so hard-hearted?

Let me join with your mamma, [responds Grandison,] with your brother, to entreat it: For your father's sake! For—

For *your* sake, Chevalier?—Well, will it do you good to see me bleed? (2.193)

This direct question, which conjures up defloration as well as menstruation,[46] sends Grandison into retreat:

I withdrew to the window. I could not stand this question; put with an air of tenderness for me, and in an accent *equally* tender.

The irresistible Lady (O what eloquence in her disorder!) followed me; and laying her hand on my arm, looking earnestly after my averted face, as if she would not suffer me to hide it from her—Will it, will it, comfort *you* to see me bleed?—Come then, *be* comforted; I *will* bleed: But you shall not leave me. You shall see that these doctors shall not kill me quite. (2.193)

Clementina, intensely active in her submission, tender in her assault, refuses to let Charles hide behind her family or the doctors; because he is the cause and her blood is already on his hands, she forces him to call for more blood and to watch the ritual sacrifice take place.[47]

Although the scene is one of a series of pathetic illustrations of Clementina's disorder, it offers a troubling glimpse of a woman deploying her own body as symbolic object, wielding it with (un-conscious) intent to accuse; the scene disturbs because of the taint of masochism and the barely suppressed aggression Clementina contains. As she submits to the doctors' lancet, she directs her gaze at Charles, calling herself "Iphigenia." The fact that Charles does not actually hold the knife—just as he never wields the sword that castrates men—does not entirely let him off the hook, either in the reader's mind or, apparently, in Clementina's. The vampire doctors, "not satisfied with a small quantity," bleed her till she faints. The pathetic tears of the spectators cannot dilute the sharper tang of her blood. And yet, despite the disruptive effects of this memorable scene, in context it does more to illustrate the erotic power of Sir Charles than to define Clementina. His erotic power must be mapped on the bodies of women, so much better adapted to sexual signification than is his own body.

In a scene that functions as a pair to this one, and that discloses the buried link between the marking of women and emasculation, Lady Olivia, the hot-blooded Italian who loves Sir Charles and hates Clementina, threatens Sir Charles with a knife:[48] "She was enraged because he would not [put off his journey back to Cle-mentina] . . . and at last she pulled out of her stays, in fury, a poniard, and vowed to plunge it into his heart. He should never, she said, see his Clementina more. He went to her. Her heart failed her. . . . He seized her hand. He took it from her" (2.380). She fails in her attempt at bloodletting; the wound is transferred back to Olivia's own body in the form of a black ribbon she wears around her twisted wrist. Harriet, because she loves Sir Charles, takes the averted murder as a warning to her, not to Sir Charles. Horrified by the story, she calls Olivia "a Medusa" and worries that, if her own relation to Sir Charles were known, "I might have as much reason to be afraid of the potion, as the man she loves of the poniard" (3.388). Medusa, double symbol of castration and the defense against castration, frightens a woman, not the man.[49] Clementina goes mad and is pierced with the surgeons' knife, Oli-via is humiliated and forcibly disarmed, and Harriet suffers from suspense about one woman and fear of another, but Sir Charles seems unscathed. The women carry the burden of Sir Charles's extraordinary desirability.

Richardson does try to shift our attention to Sir Charles's suffering, but he does so primarily through the women. When Grandison returns to Italy in a last attempt to cure Clementina, Harriet reproduces the broken language of his leave-taking in indirect discourse: "How many things did he say then—How many questions ask—In tender woe—He wanted to do us all service—He seemed not to know what to say—Surely he hates not your poor Harriet— What struggles in his noble bosom!—But a man cannot complain: A man cannot ask for compassion, as a woman can. But surely his is the gentlest of manly minds!" (2.375). The codes of male behavior bar Sir Charles from courting pity, so Harriet provides the interpretation of his behavior that will elicit compassion; as a woman, by definition able to complain, she reveals what he cannot. However, the lurking suspicion that he really has nothing to reveal—that he is composed of the overflowing desires of the other character—continues to haunt our perception of Sir Charles. The novel's relentless pursuit of openness and social meaning sometimes paradoxically stops short at Sir Charles; as this passage suggests, and as Richardson's use of Clementina to signify his anguish also suggests, women often take over the performance of his feelings. The odd effect of Sir Charles's absolute adherence to duty, which becomes a form of emotional opacity, is to give his desires the qualities more usually associated with those of women; they seem fugitive, unknowable, but are the object of constant conjecture. Harriet increasingly takes on the task of interpreting Sir Charles; she is the clearinghouse for information about his shifting status and the condition of his heart, to the extent that we sometimes wonder whether he has emotions that exist outside the realm of report.

The problem of the "double Love" paradoxically becomes most pressing when it is on the verge of yielding to a "single" love; as Sir Charles and Harriet move toward union, undoing the knot that has structured the novel produces intense discursive activity. Richardson seems to want to retain Clementina as a character and as a presence in the relation between the happy couple. The novel clings to doubleness and to Clementina, bringing her on a far-fetched trip to England to invade the sphere of Harriet and to reanimate the conflict. Sir Charles almost seems constituted by the "great struggle" between his feelings for the two women, to the extent that they seem to be part of him and bound to each other. However, reshuffling the relationships involves some fancy foot-work; the stress of continuing the identification of and distinctions between the two women disrupts continuity and logic. In a contorted letter to Jeronymo, Sir Charles claims that each of the two women possesses all his heart. He awards to each a form of hypothetical priority:

There is a Lady, an English Lady, beautiful as an Angel. . . . Had I never known Clementina, I could have loved her, and *only* her, of all the women I ever beheld. It would not be doing her justice, if I could not say, I *do* love her; but with a flame as pure as the heart of Clementina, or as her own heart, can boast. Clementina's distressed mind affected me: I imputed her sufferings to her esteem for me. The farewel interview denied her, she demonstrated, I thought, so firm an affection for me, at the same time that she was to me, what I may truly call, a first Love. (3.10)

In this highly conditional and obfuscatory elaboration of his feelings, the "flame" belongs in turn to Sir Charles, Clementina's heart, and Harriet's heart; anointing each in turn, Sir Charles binds all together in a mystical union. He asserts that "the two noblest-minded women in the world, when I went over to Italy [i.e., on his return there] . . . held almost an equal interest in my heart," but that Clementina's signs of recovery led him to have no "wish but for your Clementina" (3.11). Her "esteem for me," her "affection for me" tip the scales in Clementina's favor. And yet once Clementina has bowed out, "there is but one woman in the world . . . that I can think worthy of succeeding *her* in my affections" (3.11). Simultaneity must give way to succession, doubleness to singularity, in Richardson's attempt to get past Clementina without disowning her, but it is not easy to put the novel back together around a couple instead of the triangle. As Sir Charles

worries, speaking his author's anxiety as well as his own: "Can I
do justice to the merits of both, and yet not *appear* to be divided
by a double Love?" (3.11). The double love is explicitly acknowledged at the moment of its dissolution, at the point of transfer.
But anxiety about the *appearance* of doubleness—as if the division
were not internal—sweeps duplicity under the rug again. Charlotte and Caroline offer a solution, encouraging Harriet to see Sir
Charles's division (which they too hedge with "as if" and "supposed") as an opportunity for glory, and indeed as her only opportunity for power over the all-powerful:

His difficulties, my dear, and the uncommon situation he is in, as if he
were offering you but a divided Love, enhance your glory. You are rein-
stated on the Female throne, to the lowermost footstep of which you
once was afraid you had descended. . . . And could you, by any other
way in the world than by this supposed divided Love, have had it in your
power, by accepting his humbly-offered hand, to lay him under obligation to you, which he thinks he never shall be able to discharge? Lay
him—Who?—Sir CHARLES GRANDISON—For whom so many virgin
hearts have sighed in vain!—And what a triumph to our Sex is this, as
well as to my Harriet! (3.68)

Division—or the appearance of division—brings Sir Charles to
the level of a woman and reinstates Harriet briefly on "the Female
throne." A kind of alchemical transmutation seems to be Richardson's way of presenting the sticky issue of a hero who has at
times seemed, like Macheath, capable of being happy "with
either / Were t'other dear charmer away." In fact, Harriet herself
comes to embody that mystical transformation; because she incorporates the transcendent qualities of Clementina in herself
without the disabilities, Sir Charles implies he can love both
women in her:

How nobly do you authorize my regard for *her* [Clementina]!—In *you*,
madam, shall I have all *her* excellencies, without the abatements which
must have been allowed, had she been mine, from considerations of Religion and Country. Believe me, madam, that my Love of her, if I know
my heart, is of such a nature, as never can abate the fervor of that I vow
to you. To both of you, my principal attachment was to MIND: Yet let

me say, that the *personal* union, to which you discourage me not to as-
pire, and the *duties* of that most intimate of all connexions, will preserve
to you the *due* preference; as (allow me to say) it would have done to *her*,
had she accepted of my vows. (3.125–26)

There is a delicate implication that Harriet's religion and nation-
ality render her circumstantially superior, but that otherwise the
two women are essentially the same. Their minds seem similarly
admirable and their bodies oddly interchangeable. Marriage and
sex with Harriet will bind him to her, but in a startling assertion
of the prominence of duty in personal, sexual relations, Sir Charles
underlines the fact that sex with Clementina would have done exactly the same thing.[50] The identification between and the inter-
changeability of the two women receive another endorsement
when, in a reinvocation of the mirror, Charlotte depicts as narcissistic the relation between the two women: "*Heroines* both, I
suppose; and they are mirrors to each other; each admiring herself
in the other. No wonder they are engaged insensibly by a vanity,
which carries with it, to each, so generous an appearance; for, all
the while, Harriet thinks she is only admiring Clementina; Clementina, that she's applauding Harriet" (3.418). This identification between the two women is based on considerations outside
the logic of characterization; the two actually resemble one another only in being women, virtuous, generous—and in love with
Sir Charles Grandison. Their "resemblance" is the effect of their
identity in the heart of Sir Charles. The mirror in which they are
reflected is Sir Charles. But if the two women are the same, mirrored and doubled, and Harriet incorporates Clementina, there
should be no guilt at the union of Sir Charles and Harriet; all seem
included, no one excluded.

The celebration of marriage, as the crown of the novel's impulse toward openness and social integration, thus derives in part
from an apparently guiltless doubleness. Clementina acquiesces in
her exclusion from the marriage, but she is mystically a part of
the union between Sir Charles and Harriet, one of the many members of the happy family. The joyful unity of the novel's end is

also, however, explicitly built on the expulsion of those who have attempted to destroy the hero and the heroines; *Grandison* actually concludes with the death of Sir Hargrave Pollexfen from those wounds he suffered on Mont Martre, and, a few pages earlier, Clementina's cousin, Laurana, who straitjacketed and tortured Clementina during her derangement, dies a suicide. The emphatic marking of who is inside and who is outside the charmed circle seems partly designed to distract us from any doubts about the status and constitution of those inside. But this marking of boundaries should, in fact, alert us to the interdependence of what has been cast off and what is embraced; the portrait of the "good man" is an ideological project that cannot entirely free itself from the disturbing, destructive traces of duplicity, castration, and the violent unveiling of women.

Grandison is much less obviously grounded in violence between the sexes than is *Pamela* or *Clarissa*; the threat of rape functions as a mechanical transfer point for power rather than as a nexus for investigating transformations of gender. But as *Grandison* moves toward a new ideology of masculinity, a different kind of disruption of sexuality also emerges, signaled particularly by the recurrence of castration (performed by men on men) and by the willful blindness to the costs of doubleness and to the problems that result from uncovering women. The union between Harriet and Sir Charles is enabled partly by the exposure of feminine secrets—a socially approved form of epistemological violation—and partly by the incorporation in Sir Charles of feminine desires. Sir Charles's "double Love" is as much the love the two women have for him as it is any love he has for them. Emptied of content, he contains their doubled desire for him in lieu of love. There are the ambiguously castrated bodies of Sir Hargrave, Mr. Merceda, and Jeronymo, and there are the happily domesticated women, ostensibly to warn us of the price of transgression and show us the rewards for acquiescence, but they also signify the uneasy foundations of this enlightened, harmonious, private kingdom. In *Sir Charles Grandison* Richardson puts back together the world he took apart in *Clarissa*, but the costs of the reconciliation between men and women, and of the triumphant consolidation of masculine authority, are to be read on every page.

Afterword

Richardson's novels represent a set of meditations on the construction of gender and sexuality in the mid-eighteenth century. The depiction of a reciprocal, dynamic model of gender that Richardson offers is unparalleled in its articulation; Richardson's marked interest in influencing and defining morality causes him to examine gender and sexuality in extraordinary detail so that he can solidify (if not create) a newly reformed ideology. Yet this fraught enterprise is played out in fictions whose elaboration and psychological penetration at times counter or undermine those very didactic aims that impel Richardson to write.

In his letters and novels, Richardson often portrays women's secrets as constitutive of knowledge, and it is through femininity, through the probing of women's bodies and minds, that the process of defining the fictional world proceeds. But the centrality of feminine experience in these novels is, in a sense, illusory; if women are a way to knowledge of "mankind," they are not always the objects to be known. Masculinity, and the meaning of the male body, are subjects as alluring as is the examination of femininity. For example, the trials of Clarissa, which further the project of creating a reified and heroic femininity, also have the shadow effect of constructing an encyclopedia of male fantasies—fantasies in which the author as well as the characters must be presumed to share, at least on some level. The structuring of *Clarissa* in part around these repetitive and detailed trials creates an uncomfort-

able overlap between Lovelace's (and, to some extent, the Harlowes') attempts to employ Clarissa as the test case for femininity
and Richardson's own celebration of tragically oppressed womanhood. The distinction between the moral ends of the two enterprises, while powerful, does not entirely erase or subsume the
possibility that these are parallel and mutually informed endeav-
ors. The novel's dependence on—and fascination with—the part
played by male cruelty in the creation of its heroine's exemplarity
raises questions not only about the perverse undertow of Richardson's moral project but also about the costs to women of his reciprocal model of gender.

The developing sense that men and women belong to "opposite" sexes puts pressure on these fictions; each novel sets out to
work through a plot that will conclusively delimit the meaning of
sexual difference and define the proprieties of gender for the characters and the society depicted, but each novel ultimately portrays
the high price—both personal and fictive—as well as the violence
required to establish a system of orderly and absolute opposition.
The demands of Richardson's moral system compete with the
Tiresian roots of his imagination—his equivocal and by no means
always egalitarian ability to identify with women. Tiresias is, as
I have demonstrated in the case of Lovelace, himself a problematic
inspiration for a writing man and even more problematic perhaps
for the women he portrays, and the very fact that Richardson expels and punishes the sexual aggression linked to Tiresian impulses leaves the more metaphysical results of those impulses in-
tact. Sir Charles Grandison, whose affinity with Richardson seems
paradoxically more covert than Lovelace's resemblance to his author, demonstrates the dangers to women (and to his fellow men)
of a benevolent man who apparently completely understands and
transcends femininity.

Richardson's meticulous, extravagant novels, in their quest to
detail the meanings of gender and sexuality, reveal the problematic nature of the systems they inspect and delineate. Masculinity
and femininity, read through one another, emerge as unstable,
mixed, and ultimately fragile conceptual categories. Richardson's

vast fictional endeavor to "know the sex"—a characteristically eighteenth-century enterprise—finally tells more about the pains of living within those troubled and troubling categories than about one sex or the other. The knowledge of gender that Richardson offers remains fugitive and fragmentary; ultimately unable to settle conclusively the conundrums of gender and sex, these novels remain gripping testimony to the dangers—and fascinations—of representing gender.

Notes

Notes

Introduction

1. My discussion of "gender" derives in particular from the definitions given by Ludmilla Jordanova, *Sexual Visions: Images of Gender in Science and Medicine Between the Eighteenth and Twentieth Centuries* (Madison: Univ. of Wisconsin Press, 1989), 4; Elaine Showalter, ed., *Speaking of Gender* (New York: Routledge, 1989), Introduction, 2; and Joan W. Scott, "Gender: A Useful Category of Historical Analysis," *American Historical Review* 91 (1986): 1056. See also Jane Flax, "Postmodernism and Gender Relations in Feminist Theory," *Signs* 12 (1987): 621–43; and Nancy Armstrong, "The Gender Bind: Women and the Disciplines," *Genders* 3 (1988): 1–23. For a cogent critique of gender-based analysis, see Eve Kosofsky Sedgwick, *Epistemology of the Closet* (Berkeley: Univ. of California Press, 1990).

2. Scott, 1056.

3. Parveen Adams, "Of Female Bondage," in *Between Feminism and Psychoanalysis*, ed. Teresa Brennan (London: Routledge, 1989), 247. Adams goes on to examine the interconnectedness of gender, sexuality, and sex.

4. Eve Kosofsky Sedgwick, *Between Men: English Literature and Male Homosocial Desire* (New York: Columbia Univ. Press, 1985), 15.

5. See especially Carol Houlihan Flynn, *Samuel Richardson: A Man of Letters* (Princeton, N.J.: Princeton Univ. Press, 1982); Rita Goldberg, *Sex and Enlightenment: Women in Richardson and Diderot* (Cambridge: Cambridge Univ. Press, 1984); and Jocelyn Harris, *Samuel Richardson* (Cambridge: Cambridge Univ. Press, 1987).

6. Much of the criticism of *Clarissa* focuses on sexuality from various viewpoints; among the most useful in conceptualizing the issues are Leo Braudy, "Penetration and Impenetrability in *Clarissa*," in *Modern Essays on Eighteenth-Century Literature*, ed. Leopold Damrosch (New York: Oxford Univ. Press, 1988), 261–81, which describes sexuality in the novel in terms of the Cartesian mind/body dichotomy; Linda Kauffman, *Discourses of Desire: Gender, Genre, and Epistolary Fictions* (Ithaca, N.Y.: Cornell Univ. Press, 1986), which includes a reading of *Clarissa* in the context of a feminist post-structuralist investigation of the genre of the love letter; Terry Castle, in *Clarissa's Ciphers: Meaning and Disruption in Richardson's Clarissa* (Ithaca, N.Y.: Cornell Univ. Press, 1982), focuses on Clarissa as the victim of hermeneutic violence; Terry Eagleton, *The Rape of Clarissa: Writing, Sexuality and Class Struggle in Samuel Richardson* (Minneapolis: Univ. of Minnesota Press, 1982), is by turns a psychoanalytic, Marxist, and deconstructive celebration of Clarissa's heroism; and James Grantham Turner, in "Lovelace and the Paradoxes of Libertinism," reads Lovelace's character in terms of its libertine component. His essay is in *Samuel Richardson: Tercentenary Essays*, ed. Margaret Anne Doody and Peter Sabor (Cambridge: Cambridge Univ. Press, 1989), 70–88. In *Sentiment and Sociability: The Language of Feeling in the Eighteenth Century* (Oxford: Clarendon Press, 1988), John Mullan claims that Richardson's interest is *only* in the concept of femininity, and not at all in any "actual analysis of the condition of women in eighteenth-century society" (p. 67).

Until quite recently, work on sexuality in the eighteenth century has predominantly reflected male concerns: Roy Porter, after a generally celebratory analysis of sexual "freedom" in eighteenth-century England, acknowledges that "the much-bandied freedoms were to apply principally to males" ("Mixed Feelings: The Enlightenment and Sexuality," in *Sexuality in Eighteenth-Century Britain*, ed. Paul-Gabriel Boucé [Totowa, N.J.: Barnes & Noble, 1982], 1–27). Important sources of information include David Foxon, *Libertine Literature in England 1660–1745* (New Hyde Park, N.Y.: University Books, 1965); Jean Hagstrum, *Sex and Sensibility: Ideal and Erotic Love from Milton to Mozart* (Chicago: Univ. of Chicago Press, 1980); Lawrence Stone, *Family, Sex, and Marriage in England 1500–1800* (New York: Harper & Row, 1977); Roger Thompson, *Unfit for Modest Ears* (Totowa, N.J.: Rowan & Littlefield, 1979); and Peter Wagner, *Eros Revived: Erotica of the Enlightenment in England and America* (London: Secker & Warburg, 1988). Among the most helpful of the works that explore female sexuality in the eighteenth century from an explicitly feminist viewpoint are Nancy Armstrong, *Desire and Domestic Fiction: A Political History of the Novel* (New York: Oxford Univ. Press, 1987); Marlene LeGates, "The Cult of Womanhood in Eighteenth-Century Thought," *Eighteenth-Century Studies* 10 (1976): 21–36; Ellen Pollak, *The Poetics of Sexual Myth: Gender and Ideology in the Verse of Swift and Pope* (Chicago: Univ. of Chicago Press, 1985); Mary Poovey, *The Proper Lady and the Woman Writer: Ideology as Style in the Works of Mary Wollstonecraft, Mary Shelley, and Jane Austen* (Chicago: Univ. of Chicago Press, 1984); Katharine M. Rogers, *The Troublesome Helpmate: A History of Misogyny in Literature* (Seattle: Univ. of Washington Press, 1966); and Patricia M. Spacks, "Ev'ry Woman is at Heart a Rake," *Eighteenth-Century Studies* 8 (1974): 27–46.

7. For the argument that Richardson was feminist in his attitudes, see Katharine M. Rogers, "Sensitive Feminism vs. Conventional Sympathy: Richardson and Fielding on Women," *Novel* 9 (1976): 256–70. This material also appears in Rogers, *Feminism in Eighteenth-Century England* (Urbana: Univ. of Illinois Press, 1982), 125–35.

8. Critical discussions of the body—both female and male—have been proliferating; the journals *Representations* and *Genders* have been particularly notable for focusing on the body. For example, a special issue of *Representations* was reprinted as *The Making of the Modern Body: Sexuality and Society in the Nineteenth Century*, ed. Catherine Gallagher and Thomas Laqueur (Berkeley: Univ. of California Press, 1987). Two important recent works on the sexed body that contain significant discussions of the eighteenth century are Thomas Laqueur, *Making Sex: Body and Gender from the Greeks to Freud* (Cambridge, Mass.: Harvard Univ. Press, 1990); and Londa Schiebinger, *The Mind Has No Sex? Women in the Origins of Modern Science* (Cambridge, Mass.: Harvard Univ. Press, 1989). For a relevant investigation of women's bodies in Victorian literature, see Helena Michie, *The Flesh Made Word: Female Figures and Women's Bodies* (New York: Oxford Univ. Press, 1987).

9. See Simone de Beauvoir, *The Second Sex* (New York: Random House, 1974), Introduction.

10. De Beauvoir, xviii.

11. Jordanova, *Sexual Visions*, 14.

12. Laqueur, *Making Sex*, 22.

13. Michie, *The Flesh Made Word*, 7.

14. Stinstra's question comes in a letter of Apr. 2, 1753, and the

answer from Richardson to Stinstra, June 2, 1753, both in *The Richardson-Stinstra Correspondence and Stinstra's Prefaces to Clarissa*, ed. William C. Slattery (Carbondale: Southern Illinois Univ. Press, 1969), 16–17 and 26–27.

15. Anna Howe warns Clarissa about the power over a woman that a secret correspondent can gain: "By your insisting that he should keep this correspondence private, it appears that there is *one secret* which you do not wish the world should know; and he is master of that secret" (I, 61–62) (71).

16. Stinstra to Richardson, Dec. 24, 1753, *Richardson-Stinstra Correspondence*, 61.

17. Richardson to Stinstra, Mar. 20, 1754, ibid., 71.

18. Richardson to Lady Bradshaigh, Feb. 14, 1754, *Selected Letters of Samuel Richardson*, ed. John Carroll (Oxford: Clarendon Press, 1964), 292.

19. Richardson to Lady Bradshaigh, Oct. 5, 1753, ibid., 244. This passage continues with one of Richardson's many claims of kinship with Lovelace: In the letter he has been reporting a remark made to a "Dignitary," and he tells Lady Bradshaigh, "There was Boldness!—Does not your Ladiship think that Lovelace's Observation, that the most impudent Men in the World, are the bashful ones has some Foundation in Truth?" (p. 245).

20. Laqueur, *Making Sex*, 124.

21. Richardson to Stinstra, Mar. 20, 1754, *Richardson-Stinstra Correspondence*, 71.

22. Laqueur, *Making Sex*, 133.

23. Ibid., 124–25.

24. David Robinson, though seeing male friendship as secondary to female friendship in Richardson, considers the relation between Jeronymo della Porretta and Sir Charles Grandison covertly homoerotic. "Unravelling the 'Cord Which Ties Good Men to Good Men': Male Friendship in Richardson's Novels," in *Samuel Richardson: Tercentenary Essays*, 167–87. I share Robinson's belief that Richardson's fiction involves an examination of masculinity, although I disagree with his sense that Richardson moves toward and then retreats from a focus on "passionate male friendship."

25. Richardson's fiction fits and does not fit Eve Sedgwick's paradigm of the homosocial as described in *Between Men*; the erotically charged competition between James Harlowe and Lovelace over Clarissa

seems to be a perfect example of the homosocial, for example. But, in general, while the bonds between men seem so central as to be entirely naturalized, those bonds are often represented as secondary both to relations between women—for example, the highly wrought love between Anna Howe and Clarissa, and, more oddly, the relationship between the two heroines of *Grandison*—and to the fraught, dangerous competition of men with women. Thus, in *Pamela*, Mr. B performs his assaults on Pamela with Mrs. Jewkes as goad, and Lovelace finds himself more viscerally in competition with the monstrous "mother" Sinclair and the harpylike whores than with his fellow rakes.

26. See Robinson, "Unravelling the Cord," for a discussion of castration as feminization.

27. Sedgwick, *Epistemology of the Closet*, 31.

Chapter 1

1. See Katharine M. Rogers, *The Troublesome Helpmate: A History of Misogyny in Literature* (Seattle: Univ. of Washington Press, 1966). For a more extensive survey of Restoration and early eighteenth-century attacks on women, see Felicity A. Nussbaum, *The Brink of All We Hate: English Satires on Women 1660–1750* (Lexington: Univ. of Kentucky Press, 1984).

2. Rogers, *The Troublesome Helpmate*, 165, 163. Rogers (p. 164) quotes Robert Gould's "A Satyr against Wooing" (1698?) to illustrate "stripping":

> Strip but this Puppet of it's Gay Attire,
> It's—Gauzes, Ribbons, Lace, Commode and Wire,
> And tell me then what 'tis thou dost admire?
>
> · · ·
>
> If in her Bed you e'er perceive her fast
> Mind how her Face is crusted o'er with Past,
> Or nasty Oils us'd nightly to repair
> Her skin, quite spoil'd—with taking of the Air.

3. Rogers, *The Troublesome Helpmate*, 49.

4. Richardson himself, in the scene of Mrs. Sinclair's death in *Clarissa*, explicitly revises the genre. In a footnote to the scene, he defends the propriety and morality of Belford's horrific and horrified description of the whores in dishabille: "Whoever has seen Dean Swift's *Lady's Dressing Room* will think this description of Mr Belford not only more natural

but more decent painting, as well as better justified by the design, and by the use that may be made of it" (VIII: 51) (1388).

5. The phrase is from Mary Poovey, *The Proper Lady and the Woman Writer: Ideology as Style in the Works of Mary Wollstonecraft, Mary Shelley, and Jane Austen* (Chicago: Univ. of Chicago Press, 1984), 5. The standard discussion of the "trivialization" of women under capitalism can be found in Alice Clark, *The Working Life of Women in the Seventeenth Century* (London: Routledge & Sons, 1919).

6. Marlene LeGates, "The Cult of Womanhood in Eighteenth-Century Thought," *Eighteenth-Century Studies* 10 (1976): 21–36.

7. Ruth Bloch, "Untangling the Roots of Modern Sex Roles: A Survey of Four Centuries of Change," *Signs* 4 (1978): 237–52. Bloch's discussion is complemented by the detailed analysis of bodies and sex in Thomas Laqueur's *Making Sex: Body and Gender from the Greeks to Freud* (Cambridge, Mass.: Harvard Univ. Press, 1990), and Londa Schiebinger's *The Mind Has No Sex? Women in the Origins of Modern Science* (Cambridge, Mass.: Harvard Univ. Press, 1989).

8. Nancy Armstrong, "The rise of the domestic woman," in *The Ideology of Conduct: Essays on Literature and the History of Sexuality*, ed. Nancy Armstrong and Leonard Tennenhouse (New York: Methuen, 1987), 114.

9. Nancy Armstrong, *Desire and Domestic Fiction: A Political History of the Novel* (New York: Oxford Univ. Press, 1987), 120.

10. In a review of recent work on the novel, Charlotte Sussman counters Armstrong's claim of a shift from body to mind, asserting that it is "impossible to mark an absolute shift from interest in female bodies to interest in female minds in eighteenth-century novelistic discourse, and the convoluted arguments by critics attempting to define a binary opposition between body and soul mark the futility of this gesture." Sussman further asserts that Armstrong and Michael McKeon—and Richardson's critics as a group—uncritically inherit and reproduce the limiting ideology of femininity and the body expressed in *Pamela*. While I agree with Sussman's critique of Armstrong in particular, my own argument seeks to demonstrate the ways Richardson's text itself renders as contradictory and problematic the ideology it claims to uphold. See Sussman, "'I Wonder Whether Poor Miss Sally Godfrey Be Living or Dead': The Married Woman and the Rise of the Novel," *Diacritics* 20:1 (1990): 88–102.

11. Mary Poovey says that "far from dismissing the specter of female

sexuality, in fact, the late eighteenth-century ideal of feminine propriety simply transmutes it into its opposite" (p. 19). See also Ellen Pollak's chapter "The Eighteenth-Century Myth of Passive Womanhood," in *The Poetics of Sexual Myth: Gender and Ideology in the Verse of Swift and Pope* (Chicago: Univ. of Chicago Press, 1985), 22–76.

12. To divide women into surface and interior almost always leads to the scapegoating of the surface as a trap: "Another Ground and Reason of Love, with such Love-sick Gentlemen as you, is *Apparel* and *Deportment*; this for certain is one of the greatest Baits to entrap *Fools*, that regard the Shell, and neglect the Kernel" (*Reflections upon Matrimony, and the Women of this Country. In a Letter to a Young Gentleman* [London: Printed for R. Baldwin, 1755], 29).

13. *Reflections upon Matrimony*, 30.

14. Paul de Man, in "The Epistemology of Metaphor," *On Metaphor*, ed. Sheldon Sacks (Chicago: Univ. of Chicago Press, 1978), cites this passage from Locke's *Essay Concerning Human Understanding* (bk. 3, chap. 10), and comments on the disruptive presence of the female metaphor: "Nothing could be more eloquent than this denunciation of eloquence. It is clear that rhetoric is something one can decorously indulge in as long as one knows where it belongs. Like a woman, which it resembles ('like the fair sex'), it is a fine thing as long as it is kept in its proper place. Out of place, among the serious affairs of men ('if we would speak of things as they are'), it is a disruptive scandal—like the appearance of a real woman in a gentlemen's club where it would only be tolerated as a picture, preferably naked (like the image of Truth), framed and hung on the wall." See also the discussion of this passage from Locke and de Man's comments on it, in Helena Michie, *The Flesh Made Word: Female Figures and Women's Bodies* (New York: Oxford Univ. Press, 1987), 102–3.

15. John Berger, in *Ways of Seeing* (Harmondsworth, Eng.: Penguin, 1972), has presented an influential analysis of the split consciousness of women: "Men survey women before treating them. Consequently how a woman appears to a man can determine how she will be treated. To acquire some control over this process, women must contain and interiorize it. . . . Women watch themselves being looked at. This determines not only most relations between men and women but also the relation of women to themselves. The surveyor of woman in herself is male: the surveyed female" (pp. 46–47). This sympathetic and suggestive description of the effect of "surveillance" on women, however, rep-

resents as a simple incorporation the complex cross-identifications that traverse the female body and mind. Berger's explanation of men's investment in women's vanity as portrayed in visual arts tries to stabilize the problem of feminine doubleness partly by ascribing hypocrisy to the male artist and viewer: "The mirror was often used as a symbol of the vanity of woman. The moralizing, however, was mostly hypocritical. You painted a naked woman because you enjoyed looking at her, you put a mirror in her hand and you called the painting *Vanity*, thus morally condemning the woman whose nakedness you had depicted for your own pleasure" (p. 51). But, as I will show, hypocrisy does not cease to be a problem when men are presumed guilty of it.

Despite the limits of Berger's analysis particularly as a way to examine masculinity, I am indebted to his work, and to Tania Modleski's use of his ideas in a few pages devoted to *Pamela* in her book, *Loving with a Vengeance: Mass-produced Fantasies for Women* (New York: Methuen, 1982).

16. "The Universal Spectator. Nov. 25. No. 529," *The Gentleman's Magazine: And Historical Chronicle* VIII (London: Printed by Edward Cave, jun., 1738).

17. Here I differ from Terry Castle, who, in *Masquerade and Civilization: The Carnivalesque in Eighteenth-Century English Culture and Fiction* (Stanford, Calif.: Stanford Univ. Press, 1986), sees Richardson as refusing identification: "In the rationalized moral cosmos of Richardson and Burney (two authors particularly concerned to enclose and neutralize the unstable realm of the masquerade), otherness remains the object of charity, but never of identification" (p. 107). This chapter shows the crucial status of identification in Richardson's work.

18. See my discussion in " 'Like Tiresias': Metamorphosis and Gender in *Clarissa*," *Novel* 19 (1986): 101–17.

19. Edward Young, "Love of Fame, The Universal Passion," *The Works of the Author of Night-Thoughts*, in 4 vols. (London: Printed for J. Buckland, 1744), I: 144.

20. For an illuminating discussion of the meaning of the veil, see Eve Kosofsky Sedgwick's chapter, "The Character in the Veil: Imagery of the Surface in the Gothic Novel," in *The Coherence of Gothic Conventions* (London: Methuen, 1986).

21. For a valuable analysis of the implications of modesty for English fiction, including a discussion of *Pamela* that complements this

chapter, see Ruth Bernard Yeazell's *Fictions of Modesty: Women and Courtship in the English Novel* (Chicago: Univ. of Chicago Press, 1991).

22. In *The Proper Lady and the Woman Writer* Mary Poovey explains the value conduct material has for anyone who wishes to gain access "both to the ways in which this culture defined female nature and to the ways in which a woman of this period would have experienced the social and psychological dimensions of ideology" (p. 16). My interest is less in recovering women's experience of ideology than in investigating aspects of the construction of "female nature." Poovey's revealing analysis of "the proper lady" and Kristina Straub's discussion of Frances Burney's divided relation to propriety, in *Divided Fictions: Fanny Burney and Feminine Strategy* (Lexington: Univ. of Kentucky Press, 1987), both develop our understanding of conduct's meaning for women in the late eighteenth and early nineteenth centuries.

23. Dr. James Fordyce, *The Character and Conduct of the Female Sex, and the Advantage to be Derived by Young Men from the Society of Virtuous Women* (London, 1776; rpt. Boston: John Gill, 1781), 30.

24. John Gregory, *A Father's Legacy to his Daughters* (New York: Shober & Loudoun, 1775), 23. Ruth Yeazell observes that *A Father's Legacy* "is above all an exercise in paternal wish fulfillment, and the image of the modest young woman whose innocence somehow constitutes her own protection is only one of those he would prefer not to examine too closely" (*Fictions of Modesty*, 43).

25. *The Vindication of the Rights of Woman* (Harmondsworth, Eng.: Penguin, 1975), 111. Wollstonecraft's detailed attacks on Gregory, and on Dr. James Fordyce, are at the center of *The Vindication*. Yeazell, however, points out the parallels between Wollstonecraft's project and that of the men she attacks: Like them, Wollstonecraft "set out to discriminate true from false modesty in order to nurture the true" (*Fictions of Modesty*, 62).

26. This construction recalls John Berger's description of women as split internally between viewer and viewed. The difference comes, of course, in the fact that this split is produced through a man's view. Identifying women as split offers certain equivocal pleasures.

27. Gregory, *A Father's Legacy*, 14.

28. In "Making Faces: Physiognomy and Fashion in Eighteenth-Century England," Roy Porter describes the anxiety produced by a woman wearing rouge: this "artificial blush, which (men feared) all too

readily camouflaged lost innocence, that inability to blush, hid the bare-faced cheek of the shameless woman" (*Etudes Anglaises* 38 [1985]: 385–96). See also Yeazell, *Fictions of Modesty*, chap. 5, "Modest Blushing."

29. Dr. James Fordyce, *Sermons to Young Women* (Boston: Mein & Fleming, 1767), 38.

30. Joan Riviere, "Womanliness as a Masquerade," in Victor Burgin et al., eds., *Formations of Fantasy* (London: Methuen, 1986), 35–44.

31. Ibid., 43.

32. Luce Irigaray, *This Sex Which Is Not One*, trans. Catherine Porter with Carolyn Burke (Ithaca, N.Y.: Cornell Univ. Press, 1985), 76.

33. My use of the term "masquerade" owes more to Irigaray and Riviere than to Terry Castle. Castle sees the "controlling figure" of masking as antithesis: "One was obliged to impersonate a being opposite, in some essential feature, to oneself. The conventional relationship between costume and wearer was ironic, one that replicated a conceptual scandal" (*Masquerade and Civilization*, 5). Castle's focus on the world turned upside down is not mine; my interpretation of the masquerade of gender in Richardson suggests that impersonation is more likely to explore the body's desires and meanings through a play of surfaces than through an inversion.

34. Fordyce, *Character and Conduct*, 42.

35. [Richard Allestree,] *The Ladies Calling. In Two Parts* (Oxford: Printed at the Theatre, 1673), 12.

36. Bernard Kreissman, *Pamela-Shamela: A Study of the Criticisms, Burlesques, Parodies, and Adaptations of Richardson's "Pamela"* (Lincoln: Univ. of Nebraska Press, 1960), 15–16.

37. Quoted in Kreissman, 53.

38. Yeazell sees the attempt to reduce Pamela to Shamela as having a teleological logic; it is, she says, a way "to sort out all the contradictions and confusions in her account of herself in light of their end" (*Fictions of Modesty*, 87).

39. Michael McKeon has produced an important reading of the politics of *Pamela* in his monumental *Origins of the English Novel 1600–1740* (Baltimore, Md.: Johns Hopkins Univ. Press, 1987). As my discussion shows, I disagree with McKeon's depiction of *Pamela* as containing a "utopian achievement" of social "empowerment" (p. 380).

40. Kreissman, 28–29.

41. Quoted in Kreissman, 29.

42. Martin Battestin's introduction to Henry Fielding, *Joseph An-*

drews (Boston: Houghton Mifflin, 1961). An interesting permutation of this argument appears in the exchange in *Novel* about whether Richardson or Fielding has the better feminist credentials. See Katharine M. Rogers, "Sensitive Feminism vs. Conventional Sympathy: Richardson and Fielding on Women," *Novel* 9 (1976): 256–70; and Anthony J. Hassall, "Critical Exchange: Women in Richardson and Fielding," *Novel* 14 (1981): 168–74. For an account of the ways Ian Watt, in *The Rise of the Novel*, edgily associates Richardson with femininity, see Laurie Langbauer, *Women and Romance: The Consolations of Gender in the English Novel* (Ithaca, N.Y.: Cornell Univ. Press, 1990), 26–27.

43. In *Shamela*, Fielding scarcely needs to twist this language to "reveal" its potential for sexual meaning: " 'The Thought is every where exactly cloathed by the Expression; and becomes its Dress as *roundly* and as close as *Pamela* her Country Habit; or *as she doth her no Habit*, when modest Beauty seeks to hide itself, by casting off the Pride of Ornament, and displays itself without any Cover;' which it frequently doth in this admirable Work, and presents Images to the Reader, which the coldest Zealot cannot read without Emotion. . . . Oh! I feel an Emotion even while I am relating this: Methinks I see *Pamela* at this Instant, with all the Pride of Ornament cast off" (Henry Fielding, *An Apology for the Life of Mrs. Shamela Andrews* [London, 1741; rpt. New York and London: Garland, 1974], 2).

44. Anne Hollander, *Seeing Through Clothes* (New York: Avon, 1980), 441.

45. Annette Kuhn, *The Power of the Image: Essays on Representation and Sexuality* (London: Routledge & Kegan Paul, 1985), 53.

46. Castle, *Masquerade and Civilization*, 5.

47. See Carey McIntosh, "Pamela's Clothes," for an analysis of clothes as a "symbolic leitmotif" in the novel (*ELH* 35 [1968]: 75–83). McIntosh catalogs the allusions to clothing, categorizing them as either emblems of social standing or sexual symbols. Sheila C. Conboy looks at Pamela's interest in clothes and needlework as indications of an "artistry [that is] the key to the novel's progress toward an androgynous vision" ("Fabric and Fabrication in Richardson's *Pamela*," *ELH* 54 [1987]: 81–96). Describing Richardson's attitudes to gender by recourse to the concept of androgyny represents in my view a false "solution" to and oversimplification of complicated structures of cross-gender identification. Caryn Chaden elaborates on the "new, complex relationship between class affiliation and characterization" evidenced through Pamela's

use of the clothing of different classes. Chaden also usefully locates the details of Pamela's clothing in their historical context. "Pamela's Identity Sewn in Clothes," in *Eighteenth-Century Women and the Arts*, ed. Frederick M. Keener and Susan E. Lorsch (New York: Greenwood Press, 1988), 109–18.

48. The conversion of Lady Davers does not simply reproduce Mr. B's conversion, of course; as a woman and an aristocrat, she is mirror and foil for the newly risen Pamela. While Lady Davers attempts to see herself as more like B than like Pamela (i.e., an aristocrat), Pamela asserts that Lady Davers is more like her (i.e., a woman). B brutally underlines the asymmetry of gender relations in light of class distinction when he demonstrates to Lady Davers the radically different consequences of the marriage of an aristocratic man to a woman of lower class and the marriage of an aristocratic woman to a "groom"; the first woman rises, the second is brought low.

49. Charlotte Sussman focuses on Sally Godfrey as "a displaced part of Pamela's identity" and as "the means by which the text transports the female body to the margins of the story" while ensuring that it not be forgotten (Sussman, " 'I Wonder Whether Poor Miss Sally Godfrey Be Living or Dead' "). In my view, Sally and the other figures produced as parallels to Pamela more clearly represent, through Richardson's display in them of qualities supposedly eliminated from Pamela herself, the novel's *inability* to sustain the marginalization of the female body and that body's attendant disruptions.

50. Modleski, *Loving with a Vengeance*, 53.

51. *Pamela Censured*, printed with *Shamela* in *Richardsoniana* (New York: Garland, 1974; 25 vols.), II: 28.

52. *Pamela Censured*, 31. It is important to note that the "luscious and warm Description" and the "fondest Imagination" belong to *Pamela Censured*, not to Richardson.

53. *Pamela Censured*, 31.

54. Ibid., 31–32.

55. Terry Castle, in her chapter on *Pamela*, Part 2, in *Masquerade and Civilization*, also notes the repetition in this scene; she sees in it "Richardson's artificial means of asserting once more the nonrepeatability of the plot of metamorphosis" (p. 147). Castle analyzes *Pamela*, Part 2, in terms of an attempted but failed decarnivalization—a repression of the plot of metamorphosis that comes unglued with the entry of a literal masquerade.

56. Terry Castle, in "P/B: *Pamela* as Sexual Fiction" (*SEL* 22

[1982]: 469–89), describes Mrs. Jewkes as a phallic woman, and discusses the use of hints of homosexuality in her character. This article defines *Pamela* in terms of the heroine's psychosexual development, employing an Oedipal model to do so. While I agree with a number of Castle's observations in this article, I am more concerned with the construction of a sex and gender system than with insights into Pamela's psyche.

57. Pamela is referring to B's formal proposal to make her his mistress.

58. Castle, in "P/B," discusses Mrs. Jewkes's "shrinking" after Pamela's marriage.

59. Mr. B, as principal subject of the letters, would also claim he is in some sense their father.

60. Pollak, *The Poetics of Sexual Myth*, 68.

Chapter 2

1. Although Lovelace seems to present his bashfulness as not only feminine but moral and natural, it could itself be seen as a suspect attribute of women. Ruth Bernard Yeazell cites "a brief allegory" of 1798 in which, while "Modesty's affected double appeared as 'Bashfulness' rather than a prude, . . . she appeared to similar purpose" (*Fictions of Modesty: Women and Courtship in the English Novel* [Chicago: Univ. of Chicago Press, 1991], 55).

2. In a brief discussion of libertine identification with femininity, James Grantham Turner dismisses Lovelace's Tiresian claims as "absurd" and almost purely willful: "The libertine simultaneously identifies with the female and reinforces his masculinity by projecting his most vulnerable characteristics onto her." Turner's useful focus on the "prefabricated" elements of Lovelace's libertinism complements my study; I do, however, in contrast to Turner, see Lovelace's identification with women as far more than a conventional ploy. See "Lovelace and the Paradoxes of Libertinism," in *Samuel Richardson: Tercentenary Essays*, ed. Margaret Anne Doody and Peter Sabor (Cambridge: Cambridge Univ. Press, 1989), 70–88. Other commentary on Lovelace's invocation of Tiresias appears in Carol Houlihan Flynn, *Samuel Richardson: A Man of Letters* (Princeton, N.J.: Princeton Univ. Press, 1982), 213–14; Jocelyn Harris, *Samuel Richardson* (Cambridge: Cambridge Univ. Press, 1987), 81; and Judith Wilt, "He Could Go No Farther: A Modest Proposal About Lovelace and Clarissa," *PMLA* 92 (1977): 19–32.

3. The resemblance between Lovelace's enterprise and Richardson's

project has caused some feminist critics to view Richardson's investment in Clarissa with considerable suspicion. The celebration becomes, in a sense, tainted by Lovelace's investment in Clarissa. In a wide-ranging article on feminist criticism, Myra Jehlen defines "androgyny, in the novel, [as] a male trait enabling men to act from their male side and feel from their female side"; she goes on to disagree with the "recent praise of *Clarissa* as a feminist document," describing Richardson as "a patriarch": "If nonetheless he envisioned his heroine in terms with which feminists may sympathize, it is, I believe, because he viewed her as representing not really women but the interior self, the female interior self in all men—in all men, but especially developed perhaps in writers" (Jehlen, "Archimedes and the Paradox of Feminist Criticism," in *Feminist Theory: A Critique of Ideology*, ed. Nannerl O. Keohane, Michelle Z. Rosaldo, and Barbara C. Gelpi [Chicago: Univ. of Chicago Press, 1982], 212). Jehlen sees Richardson's "interior self" in the place Clarissa ostensibly holds, but in asserting that Richardson displaces women, she relies on a spatial metaphor—femininity as interiority—that tends to reinforce problematic constructions of the gendered self. Judith Wilt, in "He Could Go No Farther," uses similarly problematic spatial metaphors to describe gender crossing. Because Wilt also identifies the feminine with masochism, her analysis of Lovelace sometimes becomes both schematic and imprecise: "It is difficult to escape the impression that for Richardson this other side that ruins Lovelace is the woman-internal, powerfully dramatized internally in the crazed servitude to obsession by which Lovelace finally achieves his own rape-death at the hands of the manly Morden, and externally in the figures of Sinclair and the harlots." Lovelace's explicit reenactment of Richardson's ambivalent identification with women renders highly problematic any attempt to read Richardson as tidily split between Clarissa as female (interior) principle and Lovelace as male (active) principle. Both figures instead cross and recross the gender lines that seem to separate them; both implicate and disturb our sense of their author's placement.

4. In an essay on narrative cross-dressing in Richardson that attempts to distinguish Lovelace's project from Richardson's, James Carson argues that the resemblance between Lovelace and his author allows Richardson to indicate "the immorality and ineffectuality of Lovelace's attempts to traffic in women, thereby creating the space of self-criticism which grants subversive potential to his own adoption of the female epistolary voice" ("Narrative Cross-Dressing in the Novels of Richardson,"

in *Writing the Female Voice: Essays on Epistolary Literature*, ed. Elizabeth C. Goldsmith [Boston: Northeastern Univ. Press, 1989], 95–113). Carson makes the point that Richardson's use of the female voice and female figure is not simply motivated by a desire to appropriate and transcend femininity, but has its grounding in his sympathy with and knowledge of women. But Carson's sociological and Bakhtinian model for Richardson's identification with women leads him to separate Lovelace's "appropriation" from Richardson's "sympathy" with too much ease. As my more psychologically based discussions of the crosscurrents of Richardson's and Lovelace's cross-gender identification make clear, I do not see this matter as susceptible to the logic of choices or alternatives, but as dependent on contradictory, duplicitous desires and fears.

5. See, in particular, William Warner, *Reading Clarissa: The Struggles of Interpretation* (New Haven, Conn.: Yale Univ. Press, 1979); Terry Eagleton, *The Rape of Clarissa: Writing, Sexuality and Class Struggle in Samuel Richardson* (Minneapolis: Univ. of Minnesota Press, 1982); and Terry Castle, *Clarissa's Ciphers: Meaning and Disruption in Richardson's Clarissa* (Ithaca, N.Y.: Cornell Univ. Press, 1982).

6. See Turner, "Lovelace and the Paradoxes of Libertinism," on the way that Lovelace uses "experiments on female virtue" to define himself.

7. See Mark Kinkead-Weekes on the idea that the rape is "a trial of virtue itself, in that it is an attempt to disprove the existence of a moral *nature*" (*Samuel Richardson: Dramatic Novelist* [Ithaca, N.Y.: Cornell Univ. Press, 1973], 230).

8. Eve Kosofsky Sedgwick discusses the implications of how a culture draws boundaries between "the sexual and the not-sexual" as well as between "the realms of the two genders": It is, she says, "variable, but is *not* arbitrary. That is . . . the placement of the boundaries in a particular society affects not merely the definition of those terms themselves—sexual/nonsexual, masculine/feminine—but also the apportionment of forms of power that are not obviously sexual. These include control over the means of production and reproduction of goods, persons, and meanings" (*Between Men: English Literature and Male Homosocial Desire* (New York: Columbia Univ. Press, 1985), 22.

9. [Richard Allestree,] *The Ladies Calling. In Two Parts* (Oxford: Printed at the Theatre, 1673), 3–4.

10. "The Universal Spectator. Nov. 25. No. 529," *The Gentleman's Magazine: And Historical Chronicle* VIII (London: Printed by Edward Cave, jun., 1738), 591.

11. This discussion also bears on the devaluation of or suspicion about women's friendships; true friendships between women were viewed either as highly unusual or as temporary alliances while the women waited for men. For an extended discussion of the implications of female friendship, see Janet Todd, *Women's Friendship in Literature* (New York: Columbia Univ. Press, 1980), especially the chapter on *Clarissa*, "Sentimental Friendship."

12. François Bruys, *The Art of Knowing Women: Or, the Female Sex Dissected* (London, 1730), 65 and 64. Bruys' remarks derive ultimately from Aristophanes' speech in Plato's *Symposium*; in that speech, Aristophanes describes the three original sexes—hermaphrodite, male, and female—each of which had two heads and two organs of generation, and which were first cut in two by the gods and then re-bisected. "Those men who are halves of a being of the common sex, which was called, as I told you, hermaphrodite, are lovers of women, and most adulterers come from this class, as also do women who are mad about men and sexually promiscuous" (*The Symposium*, trans. Walter Hamilton [Harmondsworth, Eng.: Penguin, 1951], 62).

13. Lovelace repeatedly evinces a deep fear of the submergence that "union" implies. His repeated fantasies of incorporating feminine qualities in himself seem partly designed to fend off the threat of being erased by the union with a woman that marriage represents.

14. Edward Ward, *The Secret History of Clubs . . .* (London: Printed by the Booksellers, 1709), 284.

15. [Allestree,] *The Ladies Calling*, 14.

16. See Thomas Laqueur for a discussion of the pre-1700 attitude toward hermaphrodites, which he characterizes as follows: "Maleness and femaleness did not reside in anything particular. Thus for hermaphrodites the question was not 'what sex they are *really*' but to which gender the architecture of their bodies most readily lent itself. The concern of magistrates was less with corporeal reality—with what we would call sex—than with maintaining clear social boundaries, maintaining the categories of gender" (*Making Sex: Body and Gender from the Greeks to Freud* [Cambridge, Mass.: Harvard Univ. Press, 1990], 135).

17. The rather remarkable indecision of the text as to the profession of the hermaphrodites' rescuer—doctor or lawyer?—echoes the question of whether such cases of problematic sex and gender belong to the medical or the juridical sphere. That is, what kind of authority can decide a hermaphrodite's fate?

18. George Arnaud, *A Dissertation on Hermaphrodites* (London: Printed for A. Millar, 1750), 26.

19. Julia Epstein describes the danger to "public order" and "public morality" that the state sees in sexual ambiguity: "The difficulty, of course, always returns to marriage, a consensual legal bond that is founded on the certainty that the consenting individuals are of different sexes. The taboo, the circumscribed and disruptive possibility that must be eradicated, always resides in the union of same sexes" ("Either/Or— Neither/Both: Sexual Ambiguity and the Ideology of Gender," *Genders* 7 [1990]: 99–142).

20. Lawrence S. Kubie, "The Drive to Become Both Sexes," *Psychoanalytic Quarterly* 43 (1974): 349–426.

21. "The Judgement of Tiresias," a poem from 1730, puts the question as follows:

> When willing nymphs and swains unite
> In quest of amorous delight,
> Which sex does Venus most befriend,
> Which party best obtains its end,
> Which does the greatest pleasure prove,
> And taste the sweetest joys of love?

Hildebrand Jacob's poem is in Roger Lonsdale, ed., *The New Oxford Book of Eighteenth Century Verse* (Oxford: Oxford Univ. Press, 1984), 226–27.

22. "But who can this affair decide? / 'Tiresias can,' the Thund'rer cried: / 'Tiresias either sex has tried' " (ibid.).

23. Jacob offers the following:

> I've done all that's done by man,
> And suffered all poor woman can,
> Have made myself the bold attack,
> And fought like tigress on my back;
> Now pressed the fair within my arms,
> Now died beneath the hero's charms
>
> · · ·
>
> The diff'rence lies, with due submission,
> Not in degree, but repetition. (Ibid.)

24. It is this aspect of Lovelacean "critical cross-dressing" that Elaine Showalter objects to in Terry Eagleton's analysis of *Clarissa*. See "Critical Cross-Dressing: Male Feminists and The Woman of The Year," *Raritan* (Fall 1983): 130–49.

25. *Herculine Barbin: Being the Recently Discovered Memoirs of a Nineteenth-Century Hermaphrodite*, trans. Richard McDougall, intro. Michel Foucault (New York: Pantheon, 1980), 106–7.

26. This passage does not appear in the first edition.

27. Although I disagree with some of William Warner's conclusions, I here follow in part his rich and interesting description of Lovelace's attempts to "mark" and "know" Clarissa. See Warner, *Reading Clarissa*, 50.

28. This passage does not appear in the first edition.

29. Lovelace earlier expressed the extreme view of women as property: "And whose property, I pray thee, shall I invade, if I pursue my schemes of love and vengeance?—Have not those who have a right in her, renounced that right?" (II: 492) (717).

30. For a complete survey of Lovelace's disguises in *Clarissa*, see Margaret Anne Doody, "Disguise and Personality in Richardson's *Clarissa*," *Eighteenth Century Life* 12 (1988): 18–39.

31. In the first edition of *Clarissa* much of this material appears in indirect discourse.

32. The homosocial tendencies in Lovelace, so evident here, also appear vividly in his gloating display of Clarissa to his rakish cronies; his letters to Belford further demonstrate a sense of competition with that less glamorous correspondent—a competition he feels he can win effortlessly until the period when Belford wins by having more access than he to Clarissa during her dying days. The most gripping evocation of the homosocial and the traffic in women in *Clarissa*, however, comes in the triangle of Lovelace, James Harlowe, and Clarissa; the erotically charged jealousy and antagonism between the two men are crucial components of Clarissa's tragedy. I believe, however, that the importance of male homosocial bonds, at least as strictly interpreted, pales beside Lovelace's ferocious and traumatic contention with Mrs. Sinclair and the whores over Clarissa; these women engage in a traffic in women that is most blatant and pernicious. Ultimately it is with the whores that Lovelace competes for ownership of Clarissa, as well as, more fugitively, for the ownership of his own desires, which they seem intent upon usurping.

33. Terry Eagleton describes Clarissa as the "'phallic' woman . . . by which Lovelace protects himself from his own terrible lack of being" (*The Rape of Clarissa*, 60).

34. This passage does not appear in the first edition.

35. Judith Wilt's invocations of Lovelace's "woman's half," in "He Could Go No Farther," seem inadequate to describe this complex process.

36. Lovelace's use of classical allusion here to support his fantasy also recalls the fact that, in ancient rituals and myth, cross-dressing was often explicitly associated with marriage or intercourse. See Marie Delcourt, *Hermaphrodite: Myths and Rites of the Bisexual Figure in Classical Antiquity*, trans. Jennifer Nicholson (London: Longacre, 1961), 16.

37. This passage does not appear in the first edition.

38. Margaret Anne Doody explicates the religious imagery of this scene of Lovelace's metamorphosis, in *A Natural Passion: A Study of the Novels of Samuel Richardson* (Oxford: Clarendon Press, 1974), 234.

39. The lines from Milton on which Lovelace bases his fragment concern one of Satan's visits to Adam and Eve in the Garden (*Paradise Lost*, IV, 810–14, 819)—but the celestial eye is Lovelace's addition:

> Him thus intent *Ithuriel* with his Spear
> Touch'd lightly; for no falshood can endure
> Touch of Celestial temper, but returns
> Of force to its own likeness: up he starts
> Discoverd and surpriz'd . . .
> So started up in his own shape the Fiend.

40. William Warner focuses on Clarissa's struggle to create a unified self (*Reading Clarissa*, 26, 32). Terry Castle describes the way the "woman's body" in *Clarissa* "is broken, incomplete, motley" (*Clarissa's Ciphers*, 35). Both Warner and Castle look at the body in the context of deconstructive readings.

41. Lovelace uses Eastern monarchs to describe his own imperial designs. He likens himself to Alexander the Great (III: 26–27) (762) as well as to "the Grand Signor": "How sweetly pretty to see the two lovely friends, when humbled and tame, both sitting in the darkest corner of a room, arm in arm, weeping and sobbing for each other! And I their emperor, their then *acknowledged* emperor, reclined at ease in the same room, uncertain to which I should first, Grand Signor–like, throw out my handkerchief!" (II: 369) (637). Jocelyn Harris, who entitles one of her chapters on *Clarissa* "King Lovelace," calls attention to Lovelace's imperial fantasies. See her *Samuel Richardson*, 66–85.

42. The flamboyance of this episode has been the subject of some comment: Robert Schmitz, in a letter disagreeing with Judith Wilt's

"He Could Go No Farther," calls the fantasy "the most preposterous passage" in *Clarissa* (Forum, *PMLA* 92 [1977]: 1005); Angus Ross, in his introduction to the Viking Penguin *Clarissa*, calls the episode "a typically bravura performance by Lovelace, both as a letter and as a piece of impudent defiance, well over the top and a pity to lose" (p. 17). Although there is little question that this passage was a real "restoration," there are long-standing disagreements about whether Richardson was elsewhere "restoring" what he had originally written or was adding passages to blacken Lovelace in his later editions of the novel. See Florian Stuber's introduction to the AMS Press reprint of the third edition of *Clarissa* ("Text, Writer, Reader, World," I: 1–53), for a summary of the various positions and their implications.

43. Rita Goldberg notes that "the description expands from a hardheaded perception of Lovelace's legal position into an inflation of the external world in which the rake becomes a public figure, almost a god, accompanied by his vestal virgins, over whom only a king has authority" (*Sex and Enlightenment: Women in Richardson and Diderot* [Cambridge: Cambridge Univ. Press, 1984], 100).

44. Lovelace himself observes that "there is no fear of being hanged for such a crime as this, while we have *money* or *friends*" (IV: 260). The chances of a gentleman being prosecuted for rape were indeed extremely small; of those who were prosecuted, few were convicted, and even fewer executed. For the statistical evidence on rape convictions, see Leon Radzinowicz, *A History of English Criminal Law and its Administration from 1750*, Vol. I, *The Movement for Reform 1750–1833* (New York: Macmillan, 1948), 148. For an extended discussion of eighteenth-century rape law in the context of *Clarissa*, see Flynn, *Samuel Richardson*, 109–15.

45. This scene echoes the final prints of Hogarth's *Industry and Idleness*, which are *The Idle 'Prentice Executed at Tyburn* and *The Industrious 'Prentice Lord-Mayor of London*. In both prints, the crowd engrosses our attention; Tom Idle and the Lord Mayor are tiny, unimportant figures swamped by mobs. As Ronald Paulson says of the resemblance between the crowd at the execution and the crowd at the investiture: "Recall the old saying: The crowd that cheers him at his coronation would cheer him as lustily at his execution" (*Emblem and Expression in English Art of the Eighteenth Century* [London: Thames & Hudson, 1975], 67).

46. See Laqueur, *Making Sex*, 161.

47. Mark Kinkead-Weekes neatly paraphrases the ostensible logic of Lovelace's hopes for the rape: "If the basic nature of woman is sexual,

and her morality is only a veneer of custom and education reinforced by pride, then the physical violation which puts her at a stroke beyond the pale of custom, and is a complete humiliation, will allow her 'true' nature to emerge. The experience of sexual penetration itself should result in an irreversible change; hence 'once subdued, always subdued' " (*Samuel Richardson*, 230).

48. See Linda Kauffman: "Lovelace's seemingly inexorable logic relies on false assumptions about identity and difference; he must know the exact extent of Clarissa's similarity to and difference from other women. . . . While underlining Lovelace's obsession with *newelty*, Richardson undermines it by invariably linking it with repetition" (*Discourses of Desire: Gender, Genre, and Epistolary Fictions* [Ithaca, N.Y.: Cornell Univ. Press, 1986], 136). As I have suggested, the fact that Lovelace is in a sense searching for himself in Clarissa's body further defeats him.

49. For a discussion of this problem based on the Cartesian mind/body dichotomy, see Leo Braudy, "Penetration and Impenetrability in *Clarissa*," in *Modern Essays on Eighteenth-Century Literature*, ed. Leopold Damrosch (New York: Oxford Univ. Press, 1988), 261–81. In Braudy's view, Clarissa "turns more and more against her own body" because "physicality is the most obvious barrier to self-definition"; in my view, the female body in the novel operates more powerfully as a reflex of Lovelace's—and Richardson's—fantasies about that body, and therefore Clarissa's retreat from the body actually signifies more about masculine investment than about feminine will.

50. See Doody, *A Natural Passion*, 173–74, for the implications of Clarissa as the bride of death.

51. See Eagleton, *The Rape of Clarissa*, for the most extensive modern endorsement of this position from a Marxist point of view.

52. Carol Flynn, in *Samuel Richardson*, repeatedly notes the extent to which Richardson "ostensibly endorsed many of the sexual stereotypes of his age," but claims that "he differed radically from his contemporaries when he set out to execute his beliefs" in his creation of "heroines of integrity who raise themselves up by their own efforts" (p. 135). Flynn sees the contradiction as between Richardson's "life" and his "art": "In his life, Richardson repeatedly expressed his faith in a world of sexual differences, a world in which women had to follow their clearly defined roles. Yet in his art he created heroines who achieved success by transcending sexual and social boundaries" (pp. 285–86). This neat separation does not fully engage with the problem of Richardson's treatment

of those fictional women who are *not* heroines; furthermore, the invocation of transcendence tends to endorse Richardson's own mystification.

53. Terry Castle, in *Clarissa's Ciphers*, clearly identifies the significance of this problem: "For [Clarissa], maleness and femaleness imply different psychological predispositions—absolutely and eternally. Clarissa's naivete is again damaging: her assumptions about 'natural' male and female behavior make her perpetually vulnerable to those who suspend conventional roles" (p. 75).

54. For the history of Sally's attempt, see "Conclusion. Supposed to be written by Mr. Belford" (VIII: 251–76). Sally's life story does not appear in the first edition.

55. Doody, "Disguise and Personality in Richardson's *Clarissa*."

56. Earlier Lovelace says that "a fallen woman, Jack, is a worse devil than even a profligate man" (III: 308) (535).

57. See Wilt, "He Could Go No Farther," for the implications of "below" and "above" in these scenes.

58. Wilt's "modest proposal" takes this argument to its logical extreme: She suggests that "the rape either was not fully carried out or was carried out by the man's [i.e., Lovelace's] female 'accomplices.' " In some sense, it might be said, Lovelace pictures *himself* as a kind of dildo.

59. See William Warner: "Lovelace's dominant emotion after the scene centers on the mastery of Clarissa's art and the impotence of his own. He is fascinated with the authority she has won. . . . He revolves the components of her carefully orchestrated performance; and his awe, at the power of her act, in both senses of the word, is compared to the frothy impotence of his own once vaunted stratagems" (*Reading Clarissa*, 65).

60. Arthur Lindley, "Richardson's Lovelace and the Self-Dramatizing Hero of the Restoration," in *The English Hero 1660–1800*, ed. Robert Folkenflik (Newark: Univ. of Delaware Press, 1982), 195–202.

61. Gillian Beer, "Richardson, Milton, and the Status of Evil," *Review of English Studies* 19 (1968): 267.

62. Eagleton, *The Rape of Clarissa*, 60.

63. Ibid., 60–61.

64. Braudy, "Penetration and Impenetrability in *Clarissa*," 273.

65. According to Terry Eagleton, "It seems unthinkable that Richardson could have fashioned Lovelace without considerable unconscious

guilt: the very fact that he could think his thoughts put him beyond the ideological closure that is Clarissa" (*The Rape of Clarissa*, 84).

66. See Eagleton: "The novel's 'guilt,' then, is that the more it protects its heroine's virtue, the longer it is able to indulge its 'hero' " (ibid., 85).

67. The references to Ovid and the Ovidian models in *Clarissa* go beyond the use of the *Metamorphoses*. Linda Kauffman, in *Discourses of Desire*, for example, explores Richardson's use of Ovid's *Art of Love* and *Heroides* in *Clarissa*.

68. The translation of Ovid's *Metamorphoses* that Richardson would have been likely to know is that by Dryden, Addison, Garth, "and other eminent hands." This appears in vol. 20 of *The Works of the English Poets: From Chaucer to Cowper* (London: Sir Samuel Garth, M.d., 1717). The story of Daphne is in Book I.

69. The tale can be reread from this vantage point to become the answer to the question, Why is the laurel Apollo's tree? Daphne's transformation becomes the illustration, otherwise inexplicable, of the connection between a god and a tree.

70. Robert Erickson, in *Mother Midnight: Birth, Sex, and Fate in Eighteenth-Century Fiction (Defoe, Richardson, and Sterne)* (New York: AMS Press, 1986), 129, 116–21, also notes the reminiscences of the story of Daphne and Apollo, as well as other Ovidian echoes, in *Clarissa*.

71. See Warner, *Reading Clarissa*: "The rape is the genuine catastrophe of Clarissa's personal history. But it gives Clarissa this advantage. Lovelace can no longer deceive her, for his final intentions have been exposed. . . . For Clarissa, the rape has unalterably fixed Lovelace's meaning—he simply *is* evil" (pp. 72–73).

Chapter 3

1. "But I am teazed by a dozen ladies of note and virtue, to give them a good man, as they say I have been partial to their sex, and unkind to my own." Richardson to J. B. de Freval, Jan. 21, 1751, *Selected Letters of Samuel Richardson*, ed. John Carroll (Oxford: Clarendon Press, 1964), 174.

2. There are, of course, notable exceptions to the general lack of enthusiasm I am describing; *Grandison* was a novel highly esteemed (by readers such as George Eliot and Goethe) in the nineteenth century, when *Clarissa* had fallen out of favor. Margaret Anne Doody, in *A Nat-*

ural Passion: A Study of the Novels of Samuel Richardson, and Mark Kinkead-Weekes, in *Samuel Richardson: Dramatic Novelist*, both published in the early 1970's, began a renewal of critical interest in *Grandison*, although much of the critical work on Richardson in the 1980's focused primarily (and in the cases of Warner, Eagleton, and Castle [in *Clarissa's Ciphers*] exclusively) on *Clarissa*.

3. Richardson to Lady Bradshaigh, Mar. 24, 1751, *Selected Letters*, 180.

4. Doody finds "Sir Charles . . . so credible that he could easily be intolerable. Fortunately he does not dominate the novel. The emphasis is thrown on the female characters" (*A Natural Passion*, 274). See also Rita Goldberg: "Despite its title, the interesting characters are all women" (*Sex and Enlightenment: Women in Richardson and Diderot* [Cambridge: Cambridge Univ. Press, 1984], 25). Terry Eagleton, in his decidedly *un*sympathetic reading of the novel, grouses that "a weighty objection to Sir Charles is not just his tedious perfection . . . but the fact that he ousts the novel's heroine, Harriet Byron" (*The Rape of Clarissa: Writing, Sexuality and Class Struggle in Samuel Richardson* [Minneapolis: Univ. of Minnesota Press, 1982], 97).

5. Doody, in *A Natural Passion*, treats the social and public emphasis of *Grandison* sympathetically. Most critics, even devotees of Richardson, have lamented this aspect of the novel as a failure: Carol Houlihan Flynn, for example, locates many of the problems in the novel in Richardson's "attempts to socialize Clarissa's virtue" (*Samuel Richardson: A Man of Letters* [Princeton, N.J.: Princeton Univ. Press, 1982], 48). Jocelyn Harris connects the problems in *Grandison* to the public nature of Richardson's own method of writing the novel. Richardson sent bits of the novel to his friends as he wrote: "The fact that it was no sooner written than read meant that reconsideration or rewriting were made virtually impossible. Writing to the moment as much as his characters, Richardson could never think it out again" (*Samuel Richardson* [Cambridge: Cambridge Univ. Press, 1987], 132).

6. Richardson to Lady Bradshaigh, Mar. 24, 1751, *Selected Letters*, 179.

7. See Flynn: "In *Grandison*, Richardson makes some of his strongest statements about the war between the sexes, but he allows the war to be waged only in theory. . . . The conflict persists on the periphery of the novel, but at the center punctilio reigns" (pp. 96–97). While I

find Flynn's statements useful, my interest is directed at showing the connection of the center and the margin, the theory and the practice.

8. See John Berger, *Ways of Seeing* (Harmondsworth, Eng.: Penguin, 1972), 50–51, on the associations between women looking in mirrors and vanity.

9. Virginia Woolf suggests that women have often acted as magnifying mirrors for men: "Women have served all these centuries as looking-glasses possessing the magic and delicious power of reflecting the figure of a man at twice its natural size" (*A Room of One's Own* [New York: Harcourt, Brace, 1929], 35).

10. Chesterfield's remark is cited by Cecil Price in " 'The Art of Pleasing': The Letters of Chesterfield," *The Familiar Letter in the Eighteenth Century*, ed. Howard Anderson, Philip Daghlian, and Irvin Ehrenpreis (Lawrence: Univ. Press of Kansas, 1966), 106. Price points out that Chesterfield's famous *mot* alters Dryden's "*Men* are but children of a larger growth."

11. Harriet's already transgressive garb gains more associations with the addition, forced on her by Sir Hargrave, of a "capuchin," a hood and (red) cloak, which had "some notoriety for its use in intrigues as a receptacle of *billets-doux*" (A. S. Turberville, ed., *Johnson's England* [Oxford, 1933], cited by Jocelyn Harris, in her notes to *Grandison* [3.482]).

12. See the discussion of Pamela's clothes, and their relation to her sense of self, in Chapter 1.

13. An extended analysis of this structure appears in Gayle Rubin's influential "The Traffic in Women: Notes Toward a Political Economy of Sex," in *Toward an Anthropology of Women*, ed. Rayna Reiter (New York: Monthly Review Press, 1975), 157–210. It is also extensively employed and revised in Eve Kosofsky Sedgwick, *Between Men: English Literature and Male Homosocial Desire* (New York: Columbia Univ. Press, 1985).

14. His family history as well as the promptings of virtue set Sir Charles against dueling; his mother's death because of his father's duel justifies his distaste.

15. Anna Laetitia Barbauld, Richardson's first biographer and editor of his correspondence, skewers the contradictions in Sir Charles's refusal to duel: "Sir Charles, as a Christian, was not to fight a duel . . . ; [but] in order to exhibit his spirit and courage, it was necessary to bring them into action by adventures and rencounters. . . . How must the

author untie this knot? He makes him so very good a swordsman, that he is always capable of disarming his adversary without endangering either of their lives. But are a man's principles to depend on the science of his fencing-master?" (quoted in Doody, *A Natural Passion*, 263).

16. See Juliet Mitchell, Introduction I, *Feminine Sexuality: Jacques Lacan and the Ecole Freudienne*, ed. Juliet Mitchell and Jacqueline Rose (New York: Norton, 1985), 16.

17. Another version of this phrase appears in Charles's description of Jeronymo: "He never will be the man he was."

18. *The Gentleman's Magazine: And Historical Chronicle* XX (Dec., 1750): 532–33.

19. Doody, *A Natural Passion*, 283.

20. Judith Wilt, of course, makes a similar claim about Lovelace, in her "He Could Go No Farther: A Modest Proposal About Lovelace and Clarissa," *PMLA* 92 (1977): 19–32.

21. Several critics of Richardson have noted, usually in passing and often with a certain use of gingerly periphrasis, the presence of castration in the novel: Margaret Doody, in *A Natural Passion*, refers to Jeronymo's presumed loss of manhood (p. 261), and Juliet McMaster, in an interesting article on *Grandison*, explores the genital injuries briefly, concluding that "one suspects a delicate allegory here, and that the wounds are what Moll Flanders would call 'an admirable description, by the way, of the foul disease'" ("*Sir Charles Grandison*: Richardson on Body and Character," *Eighteenth-Century Fiction* 1 [1989]: 83–102). Carol Flynn links the emasculation of the rake with emasculation of Richardson's imagination: "In his attempt to legitimize the fantastic excursions of Lovelace, Richardson emasculates the rake figure [in *Grandison*], losing his artistic potency in the process" (*Samuel Richardson*, 231). Jocelyn Harris, in two separate comments, glances at castration: "Sir Charles is not, like Abelard, thwarted in his potency, but a certain cold rectitude in his dealings with Clementina, together with his known chastity and irresistibility to women, make them not dissimilar" (*Samuel Richardson*, 159). I believe Harris is responding to some of the same disturbances in Sir Charles that I trace here. Harris also invokes Abelard in a different context: "Richardson hints with a new harshness at Abelard's fate, castration, when Sir Hargrave expires and Jeronymo's groin injury fails to heal" (ibid., 133). The most extensive discussion of emasculation in the novel, although limited to Jeronymo della Porretta and focused on the hints of homosexuality in the novel, appears in David Robinson, "Un-

ravelling the 'Cord Which Ties Good Men to Good Men': Male Friendship in Richardson's Novels," in *Samuel Richardson: Tercentenary Essays*, ed. Margaret Anne Doody and Peter Sabor (Cambridge: Cambridge Univ. Press, 1989), 167–87. Robinson compares Jeronymo's injury to Uncle Toby's "mysterious wound," and sees it as turning Jeronymo into something like a woman.

22. Between these two quotations, another instance of the punishment of rakes appears. Charlotte tells of the sufferings of her rakish cousin, Everard Grandison. A shrewd "cast mistress" whom he mistakes for a "country Innocent" is suing him for breach of promise. In Charlotte's words, "Sharpers have bit his head off, quite close to his shoulders" (2.442). In the succinct formulation of Freud, in his essay "Medusa's Head" and elsewhere, "To decapitate = to castrate" (*The Standard Edition of the Complete Psychological Works of Sigmund Freud* [London: The Hogarth Press, 1953–74], 18: 273–74).

23. See Terry Castle, *Masquerade and Civilization: The Carnivalesque in Eighteenth-Century English Culture and Fiction* (Stanford, Calif.: Stanford Univ. Press, 1986), 41–45, for some of the reasons that a trip to the masquerade signals dangerous female desires.

24. See Robinson, "Unravelling the Cord," for the argument that Jeronymo's "emasculation . . . encourages a sexual bond with Sir Charles."

25. Doody, *A Natural Passion*, 254–55.

26. Eagleton, *The Rape of Clarissa*, 96.

27. Ibid., 98–99.

28. Richardson to Lady Bradshaigh, [1750?], *Selected Letters*, 171.

29. Eagleton, *The Rape of Clarissa*, 84.

30. For the movement to redefine the hero, see Jean Hagstrum, *Sex and Sensibility: Ideal and Erotic Love from Milton to Mozart* (Chicago: Univ. of Chicago Press, 1980), 214–15. Hagstrum is also particularly illuminating on Richardson's precursors and on the exact form of Richardson's influence on later writers.

31. In a later letter describing Sir Charles's flirtatious conversion of a recalcitrant stepmother, Harriet reports that "it [his method for coaxing Lady Beauchamp] absolutely convinces me, of what indeed I before suspected, that he has not an high opinion of our sex in general" (2.272).

32. Richardson to Lady Bradshaigh, [1750?], *Selected Letters*, 170.

33. Flynn, *Samuel Richardson*, 233.

34. Harriet writes to Charlotte: "The men are their own enemies,

if they wish *us* to be open-hearted and sincere, and are not so *themselves*. Let them enable us to depend on their candour, as much as we may on that of Sir Charles Grandison, and the women will be inexcusable, who shall play either the prude or the coquet with them" (3.121).

35. Ludmilla Jordanova, *Sexual Visions: Images of Gender in Science and Medicine Between the Eighteenth and Twentieth Centuries* (Madison: Univ. of Wisconsin Press, 1989), 92–93.

36. Lady Mary Wortley Montagu to Lady Bute, Oct. 20, 1755, quoted by Jocelyn Harris in the introduction to *Grandison*, xix.

37. Despite the enthusiasm in the eighteenth century for Clementina, few modern critics have responded to her with great fervor; according to Juliet McMaster, for example, she is "not one of Richardson's finer creations" ("*Sir Charles Grandison,*" 98), and Jean Hagstrum finds her "unredeemed by the psychological depth one finds elsewhere" (*Sex and Sensibility*, 215). McMaster and Margaret Doody locate the problems with Clementina in Richardson's failure to let her engage in extensive correspondence; Doody, however, convincingly demonstrates Clementina's importance in the novel, as well as elucidating the religious reasons for eighteenth-century readers' interest in her (*A Natural Passion*, 306–39). I would argue that Clementina performs the service of having the "psychological depth" of others (Sir Charles and Harriet Byron, in particular) written on her body.

38. Jocelyn Harris's note to *Grandison* (2.147) cites Dr. George Cheyne, author of *The English Malady* and Richardson's physician, and Robert James's *Medical Dictionary* for definitions of lovesickness in women.

39. Richardson to Lady Bradshaigh, Dec. 8, 1753, *Selected Letters*, 252.

40. Morris Golden discusses Richardson's own tendencies to imaginative polygamy in connection with Sir Charles, in *Richardson's Characters* (Ann Arbor: Univ. of Michigan Press, 1963), 21–22.

41. Richardson to Lady Bradshaigh, Feb. 14, 1754, *Selected Letters*, 288.

42. Harris, *Samuel Richardson*, 159.

43. Clementina's function as host of excess and emotion links her to the traditional English use of Italy and Italians as the repository for anxieties about violent desire. The revenge tragedy is a *locus classicus* for this use of Italy, and it is worth noting too that Jeronymo (who is the object of a specifically sexual revenge) shares his name with the central

character of one of the initiating plays in the genre, Kyd's *Spanish Tragedy*. I am grateful to Mihoko Suzuki for pointing out these connections.

44. In her discussion of the body in *Grandison*, Juliet McMaster notes that "the passionate mingling of tears, [as in] Sterne, suggests its own kind of orgasm" ("*Sir Charles Grandison*," 88). Margaret Doody describes the "sexual overtones" of this scene with less emphasis on physiology, in *A Natural Passion*, 322–24.

45. See Mary Douglas, *Purity and Danger: An Analysis of Concepts of Pollution and Taboo* (London: Routledge & Kegan Paul, 1966), especially her chapter "External Boundaries," for a discussion of the meaning of body products such as tears and menstrual blood.

46. See Sigmund Freud, "The Taboo of Virginity," *Standard Edition*, 11: 191–208.

47. Doody also offers an illuminating analysis of the mixture of "erotic and mystical" in the scene: "[Clementina's] pose, as the blood trickles down her arm, recalls the Catholic images or paintings of saints suffering martyrdom for the Faith. The erotic and mystical are mingled in Catholic symbolism, and Richardson fittingly combines the two in these passages. If Clementina is wooing Sir Charles as a possible love-object, she is also appealing to him to join the true Church" (*A Natural Passion*, 324).

48. These scenes also bear a family resemblance to what Lovelace calls "The Lady and the Pen-knife," Clarissa's use of the threat of suicide to forestall a repetition of the rape; all the scenes present the conjunction of women, men, knives, and desire.

49. For an illuminating discussion of the function of images of decapitation, see Neil Hertz, "Medusa's Head: Male Hysteria Under Political Pressure," in his *The End of the Line: Essays on Psychoanalysis and the Sublime* (New York: Columbia Univ. Press, 1985), 161–92.

50. Richardson himself was, of course, the husband to two wives (in succession).

Index

The title page, chapter openings, and section breaks incorporate decorative ornaments used by Samuel Richardson in his own printing of *Clarissa,* published in 1748.

Book design by Colleen Forbes.

Typeset in 11.5 on 13 Garamond #3 by Wilsted and Taylor, Oakland, California.

∞ Printed on acid-free paper by Braun-Brumfield, Ann Arbor, Michigan.

Library of Congress Cataloging-in-Publication Data

Gwilliam, Tassie, 1954-
    Samuel Richardson's fictions of gender / Tassie Gwilliam.
      p. cm.
    Includes bibliographical references and index.
    ISBN 0-8047-2116-5 :
    1. Richardson, Samuel, 1689-1761—Criticism and interpretation. 2. Masculinity (Psychology) in literature. 3. Femininity (Psychology) in literature. 4. Sex role in literature. 1. Title.
PR3667.G93 1993
823'.6—dc20   92-25186
                                           CIP